■ Specters of Democracy

Specters of Democracy

*Blackness and the Aesthetics of
Politics in the Antebellum U.S.*

Ivy G. Wilson

OXFORD
UNIVERSITY PRESS

Oxford University Press, Inc., publishes works that further
Oxford University's objective of excellence
in research, scholarship, and education.

Oxford   New York
Auckland   Cape Town   Dar es Salaam   Hong Kong   Karachi
Kuala Lumpur   Madrid   Melbourne   Mexico City   Nairobi
New Delhi   Shanghai   Taipei   Toronto

With offices in
Argentina   Austria   Brazil   Chile   Czech Republic   France   Greece
Guatemala   Hungary   Italy   Japan   Poland   Portugal   Singapore
South Korea   Switzerland   Thailand   Turkey   Ukraine   Vietnam

Published by Oxford University Press, Inc.
198 Madison Avenue, New York, New York 10016

www.oup.com

Oxford is a registered trademark of Oxford University Press.

Library of Congress Cataloging-in-Publication Data

Wilson, Ivy G.
Specters of democracy : blackness and the aesthetics of politics in the antebellum
     U.S. / Ivy Wilson.
     p. cm.
ISBN 978-0-19-533737-2 (cloth : alk. paper)—ISBN 978-0-19-534035-8 (pbk. : alk. paper)
1. American literature—African American authors—History and criticism.
2. African Americans in literature. 3. Democracy in literature. 4. Nationalism in literature.
5. African American authors—Political and social views. 6. Discourse analysis, Literary.
7. Rhetoric—Political aspects—United States—History.   I. Title.
PS153.N5W565 2011
810'.9352996073—dc22   2010020169

ISBN-13: 978-0-19-533737-2 (hardback)
           978-0-19-534035-8 (paperback)

9 8 7 6 5 4 3 2 1
Printed in the United States of America
on acid-free paper

■ Dành cho bà nội của Cadeo

■ CONTENTS

■ ACKNOWLEDGMENTS

In a project that seeks to limn spectral presences, I am happy to underscore the large number of people who have helped shaped this book and the ideas that animate it. Over the years, I have benefitted from conversations with Elizabeth Alexander, Kate Baldwin, Dorri Beam, Herman Beavers, Nancy Bentley, Kendall Bentz, Lauren Berlant, Hester Blum, Jason Boyte, Lori Brooks, Jayna Brown, Beverly Bruce, Kera Carpenter, Jeff Clymer, Radi Clytus, Cathy Cohen, Thadious Davis, Wai Chee Dimock, Brian Edwards, Lydia English, Cheryl Finley, Jay Fliegelman, Ed Folsom, Beth Freeman, Janet Giarranto, Luke Gibbons, Richard Gillam, Jill Goodmillow, Jennifer Greeson, Sandra Gustafson, Glenn Hendler, Sharon Holland, Sian Hunter, Larry Jackson, Virginia Jackson, E. Patrick Johnson, Diane Jowdy, Jerry Kennedy, Jay Kidd, Ferentz LaFargue, Bob Levine, David Lloyd, Chris Looby, Dana Luciano, Kate Masur, Dwight McBride, Meredith McGill, Lynn McCormack, Nellie McKay, Geneva Melvin, Bill Mitchell, Dana Nelson, Furaha Norton, Nick Pappas, Julie Park, Don Pease, Jemima Pierre, Steve Pitti, Horace Porter, Leigh Raiford, Arnold Rampersad, Cheryl Reed, Nikki Reisch, Beth Richie, Kerry Ann Rockquemore, Nancy Ruttenberg, Shirley Samuels, Valerie Sayers, Darieck Scott, Laura Selznick, Cherene Sherrard-Johnson, William Spanos, Bob Stepto, Alan Trachtenberg, Brandee Waite, Ken Warren, Bryan Wolf, Richard Yarborough, and Rafia Zafar. The model of scholarship by Hazel Carby, Michael Denning, and Paul Gilroy has informed much of my own work and I am lucky to have had them engage the project early on.

Parts of the book have been read by Erica Ball, Chris Castiglia, Russ Castronovo, Betsy Erkkilä, Peter Fenves, James Ford, Anthony Foy, Chris Freeburg, Susannah Gottlieb, Jay Grossman, Glenn Hendler, Juliet Hooker, Gene Jarrett, Bob Levine, Deborah March, Angela Miller, Imani Perry, Arnold Rampersad, Shana Redmond, Matt Sandler, and Julia Stern; the book is all the better for their perceptive comments. Amina Gautier was always ready with a keen eye and sharp wit. Anthony Foy has witnessed this project develop from its very inception and my thoughts about its ideas have profited from our frequent conversations over the years.

Along with the anonymous readers for Oxford University Press, I would especially like to thank Chris Castiglia, Russ Castronovo, John Ernest, George Hutchinson, and Maurice Wallace for reading aspects of the book at crucial junctures in its development. I appreciate the insights of all these challenging interlocutors. At Oxford, I would like to thank my editor Shannon McLachlan for her support as well as Brendan O'Neill, Jaimee Biggins, and Susan Ecklund for smoothly guiding the book into production. Before passing it off to the Press,

Stefka Mihaylova put her keen eyes on the manuscript and I thank her here. My research assistant, Louis Pignatelli, was ever helpful and ever patient with my requests.

Specters of Democracy evolved over a number of years at different institutions and academic venues. I thank audiences at the annual conferences of the American Studies Association and Modern Language Association where I gave talks on topics from the book. In another vein, students in my courses at Binghamton University, the University of Notre Dame, and Northwestern University were kind, if not unwitting, participants in early conversations about the book's fundamental ideas. A part of chapter 1 is taken from my essay in the March 2006 issue of *PMLA* (121.2) and is reprinted by permission of the copyright owner, The Modern Language Association of America. Sections of chapter 4 are taken from my essay in the special 2008 issue of *ESQ* (54.1–4) and are reprinted by permission of the copyright owner, Washington State University Board of Regents.

At Northwestern, I have been particularly blessed by the support of wonderful colleagues in African American Studies, American Studies, and English. I thank my chair Susan Manning for her guidance and enthusiasm, as well as Carl Smith and Darlene Clark Hine for welcoming me into American Studies and African American Studies respectively. My first two years at Northwestern have been hilariously enlivened and intellectually enriched by gatherings with the breakfast club: Katy Breen, John Alba Cutler, Nick Davis, Kasey Evans, Evan Mwangi, Susie Phillips, Helen Thompson, and Viv Soni. Having long admired John Keene as a writer and critic, I feel especially fortuitous to be in his presence on a regular basis. Peter Fenves and Susannah Gottlieb furnished the most finely tuned comments at the most timely moments with a care and sensitivity that reaches well beyond being merely colleagues in ways that make me feel both grateful and inspired. I stepped into an English department that has a venerable triumvirate of nineteenth-century Americanists in Betsy Erkkilä, Jay Grossman, and Julia Stern; their warmth as colleagues is matched only by the acuity of their individual and collective insights on the field. Over the years, Betsy has proved to be one of my most challenging interlocutors and an invaluable mentor.

My family, near and extended, has supported and sustained me in ways that I can only hope to repay. Kendall and Carrie tolerated my presence for an insufferable number of days on their couch while I conducted research. Priscilla and Jason provided much relief and laughter when they were much needed. Ruth Hamilton was an extraordinary scholar and I learned much about being a member of the profession from her exemplary model. This book would not be possible without Tim and Andie who challenge me at every turn about everything in ways that only people who love you can—questions I could only begin to answer in between the moments that I could spare while playing with my beautiful nephews Tre, Gavin, and Tyler.

I dedicate this book to my mom, who I feel even now and always.

■ Specters of Democracy

Introduction: In the Shadows of Citizenship

African Americans and Democracy's Alterity

Democratic polities are constituted through exclusions that return
to *haunt* the polities predicated upon their absence.[1]

JUDITH BUTLER

I sell the shadow to support the substance.   SOJOURNER TRUTH

In the "Book of Life" section of her autographical narrative, Sojourner Truth includes an excerpt from the *National Anti-Slavery Standard* describing one of her speeches at an Iowa religious convention in the 1850s. The excerpt extols the magnetic power of Truth's rhetorical acumen and recounts a moment in her speech when an allusion to the government prompts a challenge by an audience member: "Now I hears talkin' about de Constitution and de rights of man. I comes up and I takes hold of dis Constitution. It looks *mighty big*, and I feels for *my* rights, but der aint any dare. Den I says, God, what *ails* dis Constitution? He says to me, 'Sojourner, dere is a little *weasel* in it.' "[2]

Other African Americans in the antebellum black public sphere, including William Wells Brown, Charles Lenox Remond, and Frances Ellen Watkins Harper, had leveled critiques against the Constitution but perhaps none with such style. Employing both wit and analogy, Truth's retort used the example of the recent midwestern boll weevil epidemic to intimate that slavery was eating away at the Constitution and, by extension, U.S. society itself. With the use of wit and irony that was a signature aspect of the sound of her oratorical style, Truth's response puts into performance a sentiment that the Constitution offered African Americans little to no rights at all.

While Truth was already well known as a speaker on the antislavery lecture circuit, her use of *cartes-de-visite* illuminates her desire to stage herself as a proper U.S. subject (figure I.1). As Nell Painter points out, Truth's control over her physical representation in these images intimates that she would not be made "into an African or into an exotic of any kind at all"; that is, she refused to be fashioned as anything less than an American of the United States.[3] In a wider sense, her dissemination of *cartes-de-visite* is an instance of how African Americans engaged the visual codes concerning national belonging. Blacks were everywhere in the visual archives of U.S. culture in broadsides, lithographs, and newspaper sketches; Truth's *cartes-de-visite* should be thought of as a supplement, if not a response, to these various depictions.

Figure I.1 Sojourner Truth. *Carte-de-visite*, 1864.
Gladstone Collection, Prints and Photographs
Division. Library of Congress.

Truth's *cartes-de-visite* also had the effect of extending her message of liberatory politics beyond the localized setting or time of a given speech. Selling
them to support her lecturing tours, these images disseminated a trace of Truth
wherever she spoke, a shadow of her that would remain at a given place when her
body was elsewhere at another. More than simply curios and souvenirs, Truth's
cartes-de-visite were the coordinate points of an alternative constellation of political contingency. This constellation constituted a counterpublic where African
Americans created both ethereal and material forms of political agency to contest
the meanings of citizenship and democracy in the United States.

Truth's concern with self-representation exemplifies two important ways
that mid-nineteenth-century African Americans challenged the forms of U.S.

liberal democracy by engaging the art forms of rhetoric and visuality. On the one hand, her speeches represent the vernacular practices of vocal enunciation—from high diction to rude dialect—that African Americans used to develop a discourse within the larger national rhetoric about democracy. On the other hand, her *cartes-de-visite* illustrate the efforts by African Americans to exercise control over the meanings of visual representations regarding their own self-fashioning and the image of the citizen.

But more than the image itself, the printed text of Truth's *cartes-de-visite* encapsulated the liminal position of antebellum free blacks who were neither slaves nor full citizens. On each of the *cartes-de-visite* was printed the caption "I Sell the Shadow to Support the Substance." While the alliterative phrasing was in keeping with her command over the sonic impulses of language, the caption epitomizes the liminality of the selves under discussion in this book. To the extent that the "shadow" is nothing—that is, nothing material or substantial—it cannot be sold for it dissolves with the change of light. To the extent, however, that the "shadow" is taken as substance, whose instantiation and transference are signaled at the point of sale, it illuminates at the same moment that it reverses the historical conditions that politically and legally reduce the black body to something less than the nominative self. Truth's epigrammatic form represents a political equation whereby her ability to sell her "shadow" without affecting her substance prefigures the conditions under which an exchange of one's own shadow or spectral character occasions the possibility of a transformed democracy.

In a reflection on very different historical conditions—the collapse of Soviet-style communism and the emergent rhetoric of liberal market economies and liberal democracy—Jacques Derrida urges that we attend to the specters that this rhetoric is meant to exorcise and locate in these specters a democracy that transcends the limits of its current conceptualization. In this respect, Derrida's notion of a "democracy to come" is akin to Judith Butler's claim that democratic polities are haunted, and then expanded, by the return of certain exclusions as well as to the promise of Jacques Rancière's idea of "dissensus" as a radical political process occasioned by the "redistribution of the sensible" that seeks to be extended beyond the present horizons of the here and now.[4] For Derrida, attending to specters and detecting advance traces of a "democracy to come" are the Janus-faced simultaneity of the political maneuvers that will allow this coming democracy to come closer.[5] The direction of my study parallels the impulse Derrida outlines in *Specters of Marx* (1993). Attention to the politically nonmaterial elements of democracy in the antebellum United States—whether they be called "specters" or "shadows"—allows for a space where democracy is understood, discussed, and above all practiced.

My conceptualization of the "shadow" is deeply indebted to Ralph Ellison's understanding of the invisible/hypervisible dyad of blackness. In his novel *Invisible Man* (1952), Ellison describes invisibility as a "peculiar disposition" that prevents people from seeing, by which he means recognizing, blacks; they emerge as the "specters" or "shadows" whose immateriality reveals the fraught processes of (cultural and political) recognition that regulate socialities. Ellison continues by stating that black subjects are seemingly surrounded by mirrors of glass which distort their image such that, when they are approached, others see only their own "surroundings, themselves, or figments of their imagination—indeed, everything and anything" save the person immediately before them.[6] As Fred Moten has reminded us, to "be invisible is to be seen, instantly and fascinatingly recognized as the unrecognizable, as the abject."[7]

Ellison's novel is especially important in two significant respects for *Specters of Democracy*. First, *Invisible Man* correlates sound to vision, aurality to visuality. Second, *Invisible Man* makes particular use of the shadow as a metaphor for the relationship of blacks to the United States and as a predicament that ails American democracy. Ellison first stages the idea of the shadow in the novel's epigraph to intimate the social darkness produced by U.S. racial formation. The prologue and epilogue reiterate this sentiment where the protagonist has returned to live underground in a basement that is illuminated by hundreds of lightbulbs. Without mitigating the latent racial critique of Ellison's notion of the shadow, I want to accentuate the shadow as a particular kind of outline, facsimile, or replica that is produced by the different positioning of light. The concept of the shadow, in this respect, better conveys the processes by which the relationship between the first and the second, the subject and its object, takes on certain permutations and figurations. That is, the geometric outline of the shadow carries within it a graphic trace of the original and always reveals how one is related to another.

While the concept of the shadow in many respects culminates with Ellison's twentieth-century novel, it has a long and important genealogy in American letters that are preoccupied with issues of race, citizenship, and democracy. This book locates its reading of the shadow in the mid-nineteenth century when writers and artists of the period were reinterpreting how the revolutionary moment of the colonial era cast a shadow over the 1850s. One important moment at which the shadow could be said to be instantiated in U.S. political culture is when Thomas Jefferson excises the lines from the Declaration of Independence blaming King George III for the colonists' participation in the transatlantic slave trade. Another important moment would be the Three-fifths Compromise of the Constitution, which essentially rendered slaves, and hence the overwhelming majority of the United States' black population, fractional subjects. More specific to the mid-nineteenth-century period, the escalating debate about slavery put increased pressure on ideas of citizenship and saw the return of the concept of the shadow as a metaphor for the predicament of liberal democracy. The beginning of Herman Melville's short story "Benito Cereno" (1855), about a slave revolt gone awry aboard a ship, exploits this use of the shadow—"Shadows present, foreshadowing deeper shadows to come."[8] Four years later the novel *Our Nig; or Sketches from the Life of a Free Black* (1859) tells the story of Frado, a poor girl suffering in the North whom the author Harriet Wilson uses to illustrate that "Slavery's Shadows Fall Even There."

Even when the phrase itself is not invoked, the shadow remains a resonant concept in mid-nineteenth-century African American literature and political culture. It often carries a putatively negative charge, illustrated as the embodied physical spaces such as the slave auction in Frederick Douglass's novella *The Heroic Slave* (1853) and Harriet Jacobs's *Incidents in the Life of a Slave Girl* (1861) where she is trapped in the dark recesses of a garret for years. But the recesses of society often served as the spaces in which African Americans contested their own shadow status from subversive maroon colonies of runaway slaves to Northern halls where the black convention movement held its assemblies for decades before the Civil War. Indeed, in the case of the convention movements, these spaces where central to what the historian Elijah Anderson has called "shadow politics."[9] In Richard S. Newman's estimation, such instances were examples not of a strictly alternative universe but of a parallel black community that "both challenged racialized American political institutions and, at the same time, lay claim to core elements of those institutions."[10] My insistence upon reading both black and white writers and artists together for how they depict and challenge the ways that U.S. citizenship and equality have been circumscribed follows this impulse.

I use the concept of the "shadow" to conceptualize the residues and outlines of black subjectivity in political spaces where they are ostensibly fractional entities or nonentities. My readings urge that we view the shadow not simply as the figurative trace of the differential between the normative and its antithesis but as a spectacle and visual demarcation, as the very illustration of the vexed national sensibilities that have understood blackness as a kind of phantasmagoria—as something that the question of U.S. identity telescopes through the registers of the citizen and the nonhuman.[11]

Although Roger B. Taney's *Dred Scott v. Sanford* decree was in many respects the most decisive statement on the question of blacks and U.S. citizenship, prior to 1857 blacks in Northern states had access to limited rights, but in nearly every instance there was the tacit understanding that they should not be considered citizens.[12] As the political scientist Rogers Smith notes, quoting an Arkansas decision of 1846, blacks could only hope to achieve a kind of "quasi citizenship" at best.[13] Since the majority of states denied blacks the right to vote, and the right to associate became increasingly restricted—thereby changing the meanings of space for blacks, changes of space that were exacerbated by the Fugitive Slave Law—African Americans had to become even more strategic about developing the means to engage with the political sphere.

Free African Americans themselves in the antebellum United States debated the best remedy for the predicament of what I have been outlining as the liminal state of blacks living in—and as—the shadows of democracy. In an 1849 article for the *National Anti-Slavery Standard*, Charles Lenox Remond criticized the American Colonization Society and argued that it had "ever maligned the characters of the nominally free people of the North."[14] Remond was a staunch Garrisonian who urged the dissolution of the Union and disavowal of the Constitution. Five years later, in his "Political Destiny of the Colored Race on the American Continent," Martin R. Delany, noting the anomalous position of free African Americans, echoed Remond's sentiment. "We have not addressed you as *citizens*—a term desired and ever cherished by us—because such you have never been," he wrote. "We have not addressed you as *freemen*, because such privileges have never been enjoyed by any colored man in the United States."[15] A year after the publication of Delany's "Political Destiny," Frederick Douglass described the plight of the "nominally free" in his second autobiographical narrative, *My Bondage and My Freedom* (1855). "No colored man is free in a slaveholding state," Douglass wrote, for he "wears the badge of bondage while nominally free, and is often subjected to hardships to which the slave is a stranger."[16] And in her essay "The Colored People of America" (1854), Frances Ellen Watkins Harper implored her audience to sympathize with the lot of U.S. blacks by considering themselves "nominally free, [and] feel that they have only exchanged the iron yoke of oppression for the galling fetters of a vitiated public opinion."[17] But while Remond and Delany proposed that African Americans leave the country altogether, Douglass and Watkins Harper maintained that it was incumbent for free African Americans to remain in the United States and fight for their own civil liberties and act as advocates for their brethren in bondage.

Perhaps the single most trenchant mid-nineteenth-century cognate of the idea of the shadow was Douglass's notion of the "alien." In a speech delivered in May 1853 at the American and Foreign Anti-Slavery Society, Douglass lamented that free blacks had been reduced to something less than citizens: "Aliens are we in our native land. The fundamental principles of the republic, to which the humblest white man, whether born here or elsewhere, may appeal with confidence in the hope of awakening a favorable response, are held to be inapplicable to us.... We plead for our rights, in the name of the written constitution of government, and we are answered with imprecations and curses."[18] Douglass's disheartening recognition illuminates that race informed how citizenship was conceptualized and practiced, even in free states where slavery was not institutionalized, and illustrates how two of the most important definitions of citizenship—citizenship by birthright and citizenship by consent—were put into crisis when increasingly larger numbers of African Americans began to demand the full slate of their rights as citizens.

Specters of Democracy: Blackness and the Aesthetics of Politics in the Antebellum U.S. analyzes how African Americans manipulated aurality and visuality in art that depicted images of national belonging not only as a mode of critique but as an iteration of democratic representation itself. There is no dearth of studies on democracy and nineteenth-century U.S. literature.[19] This book, however, differs from much of this criticism by focusing on the mutual engagement with the national idioms by both black and white Americans and, furthermore, by illustrating how African Americans deployed artistic practices to advocate for a more egalitarian society. More specifically, I argue that black Americans used rhetoric and ekphrastic writing to articulate the meanings of their own personhood in opposition to the definitions imposed upon them by the far reach of slavery, even if one were not a slave. Such a focus on cultural production is especially necessary to recover the African American presence in political debates before the ratification of the Fourteenth and Fifteenth Amendments.

Taking as a cue one aspect of Gayatri Spivak's essay "Can the Subaltern Speak?" (1988), which draws on the work of both Derrida and Philippe Lacoue-Labarthe, this project interrogates the ways that antebellum African Americans conceived of representation in art as a proxy for their desired representation in politics.[20] In her essay, Spivak adopts Lacoue-Labarthe's distinction between *darstellen* as the re-presenting in art or philosophy and *vertreten* as the "speaking for" in politics.[21] With Derrida, Spivak, and Ellison in mind, *Specters of Democracy* interrogates the representational strategies that nineteenth-century Americans used in art and literature to delineate blackness as an index to the forms of U.S. citizenship. By exploring the permutations of rhetoric and visuality, I explore the correlation of blackness to citizenship in the age of the Civil War, focusing especially on the decade before its outbreak. The book reveals how the difficult task of representing African Americans—both enslaved and free—in imaginative expression was part of a larger dilemma concerning representative democracy. It analyzes both the politics of cultural forms and how cultural projects themselves have come to constitute the political for African Americans.

I use the term "political aesthetics" in this study to signal how various art forms put into high relief the efficacy of affect to engender and sustain collectivities of social belonging. By putting an examination of aesthetics at the center of a reading of the political, my analyses illuminate the ways that U.S. black subjects conceptualized the relationship between art and politics, a relationship that was especially heightened during the mid-nineteenth moment through their engagement with the discourses of rights, citizenship, and democracy. The question of cultural formation was especially important in the antebellum United States when most black Americans were denied access to the traditional domains of formal politics.[22] If formal politics signal certain institutional practices such as electoral processes and policy making, then a turn to culture as a particular arena where African Americans had varying levels of agency is all the more necessary in the years before they were ostensibly granted access to these structures with the passage of the Fifteenth Amendment. Or, as Richard Iton puts it speaking of a different historical period, to not engage the "cultural realm, whether defensively or assertively, would be, to some degree, to concede defeat in an important—and relatively accessible—arena."[23] The literature and art under consideration in this book focuses on the decade before the Civil War. Although I consider material from before and after the Civil War, *Specters of Democracy* is especially concerned with the fraught political debates among blacks and whites alike about democracy and citizenship because of the Fugitive Slave Law of 1850 and the Dred Scott decision of 1857.

Aesthetics has multivalent meaning. As a mode of interpretation, aesthetics encompasses evaluative judgments of artistic quality and beauty that we principally associate with the tradition inaugurated by Immanuel Kant and developed in the English-speaking space by Matthew Arnold, among others. In the Kantian tradition aesthetics is largely dominated by the idea of form, and the turn to aesthetic modes of reflection and representation therefore generally inclines toward formalism. For others, by contrast, aesthetics is more closely associated with a wide range of affects and feelings—not simply, as with the Kantian tradition, with an affectless feeling of pleasure. But, in repudiating aesthetics as a preoccupation with formalism or as a mode of evaluation, Rancière has written on the necessity of reclaiming the aesthetic and prevent it from being disaggregated from examinations of the historical and the political.[24] In the broadest sense, aesthetics is a branch of philosophy concerned with the systematic approach to the study of art that has been preoccupied with four primary issues: the evaluation of the beautiful and the sublime; the criteria and standards of taste; the nature and form of art; and acts of mimesis and representation. My own preoccupation in this book has centered on the last of these two, especially in key moments where conspicuous or failed acts of mimesis function as a metacritical polemic on the meanings of black representation in politics, where blacks hovered in a state of political being marked as non-entities at worst and nominal subjects at best.

In the context of nineteenth-century U.S. literary studies, the question of and return to aesthetics has emerged as one of the most important analytics in the study of the politics of culture in recent years.[25] This topic has been especially animated by the work of Christopher Castiglia, Russ Castronovo, and Dana D. Nelson who have insisted that questions of aesthetics are correlative with questions about democracy and liberalism more generally. The recent work of all three is preoccupied with the affective possibilities of aesthetics as a model and a means though which collectivities can fulfill the unfinished work of democracy.[26] I've attempted to situate this project in relation to these works as much as I've tried to offer a reading of a subversive black aesthetic that prefigures those later moments in twentieth-century African American political culture examined in such works as Fred Moten's *In the Break* and Richard Iton's *In Search of the Black Fantastic* on the avant-garde and the popular, respectively.

Nineteenth-century African Americans wanted their audiences to sympathize with the predicament of blacks in the country, but they also wanted their audiences to empathize with the political messages latent in their cultural production, and this twofold exploitation of aesthetics was central to their work on fulfilling the promise of democracy. Invoking the term "aesthetic" in the context of antebellum African American cultural production might itself seem superfluous, even specious, given how so many works were clearly conceptualized as political tracts rather than works of art per se. However, throughout *Specters of Democracy* I insist upon an understanding of the world of art as the realm where African Americans could render and translate their political messages: it is the "shadow" realm, as it were, that always haunts the material world of normative political activity and its agents.

Indeed, a focus on the sensory modalities of literature and art might also unveil early theories about African American art. Many of the classic statements on African American aesthetics were published in the twentieth century, including James Weldon Johnson's preface to *The Book of American Negro Poetry* (1922), W. E. B. DuBois's essay "Criteria for Negro Art" (1926), Langston Hughes's essay "The Negro Artist and the Racial Mountain" (1926), Zora Neale Hurston's "Characteristics of Negro Expression" (1934), Addison Gayle Jr.'s *The Black Aesthetic* (1971), and Albert Murray's *Blues Devil of Nada* (1996), among others. But how might we (re)construct theories of African American art when most nineteenth-century African American artists often had limited time to practice their own art and even less to postulate theories about cultural production?

The matrix of Derrida's reflection on the idea of spectrality lies in his earlier work on the concept of repetition and "iteration."[27] Repetition duplicates the original and alters it as well. And all repetition is potentially transformative, at which point it is no longer repetition but rather an original that itself becomes susceptible to a transformative repetition. By foregrounding the latent issue of repetition, this project underlines the question of how long and to what degree a peripheral subject must continually reiterate the vocabularies of the nation before she or he is recognized as a constituent of a given polity or, at least, as an influence on how these polities imagine and construct themselves. Informed by Henry Louis Gates's understanding of signifying as a trope of reversal and Homi Bhabha's understanding of the slippages and differences of colonial mimicry as a form of resistance, I interrogate the political grammars of the United States through the critical lens of what I am calling "the remix" throughout *Specters of Democracy*: the decisive mark of a "remix" is that repetition is always transformative and always solicits retransformation. The remix is, thus, not deriative but a form of active engagement.

In this vein, my earlier invocation of Spivak, whose work similarly utilizes terms drawn from Derrida's work, is meant not as a facile collapse of the histories of colonization of different imperial systems with racialized hegemony in the United States but rather as a way to illuminate how African Americans challenged the social machinations that constructed U.S. blacks as aliens. Invoking postcolonial criticism as a way to underscore blacks as a kind of subaltern class in the United States is also one way by which we might interrogate the practices that African Americans have used to enter into the discursive fields of the body politic by considering Bhabha's notion of mimicry. In Bhabha's famous formulation, he posits that the discourse of mimicry is constructed around an ambivalence that must continually "produce its slippage, its excess, its difference."[28] As a sign of "a double articulation," mimicry repeats rather than strictly re-presents and is "at once resemblance and menace" to the existing hegemony.[29] Bhabha's notion of mimicry in this regard is similar to Gates's idea of "signifying" as a practice of double-voiced repetition and reversal.[30] Equally resistant to the romanticized aphorism that acts of appropriation by subjugated peoples are always a performance of subversion as well as to the idiomatic expression that the master's tools will never dismantle the master's house, I approach the relationship between the original and its derivatives, the real and the facsimile, the primary and its repetition, as a mode of compounding that elongates a discourse over a period of time and sometimes across regions, making it resonant and intelligible precisely as a particular system of political grammar.[31]

While nineteenth-century black intellectuals like Martin R. Delany did produce separate discourse epistemologies, the maneuvers that I discuss in this book often played upon the established rhetoric of the national vernacular to modify and subvert this nomenclature for reformist, if not radical, ends. The appropriation by African Americans of conventional idioms such as Patrick Henry's "Give me liberty or give me death" phrase or the Declaration's "all men are created equal" clause is used to transform the language of revolutionary iconography into something that was not reduced and exploited for decidedly hegemonic means. U.S. black understanding of rights and liberties was not divorced from, but rather animated by, the geopolitical currents of the nineteenth-century world which allowed them to frame their discourse formations as both national and international. If this book treats liberalism with less suspicion than we might expect or otherwise want given the principal coordinates of blackness and (radical) politics, it is because most African Americans in the mid-nineteenth-century black public sphere, with the notable and important exception of emigrationists, believed in the promise of liberal democracy and that the day of their incorporation as fully embodied agential subjects was approaching on the very near political horizon. That moment may have seemed ever closer as the Civil War came into being, but it failed to concretize as a permanent condition for most African Americans. Douglass's likening of African Americans as "aliens" and Watkins Harper's identification of the "nominally free" are important prefigurations to a set of theoretical cognates in current scholarship on the dilemmas of "freedom" and/in slavery: Saidiya Hartman's notion of the "ambivalences of freedom," Walter Johnson on "agency" and the epistemic and ethical implications of New Social History, and David Kazanjian on "equivocal agency."[32] My own sense in this study has been to disaggregate the teleological underpinnings that correlate democracy with national time such that when one progresses, the other does; in this respect, I situate my readings of blackness and democracy between the material and conceptual registers of slavery and freedom, fully cognizant, as surely the subjects of this study were, that the residues and traces of slavery found an afterlife well after 1865.

In order to trace how African Americans made themselves audible and visible during this period, *Specters of Democracy* decodes the sensory modalities of how democracy is experienced through the rhetoric of aural resonances and the spatial arrangement of visual forms. The first half of the book examines a host of verbal iterations represented in fiction, poetry, and speeches as debates, oratory, and popular songs that constitute a wide cultural field of rhetoric. Throughout this half, I explore a set of terms to illuminate my understanding of the aural prosopopoeia of spectrality: echoes, dialects, quotes, and utterances. The second half of the book examines how the processes of visualization were used in both literature and genre painting to picture various images of the citizen and the nation. Throughout this half, I employ rely principally upon the trope of the shadow to interrogate the particular graphic dimensions of spectrality's visuality.

The first half of *Specters of Democracy*, "Version and Subversion: The Aurality of Democratic Rhetoric," opens with a reading of Douglass's "What to the Slave Is the Fourth of July?" (1852), a would-be commemorative speech, and his novella *The Heroic Slave*, about a revolt aboard a ship. Replete with moments of highly stylized, even overwrought, speech scenes, the novella stages its protagonist Madison Washington not only as an eloquent speaker but, importantly, as one whose techniques of persuasion effect social change. In particular, this chapter traces how Douglass stylizes repetition as the sonic device of the reverb to manipulate Patrick Henry's well-known expression "Give me liberty or give me death" to legitimate midcentury black liberation movements as specifically American. Chapter 1 outlines how Douglass deploys a series of speech acts in his Fourth of July address and novella that manipulates the accepted national idioms on the right of revolution as a means to critique slavery as anathema to democracy itself.

This reading of rhetoric is pursued further in chapter 2 on William Wells Brown's novel *Clotel*. Brown's understanding of the oratorical forms of rhetoric, including addresses, debates, and speeches, depends upon recognizing how he distinguishes "rhetoric proper" from the "merely rhetorical." By "rhetoric proper," I mean to intimate a mode of oration that self-consciously and purposefully is preoccupied with persuasion while the "merely rhetorical" is meant to intimate the forms of speech or writing that make the imperative of persuasion secondary to the art of its style. Central to my larger claims about how blacks participated in the civic sphere is Brown's use of the slave Sam's seemingly rudimentary and unskillful song—not George Green's courtroom address or any of the debates among the white characters—as a model for how Brown's own novel itself assumes the form of political discourse.

Chapters 3 and 4 continue the examination of rhetoric and sound in the poetry of Frances Ellen Watkins Harper and Walt Whitman. By examining issues of prosody, these two chapters analyze how Watkins Harper and Whitman used songs and musical cadences to translate their political messages. Examining various sonic emanations—such as muted voices, song lyrics, and instrumental airs—embedded in mid-nineteenth-century African American poetry, in chapter 3 I explore how Watkins Harper and other African American poets, including James Monroe Whitfield and Joshua McCarter Simpson, exploit the musical elements of prosody as a mnemonic device to simultaneously fashion their verse as both artful poetry and political discourse. In particular, this chapter interrogates how Watkins Harper deploys a mode of writing that creates variations on the prevailing national idioms about slavery and democracy and, more critically, reveals how African American poets used the practices of code-switching.

While chapter 3 analyzes how African American poets reinterpreted or remixed the sonic impulses of popular national idioms, chapter 4 considers three different emanations of sound in Whitman's poetry. In "Black and Tan Fantasy," I outline Whitman's use of anaphora as a form of political consensus; his reference to the Yankee fife in "A Boston Ballad" as an invocation of a national anthem; and his staging of black dialect in "Ethiopia Saluting the Colors" as being outside the registers of the language of national reconstruction. Ultimately, chapter 4 contends that Whitman uses different forms of sound in *Leaves of Grass* to enunciate one's relation to the nation.

While the first half of the book focuses on aurality, the second half concentrates on the politics and processes of visuality through paintings and ekphrastic literary texts that depict art objects. The second part "Visuality and the Optical Illusions of National Belonging" begins with chapter 5, where I elucidate how the compositional logic of American genre painting strategically organized zones in terms of centers and margins in settings as different as parlors, fields, and post offices as a means to illustrate the forms of national belonging. In works by William Sidney Mount, Richard Caton Woodville, Eastman Johnson, and Winslow Homer, this chapter analyzes the depiction of written notices, furniture, and attire as political devices that materialize space as particular social domains. This chapter pays keen attention to the ways that African American subjects are literalized as shadows in many of these paintings tucked away into corners of parlors or hovering on the outskirts of social scenes of entertainment.

I extend this critique of visuality in chapter 6 by examining the arrangement of space in Melville's "Benito Cereno." Turning away from the prevailing New Historicist readings, I argue that the text's fraught depiction of art and its proper arrangement needs to be correlated to the ambiguous social position of the African slaves.[33] In Melville's story, the Spanish ship is riddled with improperly placed tools, half-finished pieces of art, rude performances, and graffiti scrawling. "Benito Cereno" is best understood, I contend, through its staging of art; the story sets the American captain Delano's desire to restore law and order against the statelessness of the slaves whose insurrection is fashioned as a veritable example of outsider art.

In chapter 7, I turn to one of the most curious stories in all of African American literature—William J. Wilson's "Afric-American Picture Gallery," which describes a museum that is curated by one "Ethiop." "Afric-American

Picture Gallery" remains important not only as a contemporaneous account of various artworks but for its depiction of "Ethiop" as the curator who arranges the space of the museum. More theoretically, I argue that Wilson's story respatializes the antebellum black public sphere by interiorizing the museum within the recesses of the reader's mind.

An underlying claim of *Specters of Democracy* is that citizenship is experienced affectively through the cultures of everyday life as much as it is produced procedurally within political systems. African American writers used aesthetics not only to produce feelings of sympathy from their readers (and possibly affiliation with them as well) but also as a necessary corrective to the diminishment of how they were "counted" in American society. *Specters of Democracy* demonstrates how African Americans participated in civic life even when they were denied conventional access to formal political realms. By considering the ways that black Americans imagined the realm of art as an entry into the public discourse of liberal democracy, I advance a reconceptualization of our understanding of African Americans and civic identity to contend that we must examine a wide range of cultural productions to understand political sensibility.[34] I argue that a meaningful understanding of the fate of democracy in the nineteenth-century United States and beyond depends upon a fuller comprehension of the relationship of blacks to citizenship.

Specters of Democracy offers analyses of certain art forms that come together underneath the sign of blackness and democracy, an approach that attempts to analyze them ontically through the quotidian registers of their political articulations in the cultures of everyday life. If *Specters of Democracy* is to have any purchase at all, it would be that we should at least read both the shadow and the act of the nation, that we cannot allow blackness to be continually maintained as the mere shadow of democracy, as an apparitional entity separate from its substance—and as the trace of democracy to come.

PART ONE

Version and Subversion

The Aurality of Democratic Rhetoric

1

Frederick Douglass's "Glib-tongue"

African American Rhetoric and the Language of National Belonging

In the climactic moment of *Narrative of the Life of Frederick Douglass, an American Slave, Written by Himself* (1845), Douglass accentuates the description of his sensational confrontation with Edward Covey by prefiguring it as an especially calibrated rhetorical expression: "You have seen how a man was made a slave; you shall see how a slave was made a man."[1] The phrase works equally for its sense of symmetrical equilibrium whereby one half balances the other and for its sense of sound whereby words are strategically echoed and reversed. Douglass was preoccupied with issues of aurality, and his use of chiasmus was only one rhetorical device through which he stylized a critique of slavery and articulated a wider program of African American civil rights. Earlier in the same chapter of the *Narrative*, Douglass uses an epigram to mark a turning point in his consciousness and status as an American slave. Recounting his being transferred to William Freeland at St. Michael's or a second time, Douglass waxes: "By this time, I began to want to live *upon free land* as well as *with Freeland*."[2]

In his own time nearly every commentator noted Douglass's use of rhetoric, and even well after the end of slavery, he was known at least as much for his speeches as for his writings. In a June 22, 1852, lecture to the Dialexian Society of New York Central College, William G. Allen, himself an African American professor of rhetoric, regarded Douglass as the most exemplary of black speakers. "He works with the power of a mighty intellect," Allen offered, "and in the vast audiences which he never fails to assemble, touches chords in the inner chambers thereof which vibrate music now sweet, now sad, now lightsome, now solemn, now startling, now grand, now majestic, now sublime."[3] James McCune Smith, in his introduction to *My Bondage and My Freedom*, extolled Douglass's facility with words, taking particular note of their logic and effectiveness: "His were not the mere words of eloquence which Kossuth speaks of, that delight the ear and then pass away. No! They were work-able, do-able words, that brought forth fruits in the revolution in Illinois, and in the passage of the franchise resolutions by the Assembly of New York."[4]

Douglass was a keen wordsmith, but our contemporary understanding of his use of language has largely concentrated on the aspects that make it an example of literature per se rather than a sound system.[5] Returning to Douglass's speeches promises to not only restore an important discursive element of his larger political project but also underscore the sonic elements of his writings that necessitate attention to the play of sound. Such a focus on the sound of Douglass's words, furthermore, promises to underline how the artistry of his language transported the ostensible meaning of his words as political discourse, as well as outline an early understanding of a black theory of rhetoric. Allen's high esteem for Douglass's speech as an oratorical art pays particular attention to the ways it sounds, likening it specifically to music with references to chords, chambers, and vibrations.

Influenced by Carla L. Peterson and Harriet Mullen, I foreground Douglass's manipulation of rhetoric and voice as an illustration of the shadow politics through which African Americans have petitioned for their own subjectivity as citizens.[6] By examining a set of speeches and the representation of speeches in *The Heroic Slave*, this chapter interrogates Douglass's understanding of black citizenship in the pre–Civil War decade, an especially fraught period marked by the passage of the Fugitive Slave Law in 1850, intense debate among African Americans themselves about emigration, and the Dred Scott decision in 1857. In the first turn, this chapter explores Douglass's manipulation of the epideictic form in his "What to the Slave Is the Fourth of July?" oration and the latent dialectical impulse of his debates with other members of the black public sphere to illustrate a crisis in the instantiation of democratic subjectivity. In the next turn, I focus on how the story that Douglass chooses to tell in *The Heroic Slave* interpellates the genealogical implications of the American Revolution with black slave revolts as simultaneously an aesthetic and political practice—what Spviak would respectively differentiate as representation's dual possibility as the re-presenting in art or philosophy and as "speaking for" in politics.

Foregrounding the speeches contained in *The Heroic Slave*, this chapter works through the deliberate and self-conscious ways that Douglass manipulates rhetoric in his attempts to stage Madison Washington as an icon of the United States to theorize how African American activists have used oratory as a mechanism to activate the processes of visualization. In examining what she calls the "performance semiotic" of speech and text, Sandra M. Gustafson has written on the cultural shifts during the early national period where the negotiated acts between relying on texts versus departing from them represented a larger shift in the meanings of power and authenticity for emerging U.S. national identities.[7] In his 1893 book on Douglass as an orator, James M. Gregory, a Howard University–trained professor of Greek and literature, noted that such departures were a necessary and important attribute of an orator's ability: "By not being confined to his manuscript, he caught the inspiration of his audience."[8] Douglass's *Heroic Slave* might be thought of as another work where Gustafson's notion of the "performance semiotic" is manifested, but I want to call specific attention to the material conditions that have, in a sense, naturalized such departures and modifications on the standard national idioms (in either text or speech) by African Americans, from the utterings of the slave songs and field shouts in the nineteenth century to the improvisational impulses of jazz and the freestyle mandates of hip-hop of the twentieth- and twenty-first centuries.

Mapping the traces of Douglass's own speeches in his novella, then, is more than merely an illustration of his self-referentiality; it reveals something more endemic and something more allegorical about the tactics that African Americans have employed to insert themselves into the precincts of the U.S. body politic. *The Heroic Slave* functions precisely because of its use of a contrapuntal sound exchange: it must be read in conjunction with Douglass's speeches and the prevailing public idiom, with his prose and the metalanguage of the nation's founding documents. Invoking Foucault, Carla L. Peterson and Shelley Fisher Fishkin argue that Douglass used rhetoric to create a counter discourse.[9] The rhetoric of 1776 assumes a materiality in the story that saturates the text and figuratively clothes the protagonist, ostensibly functioning as a metonym for the nation—an example of what Homi Bhabha calls an "apparatus of power," which is simultaneously constitutive and a by-product of the narrative acts of nationalism.[10] Douglass's consideration of the possibility of democracy during this period was intensified by his new interpretation on constitutionalism and the right of revolution, both of which depended upon his returning to the language of the American Revolution and its aftermath to articulate a new position on blacks and citizenship.

▪ SUBVERSIVE ORATION: "WHAT TO THE SLAVE IS THE FOURTH OF JULY?"

In the years before the Civil War, Douglass made frequent use of the iconography of the founding fathers and the Declaration of Independence in his call for liberty, and there is no better example of his manipulation of that iconography than his "What to the Slave Is the Fourth of July?" His popular oration dramatizes his views on how slavery reduced democracy to a mere specter of itself. Douglass was far from the only African American to use the Fourth of July to undercut slavery. While on an antislavery lecture tour in England in 1849, William Wells Brown recalled a story about the sale of a woman and her daughter on the eve of the symbolic day: "Why, in 1847, only two years since, a woman and her daughter were sold in the very capitol of America, in the very city of Washington, by the U.S. marshal, on the 3rd day of July, the day before the national anniversary of the glorious Declaration of Independence, by which all men were declared free and equal, and the produce of the sale of these immortal beings were put into the treasury of the United States."[11] Eight years later in 1857, Charles Lenox Remond would declare that the Fourth of July was a mockery, made especially insulting in the midst of the recent Dred Scott decision: "To-day there are, on the Southern plantations, between three and four millions, to whom the popular Fourth of July in the United States of America is a most palpable insult; and to every white American who has any sympathy whatever with the oppressed, the day is also a mockery."[12]

The tone of Douglass's oration underscores the difference between him and his audience as well as between the audience and its forefathers to simultaneously illustrate how blacks have been made aliens within a larger U.S. society and how his audience has been alienated from the spirits of the past. The oration alternates continually between gestures of inclusion in the national family and those of extrication from it.[13] Douglass's opening words lay the foundation for the oration's oscillating gestures. He speaks of "your National Independence," "your political freedom," and "your nation" with such rapidity as to render ironic, by nearly divorcing, the introductory curtsey from the body of the oration, as if to present, however momentarily, what the nation should look or, rather, sound like against the presentation that follows of a bifurcated society (110). He amplifies the difference between the condition of those like him who were nominally free and those who were citizens proper by attributing this chasm to a betrayal of revolutionary principles: "I say it with a sad sense of the disparity between us. I am not included within the pale of this glorious anniversary! Your high independence only reveals the immeasurable distance between us" (116). Ironically, his very position at the lectern did in a sense include him "within the pale of [the] glorious anniversary," but he would not be placated with his personal deliverance while the masses of black Americans remained shackled.

In one of the oration's most stylistically sophisticated moments, Douglass displays a command of antithesis and irony: "This Fourth [of] July is *yours*, not *mine*. You may rejoice, I must mourn. To drag a man in fetters into the grand illuminated temple of liberty, and call upon him to join you in joyous anthems, were inhuman mockery and sacrilegious irony. Do you mean, citizens, to mock me, by asking me to speak to-day?" (117). On the one hand, he is meant to act as a representative emblem of the nation commemorating its birth. His occasional queries to the audience, then, are plaintive gestures that feign dialogue; they function precisely as rhetorical questions whose subsumed answer forecloses dialogue to illuminate the fact that the majority of blacks have been foreclosed from the realm of citizenship.

Douglass's inversion of popular political expressions from the national idiom became a signature strategy in developing his orations as a particular polyphonic discourse system through which he critiqued slavery and inequality with multiple voices. As an extension of Mikhail Bakhtin's notion of "heteroglossia," I use the term "polyphonic discourse system" to signal a field of utterances that supplement, amplify, or challenge the primary voice or voices of a text including seemingly random noises, spaced silences, echoes, music, and other sounds that, while not always legible, must nevertheless be absorbed and deciphered.[14] In this sense when Douglass references the British Tea Act of 1773 as a way to subvert the institution of slavery—"You can bare your bosom to the storm of British artillery, to throw off a threepenny tax on tea; and yet wring the last hard-earned farthing from the grasp of the black laborers of your country" he surely wants the idiomatic expression about a three-penny tax, if not the song "Revolutionary Tea" (n.d.), to echo in the minds of his original audience members and, later, the subsequent readers of his pamphlet (126). If this idiom is meant to reverberate in the chambers of the mind and the canals of the ear, the conspicuously absented statement that Douglass refuses to vocalize, the tacit sentiment that has to remain implicit, is that African Americans may indeed soon attempt to throw off the shackles of their oppression and revolt against their own tyrannous masters. Douglass's own voice abates here, halting on the precipice of a more rebellious suggestion.

Whereas the reference to the three-penny tax is generically idiomatic, Douglass also makes reference to Thomas Jefferson's specific language in developing the polyphonic structure of "What to the Slave Is the Fourth of July?" When Douglass mentions that slavery "'is worse than ages of that which your fathers rose in rebellion to oppose,'" he activates an important feature of the reverb mechanism that is central to the political critique of his oration. Jefferson first writes the words in a 1786 letter to Jean Nicholas Démeunier where he speaks of man as an "incomprehensible machine."[15] Douglass himself initially cites the Jefferson lines himself in a letter to Horace Greeley of April 15, 1846, invoking "the graphic language of the immortal Jefferson" in his effort to condemn slavery.[16] When Douglass cites and recites Jefferson, he pairs the earlier Jefferson of the Declaration of Independence with a later Jefferson of 1786. In referencing Jefferson, Douglass slightly alters his words and thus presents an echo, rather than a strict reiteration, of Jefferson's language in the context of a Fugitive Slave Law United States.[17]

As much as Douglass exploits the iconography of the revolutionary history of the United States, he also exploits examples from literature to ornamentalize his rhetoric as a mode of political critique. Predictably, Douglass quotes from both Henry Wadsworth Longfellow and John Greenleaf Whittier, two of the country's most famous and staunchly antislavery poets. Additionally, Douglass concludes the oration with a poem from his former mentor and colleague William Lloyd Garrison. While both Whittier's "Stanzas for the Times" (1835) and Garrison's "Triumph of Freedom" (1845) are explicitly antislavery in theme, such could hardly be said of Longfellow's "Psalm of Life" (1839). Douglass excises a stanza from Longfellow's poem about not living in the past and applies the lines to his antislavery message. He also quotes from Shakespeare's *Julius Caesar* (1599) and *Macbeth* (1623).

Discursively, while Douglass quotes *Macbeth* to reiterate his sentiment that the founding fathers had betrayed their principles, he strategically quotes *Julius Caesar* to change the very tone and message of his oration. The quote—"The evil that men do, lives after them, / The good is oft' interred with their bones"— acts as a volta that marks a turn in Douglass's tenor. He reaches a turning point in the oration, one where he abandons the platitudes and curtseys of the opening and turns to directly confront his audience in the main body of his delivery.

The Shakespeare references, like the Longfellow allusion, embellish Douglass's oration; that is, he recasts these references such that they act to adorn his words. These are moments when Douglass's own words, independent of their particular innate artistry, are ornamentalized.

While the discursive maneuvers of fashioning a soundscape were central to the artistic practices of his larger political project, his reference to Psalm 137 is as much an example of sampling as it is a metacritical commentary on the relationship between art and national identity. As William L. Andrews reminds us, Douglass gained his first public speaking experience in the North for black congregations and this experience inflected Douglass's tenor.[18] Comparing African Americans to displaced Jews, Douglass uses the psalm to plaintively inquire why he has been asked to sing the praises of the nation:

> "By the rivers of Babylon, there we sat down. Yea! we wept when we remembered Zion. We hanged our harps upon the willows in the midst thereof. For there, they that carried us away captive, required a song of us; and they who wasted us required of us mirth, saying, Sing us one of the songs of Zion. How can we sing the Lord's song in a strange land? If I forget thee, O Jerusalem, let my right hand forget her cunning. If I do not remember thee, let my tongue cleave to the roof of my mouth." (116)

By force of the analogy, Douglass's comparison suggests that free African Americans themselves are in a strange land; their asymmetrical political subjectivity produces a condition whereby they are made estranged from the land they inhabit, a condition that Douglass elsewhere states has made African Americans "aliens."[19]

But the functionality of Douglass's Psalm 137 reference depends less upon what is quoted than what is not, less upon what is heard than what is evoked, and it is precisely in this fabricated lacuna where he manipulates sound and aurality to telegraph a radical political critique that is more readily associated with the likes of David Walker, Henry Highland Garnet, and Charles Lenox Remond. In many respects, Douglass's particular selection from Psalm 137 gave his audience exactly what they expected to hear: that African Americans had indeed been made strangers in the United States. Had Douglass continued beyond line 6 and quoted the entire verse, his message would have been substantially different and his Corinthian Hall audience would have surely been disturbed. The last three lines of Psalm 137 have a violent tone and sentiment that speak of revenge. Like his use of the three-penny tax reference, Douglass used the biblical quote to bring his audience ever closer to a more rebellious position. But whereas the three-penny tax reference depends upon an understanding of the analogy's logic, Douglass manipulates aurality with his use of Psalm 137 to have its more defiant message intimated in the auditory chambers of his (well-versed) audience members rather than directly and explicitly with his own tongue. It is a message that is rendered, ironically, at the very moment that Douglass purses his own lips.

Douglass's use of Psalm 137 in "What to the Slave Is the Fourth of July?" is also a reminder of his complicated understanding of music and song as forms of political sensibility. In establishing the soundscape of his oration, he underscores the contrast between the sound of freedom and the sound of oppression. Earlier, Douglass invokes the archetype of the Yankee fife to note that on this day of anniversary "the ear-piercing fife and the stirring drum" will unite with "church bells" in symphony as the "nation's jubilee" (114). Immediately following the Psalm 137 reference, Douglass says that he cannot but hear the "mournful wail of millions! whose chains, heavy and grievous yesterday, are, to-day, rendered more intolerable by the jubilee shouts that reach them" (116). Here, the contrast between the sounds of these "mournful wails" set against "jubilee shouts" seems not only ironic and perverse on this day but dissonant.

Douglass's invocation of the sorrow songs was a common practice among African American abolitionists. Sara G. Stanley, in her "What, to the Toiling Millions There, Is This Boasted Liberty?" (1856), for example, deployed a similar language. Addressed to the Ohio legislature petitioning suffrage for black men, Stanley described slavery as producing only cacophony:

> Briery mountain, sparkling river, glassy lake, give back the echoes, soft and clear as if the melody was borrowed from the harps of angels. But strange incongruity! As the song of Freedom verberates and reverberates through the northern hills, and the lingering symphony quivers on the still air and then sinks away into silence, a low deep wail, heavy with anguish and despair rises from the southern plains, and the clank of chains on human limbs mingles with the mournful cadence.[20]

Likewise, Douglass had similarly written about these "mournful wails" and sorrow songs before. In his *Narrative*, Douglass writes that these songs "would do more to impress some minds with the horrible character of slavery, than the reading of whole volumes of philosophy on the subject could do."[21] Confessing that he was scarcely able to understand them himself, Douglass presents a form of political critique that depends less upon the purchase of rational discourse per se than the sensational affect of sentimentalism.[22] It is precisely their sensational affect, less so than their legibility, that instantiates their effectivity as political devices. Douglass presents an Aristotelian understanding of the sorrow songs whose latent properties as a rhetorical formation is undergirded by their sensory modalities.

Whereas Douglass manipulates the latent epideictic impulse of "What to the Slave Is the Fourth of July?" to craft his sense of irony, he was also equally adept at using humor in his speeches.[23] A little more than a month after his Corinthian Hall oration, Douglass took the stage at the Free Democratic Party in Pittsburgh, Pennsylvania, where Liberty Party men, Liberty Leaguers, and Free Soilers met to nominate candidates for the upcoming presidential contest. While Douglass's "What to the Slave Is the Fourth of July?" was prepared, his Pittsburgh speech was extemporaneous. He extended some of the themes of his earlier oration, including his critique of the Fugitive Slave Law. "The only way to make the Fugitive Slave law a dead letter," Douglass exclaimed, "is to make half a dozen or more dead kidnappers."[24] A few moments later Douglass followed with a line that the law "had the support of the Lords, and the Coxes, the Tyngs, the Sharps and the flats."[25] Both comments were met with applause and laughter. But Douglass's Pittsburgh speech remains significant not simply as an illustration of his use of humor or his dialogic interaction with his audience but, importantly, for his remixing of the founding father phrase. Extending his critique of the Fugitive Slave Law, Douglass continued: "It has been said that our fathers entered into a covenant for this slave-catching. Who were your daddies?"[26] Stylistically, Douglass's question pushes his language into the colloquial, and it is precisely this rhetorical tonality that the purchase of his speech functions as political persuasion. In moments such as the 1852 Pittsburgh event, where Douglass departs from the austere sensibility typical of many of his other deliveries, his language becomes an example of what Harriet Mullen calls a "runaway tongue."[27]

■ THE "DARK INTENT" OF SPECIOUS WORDS

If the early speeches of Douglass were influenced by his reading *The Columbian Orator* (1787) and by his being near the presence of black preachers as some have argued, the 1850s saw his speech cadences increasingly shaped by the contours of debate.[28] Among these debates, those with his African American counterparts were especially important because they illustrate a range of political thought and demarcate the lines of the black public sphere in the antebellum North. The public debate among members of the black public sphere informed not only Douglass's political ideology but also his style as a wordsmith.

One of Douglass's first formal debates was with Samuel Ringgold Ward on whether the Constitution was pro-slavery or antislavery. When the two met to debate in 1849, Douglass had become increasingly self-conscious that his early career with the Massachusetts Anti-Slavery Society had already delimited his voice too much—both his message and his intonation, his content and his style.[29] Ward was an important figure in the black public sphere who at different times acted as an agent for the *Weekly Advocate* and the *Colored American*, a lecturer with the New York State Anti-Slavery Society, and spokesman for the Liberty Party after 1844.[30] He was also a formidable orator.[31]

These debates, like the convention movement, were important spaces where African Americans tested the efficacy of their positions and developed political programs for uplifting the race by engaging a Platonic understanding of the dialectic.[32] The debating platform was one arena where African Americans met as equals to debate commonly held opinions on issues like suffrage, taxes, education, and emigration, among other topics. Thomas Van Rensselaer, editor of *Ram's Horn*, George T. Downing, Thomas Paul Smith, Henry Highland Garnet, William C. Nell, and William J. Wilson were among the African Americans who gathered in the Minerva Rooms to attend the Ward-Douglass debate. Still publicly maintaining a Garrisonian perspective, Douglass held the position that the Constitution was a pro-slavery document and frequently called for the dissolution of the Union on the grounds that dissolution was necessary to withhold economic support from the peculiar institution. Ward, by contrast, cited Article 1, Sections 9 and 10; Article 4, Section 2; and the First, Fourth, Fifth, and Eighth Amendments as examples of the Constitution's antislavery character. Furthermore, Ward placed the Fifth Amendment's due process clause next to the opening lines of the Declaration of Independence. He declared that "the sentiments of these men when writing that document" were insignificant and insisted that the nation should "go by what is written."[33]

If Ward's position was not altogether unusual, neither was Douglass's particular response that included opinions that the framers intended the Constitution to support slavery. But, importantly, Douglass's response likened the Constitution to a kind of "speakerly text," one where spectral voices were seemingly mandating directives. Referring to the Three-fifths Compromise, Douglass maintained that "every slaveholder was virtually told by that Constitution, virtually instructed by it, to add as many to his stock as possible, for the more slaves he possessed he would not only have more wealth but more political power."[34] Like Ward, Douglass read from select passages to support his position, but rather than quote directly from the Constitution he read instead from the James Madison papers concerning the 1787 constitutional convention and in so doing essentially resurrected voices of the past to overdub the language of the present reading of the Constitution.

After the debate with Ward, Douglass began to slowly diminish his association with the Garrisonians and increasingly moved toward Gerrit Smith and others who believed that the Constitution was an antislavery document eventually leading to Douglass venerating the document in his Fourth of July oration. This was an important moment in his reevaluation of the relationship of African Americans to democratic ideals and the realpolitik of governmentality. By adopting this viewpoint, Douglass essentially became a strict constructionist. In reversing his earlier position, Douglass worked against the grain of two of the most prominent members of the black public sphere: William Wells Brown and Frances Ellen Watkins Harper. In his speech before the Paris Peace Congress in 1849, Brown proclaimed he had "no Constitution, and no country."[35] Ten years later, writing for the *National Anti-Slavery Standard*, Watkins Harper lamented that she had "never [seen] so clearly the nature and intent of the Constitution before" because of the how the fugitive clause veiled its "dark intent" under specious words.[36]

The strategy of "What to the Slave Is the Fourth of July?" was to intertwine African American emancipation with the preservation of democracy for the nation—an interconnection that is disclosed when one considers Douglass's position on constitutionalism. He must appeal for the abolition of slavery by stating that the institution is anathema to the nation's idealized principles of the Declaration of Independence and the plain mandates of the Constitution. Douglass did condemn the Fugitive Slave Law, but he could not attack the entire legal infrastructure of the nation outlined in the Constitution. He knew that his final recourse for the abolition of slavery must be mandated by laws that would ultimately be guaranteed by the Constitution and, therefore, could not risk merely positioning the Declaration of Independence and the Constitution as antipodal. What Douglass is striving for here is a veritable harmonic accord in his oration that attempts to approximate—or, even more strategically, function as a proxy for—acts of political consensus. He therefore characterizes the use of the Constitution to support slavery as a betrayal of "the illustrious Fathers of this Republic": "But I differ from those who charge this baseness on the framers of the Constitution of the United States. *It is slander upon their memory*, at least, so I believe. . . . In *that* instrument I hold there is neither warrant, license, nor sanction of the hateful thing; but, interpreted, as it *ought* to be interpreted, the Constitution is a GLORIOUS LIBERTY DOCUMENT" (127).

Douglass rehabilitates the Constitution, essentially positioning it as equally "a GLORIOUS LIBERTY DOCUMENT" as the Declaration of Independence, by suggesting that its misapplication to the maintenance of slavery is an issue of hermeneutics. Slavery as an institution, he contends, can find no legal support if the document is understood "as it *ought* to be interpreted." Elsewhere, he argued, "Slavery has taught us to read history backwards, sitting at the feet of Calhoun and Taney."[37] His hermeneutic positioning of the meaning of the Constitution preserves the sanctity and authority of the governing document of the nation and shields the myth of the founding fathers. Since he fully knew that many of the founding fathers themselves owned slaves, his statement that it is "slander upon their memory" to suggest that the architects of the Constitution provided language to protect slavery is wryly furtive.

No moment better illuminates Douglass's view of the Constitution in the 1850s than his debates with Charles Lenox Remond, a staunch Garrisonian who became somewhat of a rival of Douglass and strongly advocated the dissolution of the Union. In one of his earliest speeches on the dissolution of the Union, Remond argued that it was necessary to come to terms with "the present practical workings of the American Constitution."[38] Over the course of two days in May 1857, against the backdrop of the recent Supreme Court decision in *Dred Scott v. Sanford*, Remond and Douglass held court at the Shiloh Presbyterian Church in New York City. As Ward had done earlier, Douglass now insisted upon the necessity of adhering to "the plain meaning of the language" of the Constitution: "Read, then, the preamble to the Constitution of the United States. Note how it starts: 'We the people of the United States'—not we the horses—not we the white people, but 'we the people, in order to form a more perfect union, establish justice, *** and secure the blessings of liberty to'—not the white people, but 'ourselves and our posterity, do ordain,' &c."[39] Douglass used a variation of this passage and other elements from the debate to craft a pamphlet that he later published. Importantly, the debate illustrates the necessity of both speech and print for antebellum free blacks.[40] To level his critique against Remond and the Garrisonians, Douglass had to condemn the appearance of the apparitional, in the sense that the apparitional is construed as the evidence of things not seen: "The word slave, or slaveholder, is not in the Constitution.... They tell us, though, that the framers of the Constitution had a subtle and occult meaning under their plain words. The people did not adopt occult, undercurrent meanings. They adopted the plain reading with its obvious intentions."[41] Here, Douglass militates against the "subtle" and the "occult" as things that haunt the United States and prevent the Constitution from being properly understood and democratic practices from being properly performed.

As significant as the debates between Ward, Douglass, and Remond were to African American critiques of constitutionalism, they also prompted a consideration regarding the stylistics of oratory and its efficacy as a mode of political critique. William J. Wilson, who would become an important contributor to *Frederick Douglass' Paper* and the *Anglo-African Magazine*, recorded his thoughts on the Ward-Douglass debate and published them later under the title "A Leaf from My Scrap Book" in Julia Griffiths's 1854 edition of *Autographs for Freedom*. In Wilson's estimation, Douglass's speech was too ornate, overwrought even, and its very ornamentation threatened to obfuscate the central core of his message. According to Wilson, Douglass often spoke "with copiousness of language, and finish of diction," where, even when his "ideas fail, words come to his aid—arranging themselves, as it were, so completely, that they not only captivate, but often deceive us for ideas."[42] Ward, on the other hand, was "concise without abruptness—without extraordinary stress, always clear and forcible; if sparing of ornament, never inelegant."[43] The chief distinction between Ward and Douglass for Wilson was that while Ward's appeals were directed to "understanding," Douglass's were directed to "imagination," by which Wilson means the sensational over the cognitive, appeal over logic.

Wilson's assessment of the Ward-Douglass debate reveals an important instance of how cognizant mid-nineteenth-century African Americans were of the contemporaneous discussions about oratory as a form of art. Wilson himself repeatedly assesses the Ward-Douglass speeches not in terms of their messages or discourse per se but rather as art. More specifically with respect to a theory of art, Wilson underscores the connection between orality and visuality. "Douglass' imagery is fine—vivid—often gaudily painted," he contends, whereas "Ward's picture [is] bold, strong, glowing."[44] Wilson's commentary also deploys a vocabulary that features terms like "picturesque" and "sublime" that were increasingly being associated specifically with visual artifacts.[45]

These debates were also important because they were moments when Douglass could move away from his script and speak extemporaneously, especially when challenged by a member of the audience. In these instances,

Douglass would often take an expression or question that was leveled at him and turn it on its head. Such was the case with Douglass's "Men and Brothers" speech. In the context of growing hostility toward the abolitionist movement in New York, Douglass and other Garrisonians met at the Broadway Tabernacle on May 7, 1850. There, Douglass was continually challenged by Isaiah Rynders, a gang leader in the Five Points and Tammany Hall boss who supported slavery and was antagonistic to abolitionists. Rynders repeatedly interrupts Douglass with exhortations about amalgamation, the law, and the population of blacks in the United States. But at every turn Douglass takes Rynders's words and inverts their meaning. At one point, when Rynders exclaims to Douglass, "*You* are not a black man; you are only half a nigger," Douglass responds with wit, replying, "He is correct; I am, indeed, only half a negro, half-brother to Mr. Rynders."[46] While Rynders's unruly comments were not altogether unanticipated, the *New York Herald* reported that he was adamant that should Douglass speak "disrespectfully of the South, or Washington or Patrick Henry, or of the President, then he would knock him down" himself.[47] If Rynders tracked Douglass's later speeches, he would soon learn that far from speaking disrespectfully of Patrick Henry, Douglass would continue to extol him, especially through his comparisons of Madison Washington to Henry, an analogy that itself was yet another example of Douglass's "glib-tongue."

■   TONGUES UNTIED

Rynders had good reason to fear that Douglass might take the words, if not the iconography, of national figures and contort them. By the time that Rynders confronted him at the Broadway Tabernacle in 1850, Douglass was famous on and notorious outside the abolitionist lecture circuit for his performances where he imitated pro-slavery preachers in addition to John C. Calhoun, Henry Clay, and Daniel Webster. One performance that Douglass frequently staged was the debate between Calhoun, Clay, and Webster concerning the fate of the slaves who had rebelled on the *Creole* and sailed to Nassau. As the *National Era* reported:

> Douglass put them all upon the stage before us.... There in that charmed atmosphere the magician reared the National Capitol, opened the Senate Chamber, and represented to a miracle the men we had thought were without model or a shadow. It was even terrible to our sympathies, so deeply enlisted, to witness the daring of that unlettered slave, attempting the personification of Clay, Calhoun, and Webster, in action, thought, and utterance. Gracefully athletic in his flow of thought as Clay in his happiest mood, when he presented him arguing the right of restitution—terribly concentrative as Calhoun in vindicating the international obligation, and ponderously logical as Webster in expounding the doctrine of the demand. His astounding power of transformation, his perfect clearness of discrimination, and his redundant ability in the execution, more than justified the audacity of the design. To see one man with all the varied capacity of all these three, mixing them up, without confusion or mistake,

in the puppet show of his imagination, and playing upon them at his pleasure, was verily a sight to see. But better burlesque of the American Eagle, with the Secretary's missive tucked under his wing, pouncing down upon the British Lion, and screaming in his ears "not those words of mortal terror to the tyrant beast—all men are free and created equal—so ruefully remembered; not dreadful battle cry—Free Trade and Sailor's Rights—to start his recent wounds afresh; but—but—I want my niggers!" That capped the climax.[48]

These kinds of speeches were important for their dramatic effect and for how Douglass, in the words of Andrews, began to "stage-manage his voice and adopt personae."[49] As the reviewer of the *National Era* notes, Douglass could perfectly embody the three personalities, "mixing them up, without confusion or mistake." But the review also intimates the sense of Douglass's use of alterity. The word "shadow" has a dual register here; at once alluding to Clay, Calhoun, and Webster but also signaling Douglass's own alterity. The performance was also an important part of the oral archive on Madison Washington and the *Creole* affair that prefigured Douglass's publishing *The Heroic Slave* in 1853.

As noted by much of its criticism, Douglass adapted a good deal of what was known about the Creole affair to craft *The Heroic Slave*. His story was an expanded version of the account he had often given on the lecture circuit shortly after the publication of his *Narrative*. His speeches should be thought of as shaping part of the oral archive of the transatlantic discourse on Washington. Although "Slavery, the Slumbering Volcano" perhaps contained his longest treatment on Washington in a speech, it is notable that many of his references to Washington were made while he toured the United Kingdom (e.g., in Cork and Paisley, Ireland; Edinburgh, Scotland; and London, England). Important, too, was the discourse among blacks themselves—slave and free alike—which must have passed stories of Washington below the radar on the circuits of the "lower frequencies," to borrow a concept from Ralph Ellison.[50] It is necessary to recall these voices because, even though they cannot be documented, they formed a vernacular format in the oral archive on the meanings of freedom and liberation that Douglass withholds from the words of his protagonist.

The story Douglass chooses to tell in the novella interpellates the genealogical implications of the American Revolution with black slave revolts as simultaneously an aesthetic and political practice. *The Heroic Slave* reverberates with compounded voices—speeches, dialogues, soliloquies, authorial interjections—that form the constellation of discourse underlining Douglass's wish to historicize black Americans. This more nuanced reading of the text allows us to better comprehend the author's use of speech and oratory as interventions into nationalist historiographies.

However what seems equally important to note here are the strategies that Douglass uses in *The Heroic Slave* to counteract the more commonplace representations of black Americans that threatened to reduce them to static abstractions. Douglass prefigures Washington as a prototype of the ideal democratic body fashioned in classical Greek and Roman proportions with his physical stature, his command of rhetoric, and his sense of justice. It is almost as if Washington emerges out of Douglass's head fully formed and, importantly, without the reader having to be witness to any previous scene of violence, any scene of subjection, whereby we are witness to the scarred or mutilated black body as we are in his first narrative with the horrifically graphic Aunt Hester scene.[51] In Douglass's novella, there are no moments where Washington is forced to kneel or remain supplicant, only those that accentuate his stature as being tall, upright, and stately. Douglass summarily describes Washington as being "black, but comely"; transposing one of the most well-known lines from Song of Solomon about Sheba to his portrayal of a nineteenth-century African American.

If Douglass depicted Washington's image in a manner to exemplify the idealized black body, he also underscored the tenor and sound of an idealized (African) American speech. In an insightful reading of Douglass's "aesthetics of freedom," John Stauffer has argued that Douglass conceptualized "true" art as the "accurate and 'authentic' representations of blacks, rather than caricatures such as blackface minstrelsy."[52] But Douglass also departed from attempts at strict realism, eschewing the mandates of accuracy and authenticity. Another way to consider Douglass's aesthetics, then, is not as a preoccupation with the accurate or the authentic but with the inventive, the imaginative, and the fantastic. In this respect, Douglass uses hyperbole in stylizing Washington's speeches to symbolically counteract the myriad ways that blacks had been scripted as the negative sign of U.S. democratic fulfillment.

Of the noticeable inventions that further identify *The Heroic Slave* as fiction and art, perhaps the most problematic is the fleeting portrait of Washington's wife. Jenny Franchot has argued that Douglass's novella, like his autobiographies, suppresses the presence of the feminine, even while he remained committed to women's rights in constructing his representation of political agency.[53] If little is known about Washington's life before the *Creole* affair, even less is known about his wife, whom Douglass names Susan. The *Liberator* resuscitated her presence in its June 1842 edition by speculating that she had been among the captured slaves aboard the *Creole*.[54] Brown and Child, both contemporaries of Douglass, furnished fuller character sketches of Susan, in an apparent appeal to the popular literary genre of sentimentalism.[55] Both Brown and Child have the couple reunited, but in Douglass's novella she is killed. She is more a ghost in the machine, "daguerreotyped" in the memory of Washington much as he lingers in Listwell's recollection.[56]

There seems to be a kind of inverse relationship between the functionality of the daguerreotype for Susan and Madison Washington. Douglass attaches the daguerreotype to Susan to prefigure her death (textual or otherwise), as an approximation of the early use of the daguerreotype for death portraits. With Washington, however, Douglass uses the daguerreotype as an example of the transubstantiation of the flesh and body. The only instance of Susan's voice is recalled as an auditory hallucination—dramatically, through Madison himself, as he recounts to Listwell his life after the initial flight to Canada: "At times I could almost hear her voice, saying, 'O Madison! Madison! will you then leave me here? can you leave me here to die? No! no! you will come! you will come!' I was wretched" (154).

It is revealing that, while the *Liberator*, Brown, and Lydia Maria Child all sensationalized the plot of a reunited family—so fundamental to the ends of sentimental discourse and exploited by abolitionists and (primarily) white Christian feminists—Douglass essentially reduces the presence of the wife to accentuate Washington's heroism. Why did Douglass not develop her as a character, not animate her in the realm of fiction as she was seemingly obscured in the realm of fact? The removal of the black female presence does more than simply locate the insurrection explicitly as a masculinist enterprise, as an example of coalition politics between blacks and whites, no less.[57] In a story that frequently departs from or extends the so-called historical archive, Douglass reimagines the birth of a (male) nation and its constituent (white) founding fathers (elsewhere in the Bahamas). If Washington is figured as a black founding father, then the text needs to be thought of as a site of emanation, as a repository that other writers would avail themselves of in works that could not be easily divorced from the politics and projects of national history.

Washington's association with the founding fathers depends primarily on his adoption of accepted registers of language already identified with them. As Russ Castronovo and Dana D. Nelson point out, Douglass fashions Washington to exceed rather than simply repeat "the example of his patriotic namesakes who withheld dignity and legal rights from a people they associated with a perpetual servitude."[58] Rather than being a strict example of what Mullen calls "resistant orality" what we get here with this Douglass is something closer to a "persistent orality." Replete with the exaggerated tonality of revolutionary rhetoric, Douglass describes him as having been instilled with the founding fathers' language and, as the character Tom Grant later puts it, their souls.[59] In her work on antebellum projects of resistance, Maggie Sale argues that Douglass's turn to that rhetoric redefined it by using the "language that was shared with those... [he was] trying to persuade" and allowed him to "enter into a discourse used by dominant groups and reinscribe it with a different meaning."[60] But in the 1850s he also appropriates the principles of the American Revolution to recontextualize various kinds of slave revolts from Gabriel Prosser to his own.

Unlike the classic slave narratives, which more faithfully adhered to the form of the testimonial, the written expression of an essentially verbal disclosure, the raison d'être of *The Heroic Slave*, necessitates the recognition of the discourse of 1776 as constitutively part of the public domain and therefore available to insurgent black slaves. But the novella is more than a post facto grafting of an accepted discourse onto the unsanctioned actions of black male dissidents. It suggests that the same intellectual matrix that safeguarded the institution could also provide the key to unlock the chains of slavery. Like others, Douglass would come to rely on the cultural and political discrepancies between the Declaration of Independence and the Constitution to advocate for the abolition of slavery, but his advocacy had to yield to a fundamental assumption of classic liberalism that the political apparatus should be rehabilitated rather than destroyed. *The Heroic Slave* implies that the master's house need not be dismantled, only renovated.

Although Douglass characterizes Washington as distinctly American, Washington also comes to represent the embodiment of Enlightenment ideals, something more ethereal and less contained by the boundaries of the nation. Douglass resurrects the memory of Madison Washington, the leader of a successful slave mutiny in 1841, endowing him with the cultural lineage of James Madison and George Washington. As in the classic slave narrative, which often included a preface by a reputable white person to authenticate its veracity, the qualities of Washington's patriotism are endorsed at the end of the novella by Tom Grant, the white first mate of the *Creole*: "I confess, gentlemen, I felt myself in the presence of a superior man; one who, had he been a white man, I would have followed willingly and gladly in any honorable enterprise. Our difference of color was the only ground for difference of action. It was not that his principles were wrong in the abstract; for they are the principles of 1776" (176). Through Grant's admission, Douglass is able to recontextualize Washington's campaign as something akin to that of his famous (white) namesakes. The revision of the story casts Washington as a founding father of black liberation movements and simultaneously imbricates his enterprise within accepted popular national mythologies. In the late 1840s, Douglass would return to the image of Washington as an idealized patriot. But if democratic ideals were fast spreading across the globe in the late eighteenth and early nineteenth centuries, what was intrinsically American, or even national, about Washington's crusade for liberation? How can Douglass situate Washington as both a paragon of the state and a guiding star in a global constellation of revolutionary movements?

To endow his protagonist with a readily identifiable American essence, Douglass opens his novella by recalling Virginia, the fountainhead of many early statesmen. He insinuates that Washington is of exceptional stock and perhaps also uses the commonplace assumption of the equation between birthplace and citizenship. Washington is born in Old Dominion, a state that could claim to exemplify the nation as well as any other. The narrator places Washington in the pantheon of revolutionary heroes: "Let those account for it who can, but there stands the fact, that a man who loved liberty as well as did Patrick Henry,—who deserved it as much as Thomas Jefferson,—and who fought for it with a valor as high, an arm as strong, and against odds as great, as he who led all the armies of the American colonies through the great war for freedom and in-dependence, lives now only in the chattel records of his native State" (132). The first soliloquy that Listwell overhears, in which Washington declares, "*Liberty* I will have, or die in the attempt to gain it," clearly echoes Patrick Henry's famous statement before the Virginia Assembly in March 1775.[61] But the real specter in this passage is not Henry or any of the founding fathers who are ubiquitously staged at the forefront of Douglass's imagination but rather Nat Turner, leader of the Southampton rebellion, who lingers in the dark recesses captured within the shadow lines of the novella. Harriet Jacobs, in her 1861 narrative, invokes both Patrick Henry to authorize her own attempts at securing freedom as well as Nat Turner to express her bewilderment at white Americans who were surprised about instances of black insurrection.[62]

Because Washington spends so much time in discourse, it becomes difficult to separate the character from a mouthpiece for Douglass.[63] There is a dialogic interface in *The Heroic Slave* as he imagines, writes, and edits what Washington only verbalizes. Douglass exaggerates Washington's oratorical acumen with embellishments that often approximate hyperbole. Later, at the end of the novella, Tom Grant will admit that Washington's language aided his bid for freedom: "His words were well chosen, and his pronunciation equal to that of any schoolmaster. It was a mystery to us *where* he got his knowledge of language; but as little was said to him, none of us knew the extent of his intelligence and ability till it was too late" (160). Washington gains control over his own physicality, over the *Creole*, and over the rhetorical devices that will allow him to place himself in the national narrative.

The novella intimates that it is no less Washington's rhetoric than his use of that rhetoric as a vehicle to espouse democratic ideals that makes Washington essentially American. Although the narrator will speak of Washington's strength, perseverance, and fortitude, none of these qualities are displayed; in fact, they have to be concealed to make him more palatable to his reading audience. One of the moments in the text where the reader gains evidence that *The Heroic Slave* is an exercise in liberation through literacy for both author and protagonist occurs in the closing lines of Washington's first soliloquy: "If I am caught, I shall only be a slave. If I am shot, I shall only lose a life which is a burden and a curse. If I get clear, (as something tells me I shall,) liberty, the inalienable birthright of every man, precious and priceless, will be mine. My resolution is fixed. *I shall be free*" (134). The phrasing is as noteworthy for its sounds as it is visually for the images it uses. There is a disjunction between speech and its written representation. How can Washington have a parenthetical clause in a verbal soliloquy? The natural rhythms of speech are interrupted by the intrusion of the narrator and author, who are sometimes one and the same, sometimes discrete and autonomous. There are a number of other moments where a character's speech is interrupted by such a parenthetical intrusion. It is as if the author is inserting himself into the protagonist, as if Douglass is attempting to make himself Washington. Later in the story, in the midst of blood from the revolt, Washington takes pleasure in debating with one of the white sailors about the illegitimacy of slavery and the right of revolution in a moment that illustrates what Castronovo and Nelson have called the predicament of a "cross patriotism" that limits the charge of democracy by circumscribing it to the boundaries (and discourses) of the nation.[64]

One of the ironies, or tragedies, of *The Heroic Slave* is that while Douglass wants to demand freedom for African American slaves, the protagonist can find refuge only in another country. This irony makes the work an eerie prefigura- tionof James Baldwin's notion of "another country." Yet for Douglass to appeal to his audience, he must privilege 1776 and the Declaration of Independence as constitutive elements of a specific U.S. nationalism. He therefore uses Tom Grant and Washington to position the events aboard the *Creole* as similar to those that inspired the American Revolution. Despite Grant's earlier admission that Washington and company were motivated by the principles of 1776, Washington, while laying no less a claim to the national narrative, is more conscious that the cultural apparatus that shapes the narrative is usually regulated by those in pos- session of political authority: "God is my witness that LIBERTY, not *malice*, is the motive for this night's work. I have done no more to those dead men yonder than they would have done to me in like circumstances. We have struck for our free- dom, and if a true man's heart be in you, you will honor us for the deed. We have done that which you applaud your fathers for doing, and if we are murderers, *so were they*" (161). But Douglass well knew that the underlying impulses of both 1776 and the Declaration of Independence were global. Earlier in his Fourth of July speech, he admitted that while he drew "encouragement from the Declaration of Independence," his spirit was also "cheered by the obvious tendencies of the age" (128). Hence, one of the tasks of *The Heroic Slave* is to make manifest and ubiquitous what the Declaration states to be self-evident. Philosophically, he may feel that all people are born equal or that they all possess the same right to "life, liberty, and the pursuit of happiness," but he recognizes that such ontological presuppositions must be politically guaranteed.

Notwithstanding his frequent appeals to the Declaration of Independence throughout *The Heroic Slave*, ultimately Douglass is not convinced of its proper implementation in the United States and must instead depend on the laws of another nation. The closing scene of part 4, in which Grant details the events aboard the *Creole* when the ship lands at Nassau, illustrates that one's rights must be legally inscribed by a nation. At the marine coffeehouse in Richmond, Grant informs a company of sailors that after a storm on the high seas, Washington leaned toward him and stated, "Mr. mate, you cannot write the bloody laws of slavery on those restless billows. The ocean, if not the land, is free" (162–63). The debate about state law versus natural law is articulated in a conversation between Grant and Jack Williams. Williams maintains that the events aboard the *Creole* were the result of mismanagement by the white crew. Grant's retort discloses the violent apparatuses that support the institution of slavery: "It is quite easy to talk of flogging niggers here on land, where you have the sympathy of the commu- nity, and the whole physical force of the government, State and national, at your command....It is one thing to manage a company of slaves on a Virginia planta- tion, and quite another thing to quell an insurrection on the lonely billows of the Atlantic, where every breeze speaks of courage and liberty" (161).There is almost a sense here that Douglass is signifying on his own Chesapeake Bay apostrophe from his 1845 *Narrative*. Every breeze of the Atlantic may have spoken of "courage and liberty," but the ocean turns out to be no more free than the Virginian soil, since the freedom of Washington and his company is not secured until they are within the pale of the British Empire.

Douglass depicts Tom Grant in such a manner as to recall the earlier conversion of Listwell. Whereas Listwell was captivated by Washington's rhetorical eloquence, Grant is captivated by Washington's display of physical restraint. The different forms of conversion that Douglass presents for the story's white characters hinge on the issue of pathos—Listwell sympathizes for Washington, while Grant is forced to recognize Washington by writ of the analogy of an accepted discourse.[65] Indeed, when the reader is introduced to Listwell, it is clear that Douglass wants to suggest that his heart and emotions are touched as much as his mind and rationality when he hears Washington in the woods: "The speech of Madison rung through the chambers of his soul, and vibrated through his entire frame" (135). P. Gabrielle Foreman reads this moment as an erotically fraternal version of what she calls "sentimental abolitionism." But with the word "chambers," the passage also recalls William G. Allen's assessment of effective rhetoric as being that which "touches chords in the inner chambers thereof" and, in this sense, all effective rhetoric could be said to have an affective dimensionality subsumed within its sensory properties.[66] If this is a scene can be identified as an instance of sentimental abolitionism, it is one that depends upon the registers and metaphor of music to make such a politics legible. Whereas Listwell pledged to remain true to the abolitionist crusade, Grant promises to abandon the business of slavery. Through Listwell, Douglass is able to envisage an idealized, converted white American who acts on his moral beliefs irrespective of legal codes.

Douglass does not imbue Grant with a similar sense of moral indignation concerning slavery; instead, Grant is persuaded by Washington's overwhelming physical presence. Throughout *The Heroic Slave* the size and strength of the protagonist are detailed but rarely exposed in action, as though to figure a violent black masculinity only to contain it by man's higher, more cerebral nature.[67] Despite Washington's physical presence, Douglass mitigates the violence aboard the *Creole* by refusing to describe it. Instead, he underscores Washington's benevolence. Grant's conversion is less a result of Washington's sympathy than a result of Washington's oratorical skill: "I felt little disposition to reply to this impudent speech. By heaven, it disarmed me. The fellow loomed up before me. I forgot his blackness in the dignity of his manner, and the eloquence of his speech. It seemed as if the souls of both the great dead (whose names he bore) had entered him" (161). Although Grant submits that he "forgot" Washington's blackness, the black man's speaking ability did not convince him of racial equality, as it did Listwell. Once again Douglass emphasizes the power of speech. Grant confesses that Washington's words "disarmed" him. Although conceded in a figurative sense, the disarming here parallels the earlier physical disarming of the crew. They are held captive by Washington physically and orally—equally. In Virginia, Grant subsequently announces to the men seated about him, "I dare say *here* what many men *feel*, but *dare not speak*, that this whole slave-trading business is a disgrace and scandal to Old Virginia" (159). Douglass's maneuver at this moment is subtle. Instead of having the narrator or even Washington condemn Virginia's participation in slavery, Douglass uses the recently converted Grant for such a statement.

Both Grant and Williams contest the legacy of Virginia. Astonished that the insurrection succeeded, Williams is equally concerned that the reputation of Virginian sailors will be tarnished: "For my part I feel ashamed to have the idea go *abroad*, that a ship load of slaves can't be safely taken from Richmond to New Orleans. I should like, merely to redeem the character of Virginia sailors, to take charge of a ship load on 'em to-morrow" (158; emphasis added). His frustration reveals how his disappointment regarding the disruption of the dominant racial hierarchy and his allegiance to Virginia are utterly enmeshed, and it reveals how one's regional affinities can supersede one's national affiliation. The tête-à-tête between Grant and Williams exposes more than two men vying to identify the true character of Virginia. That Listwell is a resident of Ohio—one of the free states—presumably accounts for his swift conversion, but, with Grant, Douglass offers the conversion of a man who not only had roots in the gateway to the South but was fully entangled in the business of slavery. With Grant's disavowal of slavery, Douglass implies that had the founding fathers atoned for their sin of owning slaves, they could have reemerged as rehabilitated Tom Grants. Imperfect and belated as his conversion is, Grant arrives as the son to redeem the fathers.

If Grant is furnished to redeem the founding fathers, that redemption occurs in the text only when the black body acts as a forfeiture that reifies the boundaries of the United States as a site of white hegemony. Although increasingly characterized as an American, from his adoption of certain speech cadences to being recognized (in the sense that Frantz Fanon later theorizes recognition) by Listwell and Grant, Washington ultimately is displaced from the United States. This displacement is as much textual as it is actual. Although he never assumes the position of narrator in *The Heroic Slave*, the number of lines dedicated to his words is markedly reduced in part 4. Instead, the concluding part features the conversation between Grant and Williams. Though his articulations in and of themselves are resonant, Washington speaks only four times here, and his voice is heard through and by the mouth of Grant. The effect created in this last section is the removal of the black physical presence from the United States. Only Grant and Williams are left, preoccupied with the project of narrating national history.

2 Merely Rhetorical

Virtual Democracy in
William Wells Brown's Clotel

> It is from this area between mimicry and mockery, where the reforming, civilizing mission is threatened by the displacing gaze of its disciplinary double, that my instances of colonial imitation come. What they all share is a discursive process by which the excess or slippage produced by the *ambivalence* of mimicry (almost the same, *but not quite*) does not merely "rupture" the discourse but becomes transformed into an uncertainty which fixes the colonial subject as a "partial" presence. By "partial" I mean both "incomplete" and "virtual."[1]
>
> HOMI BHABHA

In a compelling scene of the *Narrative of the Life and Escape of William Wells Brown* appended to his novel *Clotel; or The President's Daughter* (1853), William Wells Brown recounts the moment when he learns to read and write. Using a stick of barley sugar as payment, Brown convinces two other young boys to give him reading lessons. Sometime after learning to read, Brown acquires the ability to write. The scene outlines how Brown was able to ingeniously procure nearly three weeks of tutoring from the boys. It also clearly echoes a similar moment in Frederick Douglass's 1845 *Narrative* in which he describes procuring reading lessons from a few local boys after his sessions with Mrs. Auld are abruptly discontinued. For Douglass, this moment is formative because it leads him to *The Columbian Orator* (1797) and Arthur O'Connor's speeches on Catholic emancipation, among others.[2] The scene becomes central to Douglass's "formal" education as an orator on the antislavery lecture circuit.

Whereas the tutorial scene in Douglass's *Narrative* intimates the allure of rhetoric as an art and political form, the analogous moment in Brown's narrative signals a particular preoccupation with visual culture. After scribbling a few indecipherable characters, Brown learns to write by copying the script of other young boys whom he had surreptitiously persuaded to record his name:

> "Now, what do you call that?" said the boy, looking at my flourishes. I said, "Is not that *William Wells Brown*?" "Give me the chalk," says he, and he wrote out in large letters "*William Wells Brown*," and I marked up the fence for nearly a quarter of a mile, trying to copy, till I got so that I could write my name. Then I went on with my chalking, and, in fact, all board fences within half a mile of where I lived were marked over with some kind of figures I had made, in trying to learn how to write.[3]

37

With its evident focus on his name, this passage is clearly meant to mark the advent of Brown as a nominative self, one that has been transformed from an object into a subject through the virtues of education, a constitutive transformation that Robert B. Stepto has argued is fundamental to much of African American literature.[4]

But it also seems equally important to note that it is precisely fences upon which Brown scribbles his name, pieces that, taken together, might approximate a form of outsider art displayed in the public domain. If this scene is emblematic of what Stepto has called liberation through literacy, it is one that is engendered by a graffiti aesthetic, an aesthetic that progresses from being indecipherable— and, hence, more of a hieroglyphic or (un)stylized objet d'art—to one that can be perceptibly appreciated and translated through a semantic logos correlated to its proper visual notation. Considering Brown's demarcated name as an example of a graffiti aesthetic not only refers to the varying silhouettes that his name assumes in pictorial form but also, and more generically, confers upon it intrinsic value as art. The writing on the wall, as it were, might be conceptualized as outsider art not only because Brown received little formal training but because the phrase encapsulates his own status as being outside the precincts of the body politic.[5] I invoke the term here to signal both Brown's nascent engagement with aesthetic practices and the play with otherness, a key trope in outsider art. Brown is desperately attempting to vitiate his own otherness by establishing himself as a subject proper through the continuous reinscription of the letters of his name that reiterate the text of his personhood for nearly a quarter of a mile. While the question of aesthetics and politics remains relatively symbolic in this scene of *Narrative of the Life and Escape of William Wells Brown* it is addressed with even greater force throughout *Clotel*.

Replete with different visual artifacts and various modes of oratory, underlined by the overwrought nature of the novel itself, *Clotel* calls attention to its very constructedness.[6] A number of critics have noted the novel's disjointed format that makes it difficult to read as a story and to comprehend narratologically.[7] By contrast, M. Giulia Fabi and John Ernest have noted that the patchwork assembly of Brown's book was intentional and strategic.[8] Similarly, in identifying what he calls Brown's " 'excessive' aesthetic practice," Robert Reid-Pharr argues that Brown's literary technique was "proof of the complex and contradictory nature of the practice of American republicanism."[9] Rather than take *Clotel* as a novel per se, it might be more efficacious to consider how Brown uses pastiche and, especially, bricolage to reformat the novel as an objet d'art through which he accentuates different modes of political discourse.[10] In this light, Brown's incorporation of a diverse range of things, utilizing illustrations, poetry, historical records, newspaper articles, and political manifestos, underscores *Clotel* as an example of bricolage.

In an important recent essay, Deak Nabers uses *Clotel* to consider the meanings of the right of revolution on the eve of the Civil War, writing that it might be "better to register the multidirectional nature of the American Revolution, which secured both the rights slavery comprised *and* the rights slavery implied."[11] Rather than see the split between the principle and practice of the Declaration as a hermeneutical problematic, as Brown, Douglass, and other abolitionists contended, Nabers argues that this problematic is inherent to the Declaration's claim for both self-government and natural rights. While Nabers's salient analysis renders a number of acute readings, his discussion focuses on *Clotel* as a theoretical exploration of natural rights and revolution, that is best illuminated through Peck's debate with Carlton and Georgiana's understanding of the Bible's relationship to slavery and freedom. There is little discussion of Clotel and George and none of Sam; hence, notwithstanding the role of the author himself, the narrative presents these debates as primarily the preoccupation of the novel's white characters. In a sense Nabers's analysis of *Clotel* reiterates certain presuppositions about forms of deliberative democracy that fetishize rational debate and argumentative forums as the basis or model for an operable civic polity.

However, if we turn to the other *other* characters in the story—those who occupy the field of Ernesto Laclau's "constitutive outside"—then different iterations of democratic possibilities emerge on the U.S. political horizon.[12] These characters prefigure the reconstituted or extended form of deliberative democracy that Iris Marion Young calls "communicative democracy" where greeting, rhetoric, and storytelling are as necessary to political discussion as argumentative debate.[13] Young proposes some revisions to deliberative democracy by expanding the field of what constitutes communication, by which I understand her to mean both the places and forums of those discussions as well as various kinds of communication itself. In *Clotel*, this expanded field of communication includes Georgiana's personal talks with Carlton in the intimate private sphere and Sam's song performed in the slave quarters. Insofar as Brown models different kinds of political discussion in the story and the book itself constitutes a variation of Young's category of storytelling, *Clotel* needs to be thought of as a mid-nineteenth century African-American theorization of democracy.

Brown makes use of multiple forms of rhetoric to stage political discussions regarding black subjectivity and democracy in the United States. By examining the various modes of rhetoric in the text, from formal speeches to seemingly mundane songs, this chapter outlines an African American engagement with the Declaration of Independence and Patrick Henry's maxim to contest the institution of chattel slavery. More critically, by tracing how Brown characterizes slavery as a constitutional and not simply a social threat to the philosophical ideals of the American Enlightenment, this chapter outlines the discursive itineraries of black political thought that deployed the right of revolution rhetoric to contest the despotic underpinnings of the antebellum United States that many African Americans understood prevented the country from emerging as a true democracy.

■ **WORDS WITHOUT MASTERS**

Brown's story recounts the various trials and tribulations of Clotel and Althesa, the daughters of Thomas Jefferson and his former slave Currer, from their early introduction at a "Negro ball" to their untimely deaths. In developing the story of Clotel and Althesa, a host of other characters are introduced, including George Green, another "mulatto" and illegitimate son of a U.S. congressman; Sam, a caricature who ostensibly mimics his master, John Peck, at every turn; Picquilo, a black African who leads a slave revolt; and Georgiana Peck and her suitor Miles Carlton, who liberate their slaves. A number of historical figures are invoked, including Voltaire, Jean-Jacques Rousseau, Thomas Paine, John C. Calhoun, Nat Turner, and Thomas Jefferson.

Throughout *Clotel*, Brown rearranges historical events and chronology to theorize chattel slavery as endemic to the birth of the nation. In so doing, he allegorizes the mid-nineteenth-century national crisis of the peculiar institution as a crisis in the formation and interpretation of democracy in the United States. The novel illustrates how the presence of blacks shaped the very terms and limits of how liberal democracy was conceptualized and materialized in the antebellum United States and also how they engaged political discourse itself.

Brown's selection of Jefferson as the father of Clotel and Althesa was, of course, far from coincidental. As many critics of *Clotel* and scholars of Jefferson have noted, the suspicion that the third president had fathered children with one of his slaves had long been rumored, perhaps disseminated with greater authority and credibility among African Americans.[14] As Fabi has written, Brown exploited the symbolism of the "white slave" for his abolitionist audiences.[15] Beyond the sensationalist affect, Brown specifically needs the Declaration of Independence through, and against, which he can underscore chattel slavery as the fault line between discourses of liberal democracy and egalitarian subjectivities. Jefferson is the figure who most profoundly emerges as the ghost of democracy in *Clotel*. Jefferson is everywhere and yet nowhere in the novel. He does not appear as a character per se but rather as an apparition, as a presence that circulates throughout the text and haunts the story of the novel. To speak of Jefferson, then, more so than of the other historical figures of the novel, notwithstanding Nat Turner, is to come to terms with the practices that Brown deploys to vocalize the fictions of democracy.[16]

Brown uses the invocation of Jefferson to expose the lines of descent that intertwine the histories of liberal democracy with the histories of racial formation in the United States as a concomitant genealogy of the nation.[17] Mentioned at least a half dozen times, Jefferson's presence in *Clotel*, for the most part, is intrinsically yoked to the text of the Declaration of Independence. Brown's maneuver here prevents Jefferson from emerging as a fully embodied character and instead restricts him to the domain of the discursive by force of metonymy and synecdoche.

In chapters 17 and 18, Brown employs aspects of Jefferson's writings to fore-shadow a new national ideal by using the black body to demarcate a contrast between despotic privileges and democratic liberties. Nearly half of the shorter of these two chapters is composed of quotes from Jefferson, and Brown selects some of the most important ideas articulated in *Notes on the State of Virginia* (1781), including the line that the "whole commerce between master and slave is a per-petual exercise of the most boisterous passions; the most unremitting despotism on the one part, and degrading submission on the other."[18] Later in the same pas-sage, Jefferson acknowledges that slaves have rights, but that these rights are con-tinually abrogated and superseded by citizens who participate in the enterprise of slavery. One of the dangers, to Jefferson's mind, is that slavery corrupts and transforms the idea of sovereignty from being a calibrated authority over one's self into an excessive dominion over others, converting the citizen into a des-pot and, by consequence, compromising democratic potentialities. The slave, for her or his part, forsakes adopting a love of country and, with no accompanying sense of affiliation, is reduced to being merely a beast of no nation. Like the epi-graph to Melville's short story "The Bell-Tower" (1855), Brown closes chapter 17 by paraphrasing Jefferson's ruminations and a commonly held view that "slaves might some day attempt to gain their liberties by a revolution."[19]

What is remarkable about Brown's use of Jefferson as a means to contemplate the future of American democracy is that, rather than the slave, it is the master who undertakes the acts of aggression and retaliation. The first half of the chapter recounts the cruelties which the young Mary suffers at the hands of her new mis-tress, Gertude Green, the woman whom her father, Horatio Green, has married after abandoning Clotel. Gertude is particularly incensed with the "white slave girl" who reminds her of her husband's transgressions not of matrimonial laws but of the social logic of a binary racial code. Hence, she seeks to punish both husband and child by making the daughter a servant. Mary is a vestige of what Shirley Samuels has called a "miscegenated America," and Gertude is determined that the proper course of action is a readjustment of the racial logic of a split social order.[20]

In a scene comparable to Douglass's account of how slavery turned his kind mistress cruel, Gertude is described as having succumbed to base and "fiendish designs" (150). Mary is first put to work in the kitchen and then the garden "with-out either bonnet or handkerchief," and it is clear that Brown insinuates that Gertude has been overtaken by an "unremitting despotism" (158–59). Gertude determines that Horatio's violations must be punished by making his child darker and, therefore, seeks to reinforce the boundaries of racial formation against her own ocular observations that Mary looks "white" and over the codified laws that have already marked and designated the child as "black." It is not enough for Gertude to make the child a slave; she must reify Mary's blackness because black-ness is the sign in the novel of that which cannot be assimilated or incorporated. Slavery, then, induces a seductive irrationality that Brown associates with the forms of despotism, vis-à-vis his incorporation of Jefferson and his later depiction of the "true democrat" Henry Morton's diatribe against regimes, that challenges the nation's claim to a democratic sovereignty.

Framing the following chapter with the most well-known lines from the Declaration of Independence, Brown implies that the antidote to this kind of irrationality and despotism is the abolition of slavery not only to free blacks from the institution but to emancipate the nation from being held its hostage as well. By introducing chapter 18 with Jefferson's assertions concerning inalienable rights, Brown correlates the slavery crisis of the 1850s with the birth of the nation as a contemporaneous predicament regarding the development of liberalism in the United States—and the keenest indication of a democratic state turned on the idea of "liberty," which, for Brown, meant both emancipation and the full slate of rights.

Although blacks have some rights on John Peck's Poplar Farm, the fact that they are not emancipated allows Brown to deride this freedom as false and mere theory. Peck, a native of Connecticut, has long been transplanted in Natchez, Mississippi, where, among his other slaves, Currer works in the kitchen. Like Harriet Beecher Stowe's New Englander Miss Ophelia, who makes a trip down South, Brown presents Miles Carlton on a visit to his classmate Peck's plantation in Mississippi. Opposed to the notions of natural rights espoused by his schoolmate friend from the North, Peck reconditioned as a Southerner is the embodiment of a benevolent patriarch who had "early resolved that his 'people,' as he called his slaves, should be well fed and not overworked, and therefore laid down the law and gospel to the overseer as well as the slaves" (92). As William Edward Farrison notes, Brown has Peck repeat a speech that he himself had heard at the 1846 Liberty Party meeting in Rochester.[21] In Peck's imagination, the limits of constitutional affiliation are demarcated by the borders of the plantation, and once a subject tries to reconstitute his relationship with these prescribed conditions by trying to secure more rights, as with "poor Harry," he must be removed from the precincts of the plantation or eradicated altogether.

Peck's early comments on the proper management of plantations and estates quickly dissolve into an abstract debate about inalienable rights where the issue of slaves and slavery is neglected until his daughter Georgiana reinserts them into the discussion. Described as spending "too many hours over the writings of Rousseau, Voltaire, and Thomas Paine," Carlton confesses that he can see " 'no difference between white men and black men as it regards liberty' " (94, 93). By having Carlton prompt Peck to consider the Declaration and "the constitution of our own Connecticut," Brown vitiates the national authority of the federal Constitution as a text that safeguards slavery and, essentially, qualifies the concept of liberty as a problem of juridical hermeneutics rather than a self-evidentiary and self-sustaining natural right (93). Peck, for his part, maintains that the Bible is older than the Declaration and, as a governing text, that it should furnish the proper definition of liberty.

While the conversations between Peck and Carlton are staged to approximate a logical debate on the question of slavery, liberty, and rights, Peck's leisure activity as a poet reveals art's extralateral function as political discourse. Peck's poem is noteworthy because, along with Sam's song, it is the most self-evident practice of art by a character in the story and should be thought of as a metacritical commentary on art and politics. After agreeing that Carlton should visit the Jones plantation, Peck gives Carlton a poem that he has written for his sister. Entitled "My Little Nig," it is intended as a domestic piece, one that Carlton's sister can place in her album. In it, Peck offers an unduly infantilizing portrait of a young enslaved boy described in caricature as glossy dark and lazy.

> I haven't said a single word concerning my plantation,
> Though a prettier, I guess, cannot be found within the nation;
> When he gets a little bigger, I'll take and to him show it,
> And then I'll say, "My little nig, now just prepare to go it!"
> I'll put a hoe into his hand—he'll soon know what it means,
> And every day for dinner, he shall have bacon and greens. (129)

As a poem, Peck's versification is negligible, displaying little discernible meter or rhythm and obeying little of the standard poetic conventions of the day. As a work of art, the poem lacks the formal features that would readily characterize it as having artistic value, as something that is appealing if not beautiful.

Peck's intention to forward "My Little Nig" to Carlton's sister signals how the circulation of poetry could travel as political discourse. Peck presents the poem almost as a rejoinder to Carlton's comments about the sale of slaves for medical testing, about which he has read in a newspaper advertisement. Dismayed, Carlton announces that he may have to place more faith in the "hard stories" about slavery he has heard in New York from abolitionists (128). In the most immediate sense, Peck's poem is apparently meant to represent an ostensibly Southern viewpoint, another example of the competing regional perspectives between the two men. But in a more conceptual sense, the appearance of the poem compels a reconsideration of genre and how meaning is conveyed and translated through specific forms. On the one hand, the poem is expected to be consumed precisely as a "domestic piece," as an adornment or curio that is moved from one home to another. On the other hand, the poem recalls the other written pieces Peck has published in the *Natchez Free Trader* and other periodicals. Rather than consider the seeming differences between Peck's writings for the public sphere or private sphere, it seems equally necessary to ask what kind of topics can be transmitted under the code of poetry; what kind of messages can be translated through the properties of poetry; and what kind of things are better received when delivered through the aegis of a poetry self-consciously stylized specifically as art. Here, the discourse of infantilization, so central to the tenets that legitimized slavery as an institution of benevolent paternalism, is ensconced in the rhyme sequence whose lyrical aurality attenuates, if not belies, the apparent meaning of the poem as a different kind of social text.

If Peck's Poplar Farm is revealed as a space that invokes the language of the family to support a form of autocratic governmentality, stylized as the kindness of benevolent paternalism, then the sublimated language of the family in the earlier "Negro ball" scene is invoked to illustrate how the racialized and sexualized bodies of "mulattas" are at the center of the procedural transactions that allow liberalism to emerge as a particular set of social practices. Brown opens *Clotel* with a curious scene that complicates the idea of an American democratic topography. Situated between the author's own commentary on marriage and the institution of slavery and the auction block episode is a brief description of a "Negro ball":

> To bring up Clotel and Althesa to attract attention, and especially at balls and parties, was the great aim of Currer. Although the term "Negro ball" is applied to most of these gatherings, yet a majority of the attendants are often white. Nearly all the Negro parties in the cities and towns of the Southern States are made up of quadroon and mulatto girls, and white men. These are democratic gatherings, where gentlemen, shopkeepers, and their clerks, all appear upon terms of perfect equality. (64)

Currer's own impulse to see her children Clotel and Althesa suitably maintained divulges the latent sexual and racial economies of slavery. Yet it is these very economies that delineate the limits of an American democratic topography. Brown ironizes the space of these social gatherings by altogether circumventing the uneven gender hierarchies in a space where women are wholly conceived of as being thoroughly available to male suitors. His romantic portrayal of the "Negro ball," ironically, depends upon a veiling of the ball's racialized infrastructure in order to accentuate it as an environment where men and women meet, more or less, as equals.

But, more important, this portrayal of the "Negro ball" discloses how these spaces exploited the racial and gender classifications of national belonging to construct a place where a variation of participatory democracy could be formed and exercised. Brown's description of the "Negro ball" as a "democratic gathering" is indeed meant to be ironic, and this irony depends upon an inversion. If participatory democracy is a form of governance whereby all members of a political group make meaningful contributions to the decision-making process, this is one where the status of their being a political group emerges not from the necessity of public policy but rather from desire. The female body here—suspended between its discursive definition of being merely a "black body" and its sensory conception of being (at least) an approximation of whiteness—becomes a site itself where the male participants of such events are engendered as social equivalents. "Negro balls," which literalized a kind of commodity fetishism by a conversion of all-but-white bodies through the political designation of being black a priori, were governed by the imperatives of a heterosexism that fashioned these places as contingent "democratic gatherings" where white men were allowed to coalesce as a particular constituency. It is precisely here where white men of sufficient capital—from gentlemen down to clerks—are recognized "upon terms of perfect equality."

If Brown's story ironizes the "Negro ball" as a nominal democratic space, one that can only be guaranteed when mulatta women become the device that instantiates the equivalency of white men as a homosocial constituency, then the promise of mulatta women themselves gaining more rights and liberties through such "coupling conventions" or "conjugal unions" is equally fraught.[22] Even someone like Henry Morton, who proclaims the ills of slavery, fails to act in private—a failure that leads to the later reenslavement of his wife, Althesa, and their daughters. In so doing, Brown underscores how constitutional law supersedes common law, the textual over the implicit. Morton, a native of Vermont, decides to open his medical practice in New Orleans, where he sees Althesa and decides to purchase and then marry her.

His progression from being "the man of honour" in chapter 9 to the embodiment of "a true democrat" in chapter 20 passes through the white(ned) body of Althesa and therefore acts as another illustration of Brown's correlation between whiteness and democracy (116, 182). When Morton first sees her in the home of the Crawfords, he can scarcely believe that Althesa is a slave. Morton's rescue of Althesa is initially based upon the premise that "a beautiful young white girl of fifteen" should not be in the "degraded position of a chattel slave" (116). This reasoning is continued later in chapter 14, "A Free Woman Reduced to Slavery," where another white woman is sold into slavery. In this chapter, Althesa, the "virtual" white woman, helps "de genewine artekil," Salome Miller, who is "white" by appearance no less than by U.S. law (70).[23] The anomaly of white slaves, however, is expanded in the story as Morton increasingly objects to the institution as a whole.[24] Although he does not publicly call for the abolition of slavery, Morton frequently denounces the "peculiar institution" in private circles.

It is difficult to determine what precisely, beyond his marriage to Althesa, identifies Morton as "a true democrat" until one compares his language with that of the other foregrounded exponents of democratic discourse in the text: John Peck, Miles Carlton, and George Green. While at a party, Morton decries the hypocrisy of American democracy while slavery still exists in the nation, contending that the "'the native slave [is] stripped of every right which God and nature gave him, and which the high spirit of our revolution declared inalienable'" (183–84). Brown crafts Morton as "a true democrat" because he exposes the United States as being ruled by a despotic impulse that precludes the development of democracy, a proclivity of which slavery was the most severe symptom—"'But who are the despots? The rulers of the country—the sovereign people! Not merely the slaveholder who cracks the lash. He is but the instrument in the hands of despotism. That despotism is the government of the Slave States, and the United States, consisting of all its rulers—all the free citizens'" (184). Morton's logic inverts the categories of the story's earlier democrat John Peck. Peck's rationale presupposes black "citizenship" without democracy within the domain of the Poplar Farm; Morton's details a form of white citizenship without democracy within the borders of the United States.

■ "FROM THE MERE THEORY OF LIBERTY TO PRACTICAL FREEDOM"

In *Clotel*, Brown deploys a constellation of terms—including "emancipation," "liberation," and "revolution"—to translate their centrality to the nation's claims as a democratic state. Throughout the book, Brown differentiates these terms to preserve them as part of the lexicon of the national narrative. Of these forms of freedom, insurrection is the most dangerous. In the story, acts of insubordination that cannot be contextualized or sanctioned through the prescribed templates of the national narrative are deemed insurrections. Brown illustrates various attempts at independence with different degrees of viability, but the story of Nat Turner's Rebellion is used as an allegory to warn the reader of the dangers of evading a program of emancipation.

If Jefferson is the principal ghost in the machine of the novel, then Turner is the figure that most haunts the story. Brown's reading audience would have been readily familiar with the general outline of Nat Turner's Rebellion of 1831, its most sensationalist aspect perhaps being that whites had been killed during the uprising. The account of the Turner uprising is featured in the closing section of the novel, but it is the culmination of a series of descriptions about acts of insubordination. One of these includes a story that the plantation preacher Hontz Snyder shares with Carlton about a slave who rebelled and escaped to the woods before meeting his eventual death. Another is recounted by Georgiana, who describes her father's participation in a slave-hunting expedition to retrieve one of his slaves who, after being punished for visiting his wife, fled into the woods. Turner is described as having escaped to the swamps to prepare for the rebellion. These anecdotes are important because they extend a thread in the novel about the hidden alcoves of the woods and swamps as counterpublics—as spaces that furnish an alternative mode of affiliation for black subjectivity and, more critically, as locations that are the antinomies of a nominal public sphere.

More than simply an account of wanton violence, the allegory of Nat Turner's Rebellion is meant to serve as an example of that which cannot be contained within the spatial precincts of the nation or subsequently legitimized by a sanctioned discourse. In the novel, Turner is situated between Picquilo and George Green, two other (legally) black male figures. Like Turner, Picquilo is a "full-blooded Negro," but, unlike Turner, he was born in Africa, and his appearance ostensibly bears the marks of his native land: "His dress, his character, his manners, his mode of fighting, were all in keeping with the early training he had received in the land of his birth" (213–14). Picquilo is crafted as George's foil, but, in so doing, Brown ensures that Picquilo cannot be recovered as an American national. George, who participated in the revolt, exploits the discourse about the founding fathers that could serve as his "authenticating document."[25]

If George himself cannot lay claim to the national identity of being American, he certainly suggests that his actions were, and this disjunction is one of the markers that identifies his status as a "virtual American." I mean "virtual" in the sense that Bhabha uses the term in the epigraph that opens this chapter, one whose position as an avatar, facsimile, or duplicate ruptures the sanctity of a putative normative discourse and renders it violable and transformable. But George is also important for how he signals the diminishing of democratic energy that Dana D. Nelson calls "virtualization," a process whereby "constitutional order promises to eradicate the stresses of heterogeneity by distancing people from its 'dangerous' expression."[26] Following her critique of the ways in which federal democratic order abstracts the face-to-face negotiations of party politics, we might prefigure the stakes of George's demand that he be recognized as a member of the story's imagined civic polity, an emergent and contingent political subjectivity that is instantiated by his being nothing less than face-to-face with his would-be counterparts and one where he, as an example of Laclau's "constitutive outside," challenges the managerial impulses of the state which circumscribe and constitute a subset of the larger body politic specifically as "the people."

With Picquilo, however, there is no such effort to translate his actions, no attempt to prefigure him as an American, real or facsimile. The chapter titled "The Arrest" intimates that slavery transmogrified Turner, a preacher who was adored by blacks and whites alike, and disallowed him from becoming an American, compelling him therefore to fall in league with the African-born Picquilo. Turner's assault signals a split in the subjectivity of the U.S. black, more fully illuminated by the nomenclature of the term "African American" as a dialectic whereby Turner's actions ostensibly made him more African than American. Brown's rejection of insurrectionary dissent as a model for gaining freedom, however, recapitulates the racial presuppositions that undergird U.S. democracy, if not national identity altogether.

In contrast to the boundlessness and, indeed, statelessness of the insurrectionary dissent of Nat Turner's Rebellion, Brown offers Georgiana Peck and George Green as two characters who use oratory to articulate different antidotes to U.S. slavery. Georgiana is the well-heeled amalgam of the two positions between her father, Peck, and her suitor, Carlton, who wants to use Christianity as a democratizing vehicle that guarantees the fundamental aspects of the Declaration: "She gave it as her opinion, that the Bible was both the bulwark of Christianity and of liberty" (95). Tellingly, she is the one character other than George who participates in the freeing of slaves—but she does so not under the aegis of being political per se but rather from a sense of religious obligation.

Georgiana, who in some respects is a counterpart to George and whose very names echo each other, is described much like the other women in a book that oscillates between the literary conventions of sentimentalism and the literature of black (male) insurrection. Her death, which immediately arrives on the heels of her manumitting her slaves, is necessitated by the conventions of sentimentalism, not by her explicit engagement with formal politics. And her refusal to send her former slaves to Liberia—to follow the train of thought formulated in "the speeches of Henry Clay, and other distinguished Colonization Society men" as well as Stowe's bleak outlook in *Uncle Tom's Cabin*—allows Brown to present Ohio as an idealized space where political liberation and Christian salvation are equivalents (91). The problem, Brown intimates, is that the inebriating discourse of rights only compels Peck to adopt a variation of feudal orderliness and resigns Carlton to a position of stoic indifference.

Chapter 18 depicts Georgiana and Carlton pondering what to do with their slaves after her father has died and she and Carlton have married. As if to illuminate the necessity of liberties to a democracy, Brown prefigures the emancipation of slaves with Georgiana's own acquisition of rights. While it is clearly a secondary concern to the primary plot of liberating black slaves in the novel, Brown presents Georgiana's own liberation from patriarchal authority as a precursor to the necessity of contravening other normative social conventions. After the death of her father, Georgiana receives control of the estate, but "both law and public opinion" prevent her from emancipating her slaves in any manner "that she might think of adopting" (161). Notwithstanding her relatively young age of eighteen, the dominant social conventions of gender presupposed that one paterfamilias be replaced by another, and Georgiana is made aware that one of her Northern uncles is available "to come down and aid in settling up the estate" (161). But it is decided that there is only one proper way to emancipate the slaves, and this course involves Carlton. But why Carlton? Throughout the novel, Brown describes the North as an idealized space—Peck and Carlton are from Connecticut, Georgiana is educated above the Mason-Dixon Line, and Henry Morton is a native of Vermont—and the uncle would, therefore, seem to be a likely candidate to support Georgiana's inclinations. Georgiana's declaration of her willingness to marry Carlton is depicted as an instance of women's rights, but Brown ensures that these rights are used in tandem, as a proxy, to the cause of emancipating slaves.

The reference to women's rights in the chapter titled "The Liberator" is used to introduce a more sustained discussion between Georgiana and Carlton about the relationship of blacks to the nation. Carlton proposes that they be sent to Liberia, suggesting that the newly emancipated blacks would be better situated "in their native land," but Georgiana immediately disapproves: "'Is not this their native land? What right have we, more than the Negro, to the soil here, or to style ourselves native Americans? Indeed it is as much their home as ours, and I have sometimes thought it was more theirs. The Negro has cleared up the lands, built towns, and enriched the soil with his blood and tears; and in return, he is to be sent to a country of which he knows nothing'" (163). Georgiana notes other contributions of blacks during the American Revolution and the War of 1812, and it is evident that Brown is suggesting that blacks have always conceptualized themselves through the lens of the nation. And, though far from being citizens, they continually exhibit "the *amor patriae*" Jefferson believed to be absent among slaves. The primary underpinning of this passage is fairly commonplace in anti-slavery rhetoric, and Brown will later return to this impulse in his compendium *The Black Man* (1864). The most unanticipated—and, indeed, the most radical—declaration within Georgiana's speech, however, is her critique of the modes of national belonging that too often understood whites and "native Americans" to be convertible terms.

By having Georgiana and Carlton liberate their slaves, Brown develops them as models for what slaveholding Americans should do. Informing Carlton that "liberty" has always been their "watchword," she continues with a line of rhetoric about the ills of slavery in a style that is both grandiose and hyperbolic (164). Her language here needs to be read for its form no less than for its content. Similar to Madison Washington's soliloquy in *The Heroic Slave* that serves as the catalyst for Listwell's conversion, the cadence, pattern, and delivery of Georgiana's words are all stylized as rhetoric as if she were holding the floor before an assembly. Brown fashions Georgiana as an interlocutor through whom he intends to sway the public opinion of his reading audience. Significantly, it is at this point in the novel that Brown's conceptualization of liberation is increasingly differentiated.

Although often similarly invoked, the term "liberation" is contextually associated in the novel as either "emancipation" or "revolution," and, importantly, the term signals the larger crisis of how to legitimate and naturalize blacks into the body politic. In *Clotel*, emancipation is gradual and procedural; revolution is abrupt and unmanageable. Georgiana and Carlton may have wanted to emancipate their slaves immediately, but they decide upon a program of gradual manumission whereby the slaves would, in essence, earn their freedom: "They were also given to understand that the money earned by them would be placed to their credit; and when it amounted to a certain sum, they should be free" (165). But given the previous examples of black military service, which clearly were meant to intimate that slaves in the past had already earned the freedom of blacks in the present, why would Brown make Georgiana and Carlton subject their slaves to paying for themselves, after years of service? Such a system of gradual emancipation would ostensibly be necessary to afford the slaves sufficient time to prepare for freedom. Taken as a whole, Brown's depiction of a conditional liberation, one that is progressively administered, complicates his understanding of the very idea of an intrinsic freedom tied to a belief in natural rights.

While Georgiana and Carlton favor an immediate emancipation based upon universal rights, Brown needs to circumscribe their desire so that he can portray a mode of social organization based on democratic impulses rather than benevolent paternalism. Under Peck's control, the Poplar Farm is described as a relatively benign plantation, complete with an overseer, preacher, and slaves, whom Peck affectionately calls his "people." The foremost sign of their degraded position, however, is not physical abuse but rather their indoctrination, their being forced to accept their lot as part of a natural order sanctioned by Christianity. One of the central tenets of Georgiana's program of emancipation, consequently, includes reading and *explaining* the scriptures to her slaves. Brown romanticizes the blacks on the new Poplar Farm, describing them as reinvigorated with a sense of purpose and industry, hurrying to and fro without exhaustion day after day. When a bewildered neighbor asks Carlton what is responsible for the marked difference among his slaves, he informs "Parker that their liberties depended upon their work" (167). In both instances—one regarding religion, the other labor—Brown's portrayal reveals a distinction between positive liberties and negative liberties. What Brown illustrates, then, is the transformation of Poplar Farm from a small oligarchy into an ostensible liberal state in microcosm.

While Brown uses Georgiana to revise the latent presuppositions of the sentimental romanticism of Stowe's *Uncle Tom's Cabin*, George Green is the only character who explicitly adopts and deploys the iconographic language of the American Revolution to frame his polemic for black emancipation. Like Stowe's George Harris, Brown's George Green has very fair skin—so much so that he will later exploit his complexion to facilitate an escape. George literally confronts the boundaries of American liberal democracy physically and rhetorically. In a crucial scene of *Clotel*, he, speaking before the court, compares his participation in a slave insurrection to the colonials' break from England in 1776.

As an illustration of my claims about the aurality of political resonance, George contends that his actions were the direct result of his having been exposed to the Declaration of Independence: " 'I will tell you why I joined the revolted Negroes. I have heard my master read in the Declaration of Independence "that all men are created free and equal," and this caused me to inquire of myself why I was a slave' " (226). Here is an example of what Jay Fliegelman has identified as the thorough dynamism of the Declaration that Jefferson intended to be read aloud and rhetorically performed.[27] In Brown's hands, George actually collapses two documents in a manner that illustrates what I have been calling the remix. The second sentence of the U.S. Declaration of Independence reads "that all men are created equal," whereas the first article of the Massachusetts Constitution of 1780 reads, "All men are born free and equal." The expressions sound similar, to be sure, but their rearrangement and distillation into George's phrase also helps illuminate the wider political background of the United States when *Clotel* appeared in 1853. By having George sample the Massachusetts constitution, Brown evokes the state that arguably had the most progressive stance on blacks as citizens and perhaps racial egalitarianism, if one uses the right to vote as an index. The courtroom scene is one example of how, in Fliegelman's words, the "unfinished revolutionary agenda of social equality would be read back into the Declaration, a document endlessly appropriated and invoked."[28]

But George's phrasing also reveals the malleability of the national idioms, a malleability that further illustrates how deeply entrenched and fraught was the battle to define a national language. If Brown made particular use of the Declaration and the Massachusetts constitution to challenge slavery, then John C. Calhoun's 1848 speech before the Senate offered an earlier challenge to the expression to castigate the idea that blacks were anything more than subordinates to whites. In the speech, Calhoun contends that the phrase "all men are born free and equal" was unnecessarily inserted into the Declaration without any necessity and traces the central idea of the concept back to John Locke and Algernon Sidney. The speech is important not only for a counterreading of natural rights philosophy but for Calhoun's understanding of how the specters of the past have been rearranged in the present. In Calhoun's estimation, the ideas of Locke and Sidney were misunderstood by the founding fathers; exacerbating things further, this "most dangerous of all political errors" was being "widely extended" and "repeated daily from tongue to tongue." The Declaration, in this sense, was no repository of a positive charge set against the ostensible conservatism of the Constitution but instead reveals how the electricity of these documents was being defined and redefined by the political charge of the present moment as they moved from body to body, tongue to tongue.

George's speech more than superimposes the accepted rhetoric of the American Revolution onto the actions of black male dissidents. It is important that George has heard his master discuss the Declaration because it is listening— not necessarily reading—which is fundamental to the transmission of his politicized impulse. Horatio Green had earlier forsaken Clotel and his own daughter Mary for a career as a statesman that necessitated that the boundaries of formal electoral politics remain correlated to the boundaries of whiteness. George, himself the son of a congressman and a black servant, is positioned as the unacknowledged prodigal son who arrives to redeem the sins and hypocrisies of the story's father figures (Horatio Green, George Green's own father, and the founding fathers). Important, too, are the strategies that Brown employs to portray George as the inheritor of a democratic ethos.

Like Douglass's story *The Heroic Slave* published in the same year, Brown staves off describing George's participation in the revolt itself. Instead, Brown exaggerates an earlier act of George's heroism as an expression of his fundamental dedication to the state. Some weeks before Nat Turner's Rebellion, the courthouse has taken fire and its contents are rapidly burning. There being "no one disposed to venture" through the fire, George climbs a ladder to save "a small box containing some valuable deeds belonging to the city" (225, 224). After George falls from a ladder, a cadre of "white men took him up in their arms, to see if he had sustained any injury" (225). The "deeds"—some of which may have been official papers of the state—become veritable "authenticating documents" for George. On the one hand, the saving of these documents becomes the basis of a temporary moment of recognition from the city authorities, who "passed a vote of thanks to George's master for the lasting benefit that the slave had rendered the public" (225). It is George's "'meritorious act'" that allows him to speak in court. George—whom Brown describes as "as white as most white persons"—can only be recognized by the state as an ancillary of his master, the father of Horatio Green, as a facsimile of whiteness. George's heroism is divorced from the black body (whose very "blackness" is reinforced by the category of "slave") and transferred as a concomitant act of democratic virtue to his master. On the other hand, these documents symbolize the codified laws that literally hold George in suspension, awaiting death after being convicted of high treason for violating the state. George's initial act of heroism recovers the texts that guarantee that his second act is understood under the juridical valences of rupturing the state.

Unlike Douglass's "full-blooded" black Madison Washington, Brown is keen to distinguish George from his (visually) black counterparts. When the reader is first introduced to George in chapter 26, the reader learns that he is the sole remaining prisoner from the revolt led by Nat Turner described two chapters earlier. This insurrection, led by the "full-blooded Negro" Nat Turner, was joined by another "full-blooded Negro" slave, Picquilo, who had been taken from Africa at age fifteen to Cuba and then transported to Virginia. Brown's description of Picquilo, in particular, exploited the nation's fear of slave insurrections as a looming possibility produced by the continued maintenance of slavery, but in doing so, Brown reiterated conventional stereotypes of Africa as a place of barbarous tribes. Rather than portray the insurrection as an explicit example of transnational black political radicalism, Brown portrays it as a demand for universal human rights, beyond specific racial politics. To do so, he creates a fissure in the text that ensconces George in a narrative non-space, away from the center of violent action between chapter 24 and chapter 26, only to emerge before a court in a display that is more akin to an elected representative giving a speech in Congress. Brown, in essence, removes George from the transnational black space of Southampton's "Dismal Swamp" and ushers him to the (white) precincts of the state apparatus. By moving George from the heart of darkness into the pale of whiteness, Brown is able to preserve the concept of insurrection in the national narrative about the American Revolution. Black insurrection, however, is re-repressed, relegated to the underground of the text that is the unrepresentable space that remains unilluminated by democratic discourse.

It is George's command of the rhetoric of the right of revolution, however, that Brown accentuates as particularly democratic. In a speech where nearly "every one present was melted to tears," George underscores that he and the other insurrectionists had a greater claim to the democratic impulses that motivated the American Revolution than did even the early colonials themselves:

> "The grievance of which your fathers complained, and which caused the Revolutionary War, were trifling in comparison with the wrongs and sufferings of those who were engaged in the late revolt.... You say your fathers fought for freedom—so did we. You

tell me that I am to be put to death for violating the laws of the land. Did not the American revolutionists violate the law when they struck for liberty? They were revolters, but their success made them patriots—we were revolters, and our failures makes us rebels. Had we succeeded, we would have been patriots too." (226)

George's language here, which invokes the ghosts of the founding fathers, is part of a lexicon of democratic rhetoric exploited by other "heroic slaves," including Stowe's George Harris and Douglass's Madison Washington.[29] At the conclusion of George's speech nearly "every one present was melted to tears" (227). By interpolating the right of revolution discourse with the language, or at least the tear ideograph, of sentimentalism Brown's text suggests that logic necessitates an element of emotion to fulfill the promise of democratic rhetoric.[30]

Brown may have believed in the political necessity of dissent, but, ironically, he could characterize such tactics as legitimate only by attenuating George's presence in a virtual act of transubstantiation where the black male body is continually displaced by the white male body. Brown characterizes George as the conventional hero of the story and thus illustrates Nancy Bentley's contention that black heroes who physically confront slavery are almost always visually depicted as virtually white.[31] As an episode, then, the chapter titled "The Escape" exploits the iconography of revolutionary rhetoric to align the (chronologically) earlier courthouse scene with Nat Turner's Rebellion as parallel enactments of preserving and expanding the state.

A principled participant in Nat Turner's Rebellion, George can move from the underground space of slave insurrection to the generative site of democratic discourse—its hallowed institutions—with his corporeality intact. In this site, he concretizes the spectral presence of the founding fathers. Materialization, though, has its requirements even in a text meant to demystify the signifying power of a body's color: here it allows the speaker of democratic truths to be black as long as his body is white. The disembodied character of the rights-bearing individual under liberal democracy is here ameliorated, but the potential for its theoretically unlimited extension is racially contained.

■ BEYOND THE PALE

The novel's preoccupation with democracy, depicted as a series of increased engagements with freedom and liberation, is filtered for the most part through the white body.[32] The dual genre of the book's architecture, which unevenly combines sentimental fiction with the literature of black slave insurrections, produces two modes of gendered identification—one that follows the white(ned) female body (Clotel and her children, Althesa and hers, and Georgiana) and another that traces the white(ned) male body (Horatio Green, John Peck, Miles Carlton, and George Green). George's participation in a black slave insurrection, by contrast, gets (temporarily) recontextualized as analogous to the American Revolution

LEAP OF THE FUGITIVE SLAVE.

Figure 2.1 "The Death of Clotel" from *Clotel*. Manuscripts, Archives and Rare Books Division, Schomburg Center for Research in Black Culture, The New York Public Library, Astor, Lenox, and Tilden Foundations.

through a textual act of telescoping that is meant to encourage the reader to associate such acts with the white male body. The most conspicuous example of a white female body entering into political discourse occurs when Georgiana is devising a plan to gradually emancipate her slaves.[33]

If George and Georgiana become the vehicles through which Brown explicitly ventriloquizes the iconographic language of the American Revolution, then he uses Clotel and Sam to limn its figurative alterity. As Reid-Pharr contends, Clotel is "less a paean to the long-suffering slave than an encomium for a stifled democracy."[34] As perhaps the most graphic aspect of the book, the featured illustrations of *Clotel* provide an occasion to think about the interrelation between aurality and visualization, as well as the social practices of imagining a particular civic polity. Of all the illustrations featured in Brown's text, the fourth image—the one where Clotel leaps to her death into the Potomac River—offers the most acute indictment of slavery as a system that threatens the institutionalization of democracy in the United States (figure 2.1). The illustration, which accompanies the aptly entitled chapter "Death Is Freedom," displays a sensational still—sensational because of its latent deployment of the tenets of sentimentalism and for its dramatic theatricality.[35] Surrounded on both sides by slave catchers, Clotel is pictured leaping over a rail into the river. The sketch deploys religious symbolism by depicting her leap less as a jump into the Potomac River than a hovering above it, making her presence as much ethereal as material, as much spectral as social.

But the most fraught aspect of the image's concern with a political aesthetic and the problem of representation is not how it depicts religious symbolism but rather how it encodes the body to stage the question of civic identity. In the image, Clotel's face is clearly shadowed to be perceptibly and identifiably black, an anomaly that works against the visualization mechanics of the novel, where she has been continually described as fair and seemingly unidentifiable—an aspect borne out in the scene before the chapter titled "Death Is Freedom" that has her masquerading as a Spaniard or Italian. In an astute reading of the scene, Russ Castronovo marks Clotel's leap into the Potomac as an example of the national decree of making the body available to death as a precondition of transmogrifying the subject into a citizen, a decree announced by Patrick Henry's famous proclamation.[36] I want to extend Castronovo's compelling idea of "necro-citizenship" slightly by thinking through the question of blackness and the formation of civic polities—a question that is illustrated in rather stark terms with "The Death of Clotel" sketch in Brown's story.

Although the chapter is entitled "Death Is Freedom," it seems urgent to consider how freedom becomes palpably embodied in the novel and what these embodiments mean in relation to how civic polities are imagined and constructed. In addition to the shading practices that work to color and encode her as specifically African American, the contortions of Clotel's body translate the bifurcated registers of her political affiliation and social belonging. The image is meant to reiterate the religious underpinnings of Brown's language, ostensibly announcing her impending entrance into the coming community of a providential commonwealth: "She clasped her *hands* convulsively, and raised *them*, as she at the same time raised her *eyes* towards heaven, and begged for that mercy and compassion *there*, which had been denied her on earth; and then, with a single bound, she vaulted over the railings of the bridge, and sunk for ever beneath the waves of the river!" (219).

The sketch portrays something slightly different, however—and it is precisely the differential between the written narrative and its visual counterpart that illustrates the question of citizenship. Rather than remain looking at the heavens or staring into the ominous waters below, Clotel's body is maladroitly configured with her face turned to a profile position and, more important, with her eyes directly engaging one of her pursuers. What is captured in this image is not the would-be refuge of a religious sanctuary in death but instead a moment where Clotel's directed gaze demands that her pursuers recognize her as their equivalent. In the narrative, which depicts the leap itself as one quicksilver movement, there is no description of this fleeting moment of social interaction between Clotel and her pursuers. The visual impression, however, registers a different representation of black political agency.

The most problematic visual rendering of the image is how it illustrates the question of gender and citizenship through its depiction of the feminized body. In narrating her escape, Brown has been at pains to note her appearance as a male. Her appearance in this guise was as much a product of her cross-dressing masquerade as the cutting of her hair, which was initially a form of punishment she received from one of her mistresses. Yet, with her attire and her long tresses well below her shoulders, the image belies the narrative of Brown's novel. In one regard, the incongruence between the image and the novel begs the question not only about the indexical relationship between illustration and narrative but also about the processes of visualization as parallel interiorized acts of reading. In another regard, the image begs the question of why the artist felt compelled to racialize and gender Clotel's body as black and female, respectively.[37]

In other words, what would be at stake if the visual image corresponded more precisely to the narrative by having it look as if it were a white male leaping off the bridge surrounded by pursuers? Might it signal the symbolic death of democracy; the death of a material democracy on earth placed in contradistinction to the ethereal democracy Clotel is expected to join in heaven? Within the story line, Clotel's death intimates a kind of literalization of Patrick Henry's binary calculus of U.S. political subjectivity, one where she is, in the most perversely ironic sense, a constitutively national body at the same moment that the status of the citizen cannot be conferred upon her. The visual image threatens to elide the complexity and contradictions of that convoluted subjectivity by reducing the body to the zero degree of the corpus.

Rather than an indicative, declarative statement, Clotel's muted articulation in this sketch might be understood as a variation on the politics of recognition as well as a critique of the gendered presuppositions that make those forms of agency translatable and perceptible within the idioms of the national lexicon. The image of the drowned body of Clotel returns us to what would seem a stubborn liminality: simultaneously embodied and disembodied, and a speaking through her very unspeaking.

If Clotel's language necessitates translation because of how it becomes figuratively embodied, then Sam's critique demands translation because it is rendered in dialect. Throughout the novel, Sam is parodied as a caricature who fancies himself a doctor and who desires nothing more than to be an imitation of his master John Peck. In chapter 12, "A Night in the Parson's Kitchen," he is described as aspiring to be a poet like Peck and singing doggerels of his own creation. After Peck dies, Georgiana and Carlton pass by the slave quarters, where they overhear Sam and others singing about their deceased master. Georgiana insists that they remain to hear the song in its entirety, even after it has become apparent that far from mourning Peck, the slaves are indicting him. In outlining how Brown manipulated the ambivalence of minstrelsy's form, Paul Gilmore notes how Brown rewrote Stephen Foster's "Massa's in De Cold Ground" (1852) for antislavery purposes.[38]

What happens to our understanding of Sam's subversive sermon in the chapter titled "Death of a Parson" (a kind of politics of the lower frequencies) when we refuse to relegate it to outside the domain of democratic discourse because of its exaggerated dialect form? Lyrically, the two middle verses of Sam's song read almost as if they are mock occasional poems, while the first and fourth verses offer sober critiques of chattel slavery. But while both the first and the fourth verse recount the violent horrors of slavery, the fourth begins to castigate it especially as a particular kind of political system:

> We'll no more be roused by the blowing of his horn,
> Our backs no longer he will score;
> He no more will feed us on cotton-seeds and corn;
> For his reign of oppression now is o'er.
> He no more will hang our children on the tree,
> To be ate by the carrion crow;
> He no more will send our wives to Tennessee;
> For he's gone where the slaveholders go. (155)

By having Sam pronounce the phrase "reign of oppression," Brown characterizes Peck as a despot who, despite announcing his own benevolent paternalism, brutalizes his slaves. The language encapsulated in Sam's phrase is meant to illuminate the brutality of slavery not only as an illicit system that tears the body asunder but also as a defective mode of political governance that is anathema to an ostensible democracy. The phrase clearly echoes Jefferson, notably his tract "A Summary View of the Rights of British America" (1774) where he writes that "single acts of tyranny may be ascribed to the accidental opinion of the day; but a series of oppressions, begun at a distinguished period, and pursued unalterably through every change of ministers, too plainly proves a deliberate, systematic plan of reducing us to slavery."[39] Whereas Sam's speech is rendered in dialect everywhere else throughout the novel, Brown further accentuates the meaning of Sam's words here more expressly as political discourse by having them conspicuously rendered in standard tongue and also in poetry.

This scene remains important as much for the content of the message per se as for the forms of its delivery and the stylized manner that Sam and his party deploy to contest the meanings of their uneven subjectivity on the Poplar Farm. Presented with Sam as the lead singer and joined by a chorus, the songs are prefaced as "the unguarded expressions of feelings of the Negroes," as an inside view of slave life underlined by the image of Georgiana and Carlton watching the performance from a distance (156). The songs are impromptu and spontaneous and, as such, might be thought of as unduly transitory. The song that Sam leads is marked by its antiphonal quality and the mechanics of a call-and-response structure that produces an even calibration between the verse and chorus. Artistically, the final chorus is both an anomaly and the song's very apotheosis. It is an anomaly in terms of form because it repeats the words in the first two lines only to depart from them in the final three and thus modifies the anticipated form with an unanticipated freestyle. But, in a sensory capacity, it also becomes the song's apotheosis when the chorus assumes Sam's improvisational style in a moment of shared unison. The stylization of this musical unison is itself a metaphor for political unanimity, one where a black constituency coalesces less by consensus than by impulse.

Whereas George's words exemplify a speech proper, Sam's are impromptu; where George's are formal, Sam's are vernacular; where George's are delivered in the state forum of a courthouse, Sam's are rendered in the private recesses of the slave quarters. George's speech might be thought of as an example of what James C. Scott calls "public transcripts" that describe the open and exposed interaction between dominators and the oppressed, while Sam's song might be thought of as an example of a "hidden transcript" that critiques the dominant class offstage as it were.[40] In this sense, the novel not only contains a scene within its storyline that constitutes a "hidden transcript" but the novel itself becomes a meta-fictional "public transcript" that acts as a social text of political discourse. But insofar as both have audiences that are subject to persuasion, even though Sam is unaware that Georgiana and Carlton watch from a distance, both are examples of rhetoric, a fact all the more pronounced when one recalls that Sam's song alone is the sole example in the story wherein the discourse of an African American character eventuates a social change. The songs are not simply "unguarded expressions" of an African American interiority but become the very vehicles that induce Georgiana to finally take action. The songs, then, model a form of participatory engagement that symbolizes how constituencies can be organized into a political bloc as the song moves from entertainment and recreation into the discursive, from black to white America.

3 Rhythm Nation

African American Poetics and the
Discourse of Freedom

Ethiopians speak / Sometimes by Simile...[1]   PHILLIS WHEATLEY

The vocabulary of Enlightenment rationalism, although it was
essential to the beginnings of liberal democracy, has become
an impediment to the preservation and progress of democratic
societies.   RICHARD RORTY

In his book *The Anti-Slavery Harp* (1848), William Wells Brown included a piece
entitled "A Song for Freedom." Thematically, it was much like others in the collection. But "A Song for Freedom" was exceptional in the sense that its lyrics,
like the character Sam from his novel *Clotel*, were rendered from the perspective of an enslaved African American. It tells the story of a group of slaves who
gather around one of their own to recount the hypocrisies of slavery that they are
expected to accept.

He tells us of that glorious one,
I think his name was Washington,
How he did fight for liberty,
To save a threepence tax on tea.
(Chorus)
My old massa tells me O
This is a land of freedom O;
Let's look about and see if't is so,
Just as massa tells me O.
And then he tells us that there was
A Constitution, with this clause,
That all men equal were created,
How often have we heard it stated. (58)

"A Song for Freedom" is a metaliterary example of how conscious African
Americans were of the ways that slavery problematized the concepts of freedom and liberty as they are related to the particular history of the United States
as a democratic space. More than a mere anecdote, the song is an instance of
how political discourse is circulated and translated on the sonic frequencies
of popular culture. Misidentifying the Constitution for the Declaration of
Independence, "A Song for Freedom" riffs on its most idiomatic phrase that "all

men are created equal" and challenges the purchase of both the Declaration and the "threepence tax on tea" as rhetorical elements of what Lauren Berlant has called the "national symbolic," which undergirds and delimits civic polities by regulating a set of discursive icons.[2] Furthermore, like Frederick Douglass's "What to the Slave Is the Fourth of July?" speech, "A Song for Freedom" invokes the threepence tax phrase to suggest that enslaved African Americans have greater cause to revolt.

"A Song for Freedom" is as noteworthy for *how* it delivers its message as much as for the content of the message itself. It opens as a call for other slaves to join together to put "a song in massa's ear," and it is this embedded song that makes up the majority of the poem. The visual image produced by "A Song for Freedom" is a clandestine scene of men gathered around one figure, listening intently to memorize the words and rhythms of his speech. The narrative of "A Song for Freedom" is not simply descriptive but prescriptive; it calls for each of its enslaved black listeners to memorize its words and transmit them to the different locales of their own respective plantations. It expects that these words will migrate from the private recesses of an enslaved black community into the ears of slave masters and, in a more figurative sense, move from one body to another.

"A Song for Freedom" conceptualizes one way that U.S. blacks, without access to the formal domains of political action, strategically exploited cultural convention to reorganize the precincts of civic participation. The song's communal nature as a social text is underscored by the use of the chorus, as if the song was or, further still, *had* to be a mutual enterprise. Subsumed within "A Song for Freedom" is a mode of political dissemination, one that circulates along the routes of music and (re)constellates a black public sphere to challenge the authority of the slaveocracy.

As prolific as Brown was, *The Anti-Slavery Harp* was only one among many songbooks that mobilized popular music as an intervention into the contemporary political moment. Like Jairus Lincoln's *Anti-Slavery Melodies* (1843), George Washington Clark's *Liberty Minstrel* (1844), and Joshua McCarter Simpson's *Original Anti-Slavery Songs* (1852), Brown's collection appropriated popular songs by taking their instrumental musical components and adding different lyrics. Some of these lyrics were created especially for newly rearranged songs; others were imported poems set to music.

Music was central to nineteenth-century African American poetry. Beyond some of the formal properties such as rhyme and meter that make poetry akin to music, nineteenth-century African American verse is replete with allusions to harps, lyres, lutes, and songs. Yet what seems pressing to note is how African American writers both use the instrumentality of music to create poetry as well as manipulate the function of music within poetry to reimagine socialities through the political aesthetics of the remix. In the collections by Brown and Clark, for example, "A Song for Freedom" appears in both, set to the (musical) air of "Dandy Jim."[3] Black Americans were acutely cognizant of the rhythms of the nation, and poets of the first half of the century certainly rearranged—or, more aptly, remixed—these songs.

Brown's text offers an occasion to begin considering a theory of African American poetics during the mid-nineteenth century. Like her contemporary Brown, Frances Ellen Watkins Harper used a sonic revamp within the broader literary field of revision in her poem "Freedom's Battle" (1858). Watkins Harper's piece was crafted specifically to be included as part of William C. Nell's program that took the anniversary of the Boston Massacre as a moment to protest the recent Dred Scott decision. Staged at Faneuil Hall, the program included speeches by Wendell Philips, William Lloyd Garrison, and Charles Lenox Remond interspersed with songs from musical clubs. Watkins Harper's poem "Freedom Battle," which itself was a distillation of her own earlier "Be Active" from 1856, was transformed into a song for the occasion and performed by Hester and Phebe Whitest, Ariana Cooley, and John Grimes. As significant as Watkins Harper's selection of key stanzas from her earlier poem was to their new use as song verses, so too was her selection of the musical air "Greenville" carry her lyrics. Both of these strategies were important aspects in developing a recombinant cultural form.

What I am concerned with here is not so much how precisely African American writers appropriated the idioms of the national language but instead with the deviations, the schisms, and the slippages between (at least) two forms or compositions—differences that might be too easily dismissed as incongruent or dissonant. For it is precisely in these moments in which African American poets are manipulating the anticipated chords of the nation that they are making some of their most acute critiques and, simultaneously, offering poems that are not simply documentary signs of the times but rather constitute a different soundtrack to America altogether. It is these ostensible anomalies, yielding varying degrees of dissonance and harmony, that African American poets exploited to articulate their own notations onto U.S. political discourse.

Through readings principally of Watkins Harper's antebellum verse, this chapter underscores how she interrogated the gendered political subjectivity of black women (and, specifically, black mothers) to explore the claims of democracy. In turning to the formal qualities of her poetics—notably her manipulation of resonance, allusion, and prosody—I want to suggest that Watkins Harper rearranges aurality in many of her early poems to produce reconfigured sound patterns that challenge the latent meanings of popular and commonplace political idioms.

■ "LET ME MAKE MUSIC"

In a career that encompassed the entire second half of the nineteenth century, Watkins Harper repeatedly explored in essays, novels, and poetry the dilemmas of national subjectivity for African Americans. Although she was well known as the author of the novel *Iola Leroy* (1892) her antebellum poetry has remained relatively neglected.[4] As much as she needs to be read with turn-of-the-century writers such as Pauline Hopkins and Charles Chesnutt, she also needs to be contextualized with earlier authors such as Harriet Wilson, Harriet Jacobs, Martin Delany, and William Wells Brown. More specifically, Watkins lengthened the continuum of African American poets who arrived after Wheatley, including George Moses Horton, Charles Lewis Reason, Ann Plato, James Monroe Whitfield, and Elymas Payson Rogers.[5] Equally important, too, is reading Watkins with her other early contemporaries, such as Harriet Beecher Stowe and Walt Whitman. Influenced the foundational work of literary critics like Frances Smith Foster, Carla L. Peterson, and Hazel Carby, I hope to complement the work by feminist historians like Evelyn Brooks Higginbotham, Deborah Gray White, Glenda Gilmore, and Martha S. Jones who have recovered the presence of African American women in nineteenth-century U.S. political culture.[6]

Given the dearth of studies of African American verse of the period, it has become almost de rigueur to begin any discussion of black poetry and poetics with Phillis Wheatley. Her poem "America" (1768) prefigures a theory of African American poetics, pronouncing that "Ethiopians speak / Sometimes by Simile" (ix–x). Wheatley's lines here need to be reconsidered for how they signal a mode of writing that creates variations on standard languages and idioms as a strategy to interpolate an alternative, if not oppositional, meaning. These variations, from slight alterations to elaborate rearrangements, underscore how utterly attuned African Americans were to the idioms, if not the larger political discourses of which they are a part, and how well-versed they were in practices of code-switching.

Published in 1854 with a preface by William Lloyd Garrison, *Poems on Miscellaneous Subjects* underlined Watkins Harper's investment in various social causes, including the antislavery, temperance, women's rights, and Christian movements. The form of much of Watkins Harper's early poetry was influenced by oratory, and it displays as much attention to rhetoric as to versification. Beginning her career as a public speaker for the Maine Anti-Slavery Society in 1854, Watkins Harper was highly regarded for the eloquence, if not the cogency, of her speeches.[7] Among the numerous accounts of her speeches, the *Christian Recorder* took note of her lecture on the Civil War commenting that her delivery was both filled with depictions of "slavery in all its horrors, at times causing the audience to weep" and "so replete with logical reasoning and rhetorical diction, that those who heard her said that it was one of the most masterly productions that they had ever listened to on the subject."[8] In *Disgarded Legacy*, Melba Joyce Boyd praises how Watkins Harper's use of the ballad form was informed by the tenets of elocution.[9] However, in his assessment of Watkins Harper, J. Saunders Redding notes, disparagingly, that her verse was "led into errors of metrical construction" because it was primarily composed to be recited.[10]

Frances Smith Foster, has reiterated the necessity of remaining cognizant of the conventional standards of nineteenth-century verse to more fully appreciate Watkins Harper, and Peterson has argued that dehistoricizing Watkins Harper's poetry threatens to ignore "the cultural work that it performed."[11] As was typical for a popular speaker on the antislavery circuit, Watkins Harper's addresses routinely included both speeches and poems. Two of her first books sold more than 50,000 copies, and her public speaking most likely enhanced the sale of her work. Likewise, Watkins Harper's early verse necessitates close attention to the mechanics of aurality, especially given the particularity of her poetry's genre and the modes through which it was disseminated on the antislavery lecture circuit.

Although she wrote in several genres, including the novel, nonfiction prose, and oratory, the themes and form of her poetry were consistently characterized by a reformist mandate and a penchant for the quatrain. Her poems, whether recollected in whole or simply in fragments, were disseminated wherever she toured, and her poetry, consequently threaded a constellation of the discourses of democracy and blackness. The rhyme sequences allowed the poems to be not only consumed and internalized but recalled and reiterated, a practice that was more commonplace during an era when readers frequently committed to memory long sections of Henry Wadsworth Longfellow and John Greenleaf Whittier. Watkins Harper's use of the quatrain to embed and transplant her critique of the nation vis-à-vis a rhythmic reverberation is extended by the narrative form of much of her poetry that often depicts a solitary subject, as if to approximate a recitative. The conceit of Watkins Harper's poetry sought to ventriloquize her voice through other bodies and form a cadre of interlocutors, thereby pushing the very meanings of the terms "speaking in tongues" and "body politic" beyond their conventional conceptual formations.

■ MOTHER AND CHILD REUNION

All of Watkins Harper's antislavery verse sought to disclose the evils of the peculiar institution, but to do so they had to mediate the phantasmagoric. The "dynamics of the spectacle," as Carolyn Sorisio has called it, necessitated that antebellum antislavery writers develop "textual strategies to reveal slavery's corporeal nature without soliciting readers' voyeuristic spectatorship upon the bodies of slaves."[12] Slavery was at once eminent and pervasive, so deeply suffused as to be pushed into the recesses of society where the unimaginable could indeed occur—what Toni Morrison has called "unspeakable things unspoken."[13] If certain sensibilities about decorum and propriety prevented writers like Douglass, Watkins Harper, and Jacobs from detailing specific incidents in the life of a slave such as rape, then the diacritics of antislavery logic depended upon translating the sensations and experiences of slavery not into the graphic and explicit but rather into the veiled and muted.

Three of her most well-known poems—"The Slave Mother," "Eliza Harris," and "The Slave Auction"—all typify the maneuvers of Watkins Harper's writing that transported her critique of the nation well beyond the walls of lecture halls, engendering her poetics of freedom. Furthermore, all three poems are examples of sentimental literature.[14] Like many of the other selections in *Poems on Miscellaneous Subjects*, these poems are composed in quatrains, usually totaling no more than eight per title. The quatrain, with its various rhyme schemes, allowed Watkins Harper to transmit her message through a mnemonic practice of converging the poetic with the discursive. Perhaps more so than the lectures themselves, her poetry exploited a form that allowed them to be inculcated, if not memorized, by her audience.

In "The Slave Mother," Watkins Harper details the relationship between mother and child as a "joyous light" or lyrical "music" to intimate a harmonic accord. The forty-line poem, consisting of ten quatrains with a rhyme scheme of *abcb*, is written in ballad stanzas. However, the structural design of the poem developed in this format, suggesting love as the theme, is vitiated by the overwhelming image produced therein of violent separation—which essentially makes the poem a veritable elegy and, perhaps, if we think of slavery as a social death, a eulogy as well. Such a modification on the conventional themes of the ballad form anticipates later African American poetry such as Langston Hughes's "Ballad of the Landlord" (1943) and Gwendolyn Brooks's "Last Quatrain in the Ballad for Emmett Till" (1960). The first three stanzas of "The Slave Mother" activate a systemic operation of the poem whereby the reader is brought ever closer to the narrator. The plaintive queries that open each of these stanzas—"Heard you that shriek?," "Saw you those hands so sadly clasped," "Saw you the sad, imploring eyes?"—pull the reader into the poem's domain, instantiating its ethical hermeneutics by translating the echo and spectacle of violence from a merely descriptive scene into an interactive and participatory engagement (1, 5, 9). As an approximation of Aristotelian aesthetics, the poem's ethical hermeneutics oblige the reader to question whether he or she can continue reading without being compelled to action.[15]

"The Slave Mother" depicts one of the supreme offenses conceivable under the tenets of sentimental discourse—the forced separation of mother and child—but it does so by a split register of the unimaginable and the commonplace, the gothic and the actual. Refusing to specify the mother as "black" in the lines of the poem itself, Watkins Harper wanted to universalize the travesty as something that could befall any mother. As Watkins Harper later wrote to Thomas Hamilton, the editor of the *Anglo-African*, in 1861, "If our talents are to be recognized we must write less of issues that are particular and more of feelings that are general. We are blessed with hearts and brains that compass more than ourselves in our present plight."[16] Attempting to suspend the particularity of her enslaved condition, Watkins Harper accentuated the generic identity of the mother figure:

She is a mother pale with fear,
    Her boy clings to her side,
And in her kirtle vainly tries
    His trembling form to hide (13–16)

Watkins Harper's convention underscores the generic position of the poem's subjects by heightening the threat as imminent at the same moment, however, that she renders it unassignable. It is almost as if the child were being abducted from the mother by a gothic apparition, represented in the poem by the disembodied cruel hands that seemingly appear from nowhere and everywhere. The poem's dominant visual depiction of a mother hovering over her child is repeatedly contested by the poem's aural soundscape that is saturated with pervasive "shrieks" that linger in the reader's ear as a continuous echo. Mindful of John Hollander's claim that poetry is "hearing and vision joined" that works "midway in the mind between eye and ear," the political aesthetics of Watkins Harper's poetry employs sentimentalism to intimate that language should pass through the heart as it oscillates between the ear and eye.[17] The language used to describe the mother's physicality—"clasped," "bowed," "circling arms," "embrace"—illustrates her efforts to shield the child, as if she is attempting to reincorporate him to stave off their separation.

And it is precisely this contest over "incorporation" that drives the central crisis of the poem. The poem tries to insist that the child belongs to the mother as a natural and providential right. But the titular announcement of "The Slave Mother" interjects a specific political economy that challenges her claim to such rights and governs how the action will unfold. The body of the poem, however, makes no direct references to the peculiar institution, no explicit notation about the race of the child or mother. The intimated political economy of chattel slavery, which politically registers the child as fractional and economically quantifies him as a commodity, is rendered through allusion in the poem. The child was already, it seems, *corps perdu*.

> He is not hers, although she bore
> For him a mother's pain;
> He is not hers, although her blood
> Is coursing through his veins! (17–20)

If this quatrain is emblematic of how Watkins Harper intertwines the female and male subject positions, it is also the place where the poem moves from the generic to the specific. For it is here that the customary law of *partus sequitur ventrem*, meaning that the condition of the child follows that of the mother, scripts the mother expressly as "black mother."[18] Though never explicitly cited, it is this law that legally and, ultimately, juridically codes the female subject in "The Slave Mother" poem as "black mother." In other words, it is this law, coupled with a labor system of chattel slavery, that policed her body in terms of a sexual economy and where the body becomes part of a constitutively public discourse on the law. The black body, and specifically the black female body, not only enters into the public arena but essentially carries that very domain on her person through which others can imagine their political claim to the nation and the machinations of cultural belonging through the economies of race, sex, and gender.[19]

It is in this latent political meaning of the poem, lurking as it were, that we find the greatest achievement in Watkins Harper's poem; for it is against this law that she continues to insist upon the interiority of African Americans—something that is not achieved in similar poems by others such as Longfellow and Whittier. More specifically, Watkins Harper is able to bring forth the interiority of African Americans by reimagining the home. Making a distinction between "home" and "house," along the lines that Morrison has in an important essay, prompts a reconsideration of what the "public" and "private" could possibly mean conceptually to blacks in the antebellum United States.[20] Watkins Harper uses the idea of home as a way to evince the private lives of blacks, even in the midst of often not actually possessing the material structures of houses themselves. This maneuver is translated in the following stanza where "love" is represented as a pathetic fallacy, as a version of "home":

> He is not hers, for cruel hands
> > May rudely tear apart
> The only wreath of household love
> > That binds her breaking heart. (21–24)

Not only does Watkins Harper use metaphor to produce a distinction between "house" and "home" here—whereby the "home" is imagined as something that is internal to one's person—but, in so doing, she also manipulates the ideas of space and spatialization in a subversive fashion. As cultural critic Marc Anthony Neal has argued, "The practice of polytonal expression, particularly when premised by the type of public/social formations and surveillance that accompanied slave labor, created the context for the creation of covert social space(s) in which the parameters where not physical, but aural."[21] But Watkins Harper's insistence upon the interiority of black lives here, her insistence that "home" metaphorically and literally is where the heart is, creates a political counternarrative that African Americans can invent and indeed *own* their own home even when the physical custody of such a space was made consistently untenable. Watkins Harper's reconfiguration of "house" versus "home" is a conceptual maneuver that might be thought of as a variation on John Locke's idea of "possessive individualism."[22]

But whatever predilections African Americans might have for claims to either "possession" or "individualism," such claims were being constantly abrogated—and perhaps no other place ironized the meanings of these terms in the nineteenth-century United States more than the auction block. As a site, the auction block presented enslaved blacks as a spectacle, simultaneously registering them as material and apparitional, undifferentiated and individuated. Watkins Harper was not unaware of the debates about slavery and free labor that later circulated in books like George Fitzhugh's *Cannibals All!* (1857) and lingered in the footnotes of Karl Marx's *Capital* (1867). After reading Solomon Northrup's *Twelve Years a Slave* (1853), for example, she quoted from her own poem "The Slave Mother" in composing "Free Labor," published twenty years later in 1874.[23]

Watkins Harper's poem "The Slave Auction" translates the language of sentimentalism into an implied critique of the political economy, not simply the immorality, of slavery. In a letter to William Still from October 20, 1854, Watkins Harper asked, "Oh, how can we pamper our appetites upon luxuries drawn from reluctant fingers? Oh, could slavery exist long if it did not sit on a commercial throne?"[24] Watkins Harper's depiction is part and parcel of a discussion, including the scene in Brown's novel where Clotel is inventoried and tallied and the episode where Georgiana reminds Carlton that slavery takes "from a man his earnings," that was considering the relationship of slavery to the emerging forms of liberal capitalism.[25] By invoking a tenor of feudalism, Watkins Harper characterizes the sale site as anachronistic:

> And mothers stood with streaming eyes,
> > And saw their dearest children sold;
> Unheeded rose their bitter cries,
> > While tyrants bartered them for gold. (6–8)

Watkins Harper suggests that such episodes belong to an older modality of social organization and the poem depicts the dissolution of a fundamental unit of societies: the family. Although the mother and child are on the block together, Watkins Harper delays the presentation of the mother and child as a unit by introducing them singly in different stanzas as a way to accentuate their imminent separation. And like "The Slave Mother," "The Slave Auction" is delineated by a shift that begins with a sympathetic but nonetheless detached tone to one that directly interrogates the reader.

In the same volume of poetry in which "The Slave Mother" and "The Slave Auction" appeared, Watkins Harper also included "Eliza Harris." The poem was twice published in December 1853, first in Garrison's periodical and then in *Frederick Douglass' Paper* a week later. Like other responses to *Uncle Tom's Cabin*, Watkins Harper's poem lengthened the discursive limits of Stowe's novel. Robert S. Levine has mapped the circulation of Stowe's most famous novel in Douglass's periodical.[26] What might Watkins Harper's poem suggest about the intertextual strategies that disseminated the representation of Eliza Harris from one genre to another? Derrida's notion of the "supplement," as a practice of accretion and not simply repetition, is useful here; for Watkins Harper's poem adds a different dimension to the figure of Eliza Harris, one that was shaped as much by Watkins Harper being African American as it was by Stowe being white.[27]

Watkins Harper's portrayal of Eliza Harris was one of her three responses to *Uncle Tom's Cabin*, including "To Mrs. Harriet Beecher Stowe," which appeared in the January 27, 1854, number of *Frederick Douglass' Paper*, and another entitled "Eva's Farewell," which was the closing poem of the original edition of *Poems on Miscellaneous Subjects*. As Robert B. Stepto has noted, Stowe's development of Eliza's characters was indebted to the narratives of Douglass and Henry Bibb, published in 1845 and 1849, respectively, especially Stowe's characterization of George Harris.[28] And Stowe's George Harris influenced Brown's characterization of his George Green in *Clotel*. The multiple revisions on the original figure of Frederick Douglass, echoed in other works, reiterates him as a stereotype whereas, with the character of Eliza Harris, both Stowe and Watkins Harper wanted to suspend her exceptionality to fashion her as an archetype of the mother figure.

Watkins Harper's "Eliza Harris" represents two transitions to freedom: one material, the other spiritual. The poem itself describes a key moment in the story of Watkins Harper's escape—her leap over the Ohio River into freedom. In *Uncle Tom's Cabin*, a great deal of emphasis is placed on the difference between Kentucky as a slave state and Ohio as a free state to underscore Stowe's opposition to the spread of slavery as a result of the Missouri Compromise. In Stowe's characterization, Eliza is being pursued by Haley and Sam, a slave from the same plantation. Sam's presence in the company is what initially allows Eliza to get an early jump on her escape as he alerts her to Haley's approach. In Stowe's version, Eliza is helped to shore by a newly transplanted Ohioan from Kentucky—already a symbol of that transition from slavery to freedom. Important, too, is the fact that a former slave owner himself comes to Eliza's aid. Stowe was surely trying to accentuate that the transition from slavery to freedom (taking the personal as synecdochic of the national) was part of a conversion of the soul—that the peculiar institution, in essence, enslaved black and white alike.

The poem initially appears as if it is composed in regularized meter, formed in stanzas composed of rhymed couplets. The architecture of the poem, however, shadows the action of the poem's central character. Its uneven sense of rhythmic calibration parallels Eliza's own sense of discombobulation as well as her physical movements across the Ohio River. Where the reader might have anticipated standardized stanzas comprising heroic couplets, Watkins Harper presents lines with an inconsistent number of syllables. The irregular meter in "Eliza Harris" underscores the action and flight in the poem to characterize the impulsive movement of the runaway slave. Although the meter is irregular where the reader might have expected iambic pentameter to produce a governing cadence, the rhymed couplets nonetheless create a rhythm that pushes the movement of the poem forward at the same moment that Eliza is moving forward in her travels. It is as if the poem itself wants to obey formal and standardized poetic conventions but is continually prevented from reaching such an apotheosis. Even at the end of the poem when Eliza is on free ground, suggesting that while slavery may have been temporarily jettisoned, other social ills will only grant her something less than poetic justice, as intimated by the lines "Oh! Poverty, danger and death she can brave, / For the child of her love is no longer a slave!" (47–48).

The poem prefaces the generic category of a mother to allow for greater identification and empathy before specifying the nuances of Eliza's particular political existence that construct her socially as "black" and economically, quite literally and figuratively, as the means of production. Eliza's leap to freedom is witnessed in Watkins Harper's version by at least two others, one of whom narrates part of the poem: "Like a fawn from the arrow, startled and wild, / A woman swept by us, bearing a child" (1–2). With no detached narrative voice, the opening lines of the poem telegraph the act of reading with the narrator's own witnessing of the escape and, like "The Slave Mother," reconstitute the meanings of "bearing witness" to move beyond mere spectatorship into the formation of an imagined community through affective sensibilities.

Watkins Harper's maneuver here depends upon privileging the instrumentality of the spectacle—the vision of the narrator as well as the inner vision of the reader—such that the spectacle serves as a precursor to the poem's latent political discourse. The poem creates an imagined community between the narrator and the reader that is instantiated by the equivalency of their positions precisely as spectators. But the sustainability of that belonging is tested by their participation in a parallel discursive exercise. The poem anticipates that the reader will not only visualize what the narrator sees (as the re-presenting in art figured as *darstellen*), but will be compelled to speak out (as in politics figured as *vertreten*) against the nation as does the narrator. If affective sentimentalism is to mean anything here, then it must at least mean that communities of belonging premised on sensory modalities of association cannot afford to split the representational capacity of metaphor and translation by disaggregating the visual from the discursive, sight from sound, and, ultimately, the abstract from the specific.[29] Watkins Harper's poem requires that its reader identify with the narrator as much as the poem needs to have the reader associate with—that is, to *feel* for—Eliza. If the act of translation that ostensibly transposes the reader and Eliza is forestalled, then the purchase of sentimentalism is reduced, producing an asymmetrical domain of vision that diminishes the field of recognition as both a sensory and a political entailment.

Notwithstanding the emphasis on Eliza's gendered position as "mother," Watkins Harper invokes Eliza's near whiteness as a medium through which her readers might otherwise sympathize with the escaped slave. If, as Nancy Bentley has argued, the antebellum "Mulatto" is the "figure who most distinctly locates the internal contradictions of domestic ideology and its subtext of the body," how might we read the figure of the antebellum mulatta who may have suffered through a life that was indeed tragic but had not yet been formalized as the "tragic mulatta" of the later fiction by Watkins Harper, Chesnutt, and others?[30] How might we recognize the latent political meaning of a social position that is being continually scripted through the valence of domesticity but whose body bears the supratext of publicity? "When you are born into a national symbolic order that explicitly marks your person as illegitimate, far beyond the horizon of proper citizenship," Berlant writes, "and when your body also becomes a site of privileged fantasy property and of sexual contact that the law explicitly proscribes but privately entitles, you inhabit the mulatta's genealogy, a genealogy of national experience."[31] In Watkins Harper's poem, whiteness emerges as the shadow of the gothic—as in the paleness of Eliza's face which produces a "vision to haunt us" (9). But it also functions as a claim to the normative position of the citizen-subject, a claim that is being contested by the taint of that very whiteness: "How say that the lawless may torture and chase / A woman whose crime is the hue of her face?" (20–21).

The efficacy of her whiteness as a corporeal index that the senses can register is abrogated by an unstated "fiction of law," as Twain later portrays it in *Pudd'nhead Wilson* (1894), that supersedes the senses. Eliza's body not only becomes a site of a public discourse on the understanding of law and citizenship in antebellum America but also symbolizes a hermeneutical crisis of interpretation itself, of compelling the senses (especially the ocular) to be reorganized around a set of social logics. In Stowe's *Uncle Tom's Cabin*, Mr. Symmes helps Eliza onto the riverbanks of the Ohio shore and rationalizes his actions as helping the downtrodden rather than conspicuously undermining the law. In fact, the narrator discloses that had he been "instructed in his Constitutional relations," he would not have been "betrayed into acting in a sort of Christianized manner."[32] Stowe surely meant to suggest that Christianity could reform the nation. But this scene also intimates that other modalities of belonging were challenging the national mandate of presupposing a civic identity by imagining alternative ideals of interstitial communities.

In Watkins Harper's "Eliza Harris," Mr. Symmes is nowhere to found, being replaced instead by providence. Watkins Harper's devotion to Christianity shifted the realm of affect here—instead of explicitly depicting a reconfigured racial community of black and white (as had Douglass in "The Heroic Slave"), Watkins Harper presents a community based on spirituality, suggesting that a community of faith could transcend national affiliation. As with Stowe, Watkins Harper wanted to underscore that certain Christian laws should inform U.S. national laws.

> With her step on the ice, and her arm on her child,
> The danger was fearful, the pathway was wild;
> But, aided by Heaven, she gained a free shore,
> Where the friends of humanity open'd their door. (25–28)

In *Uncle Tom's Cabin* Eliza is welcomed into the home of a senator and his wife who have been discussing the passage of the Fugitive Slave Law when Eliza appears at the door. They remain unnamed in Watkins Harper's poem, replaced instead by the generic "friends of humanity." The scene illuminates Stowe's and Watkins Harper's commitment to what Susan M. Ryan has called the "forms of benevolent citizenship."[33] In doing so, Watkins Harper enlarges the problem of chattel slavery from one of the national to the spiritual. The abolition of slavery, the poem implies, is as much about the fate of liberal democracy in the United States as a political system as it is about the viability of Americans joining a global community of virtuous citizens who are governed principally by the mandates of Christian law. This inference that state law should intersect with Christian law echoes an earlier illustration by Whittier where democracy is understood to be undergirded by the well-known maxim from Matthew that you should do unto your neighbor as you would have them do unto yourself.[34]

■ NATIONAL ANTHEM REMIXED

Eliza Harris, in both Stowe's and Watkins Harper's versions, does not herself participate in political discourse—she is, alas, representation's representation. In the chapter of Stowe's novel titled "In Which Property Gets into an Improper State of Mind, George Harris has a lengthy conversation with Mr. Wilson, his former employer, where he pronounces his recognition of the discrepancy between the promise of democratic principles and the contradictory embodiment of their materialization in the United States. Eliza renders no such explicit articulation in either the novel or the poem, but Watkins Harper rearranges the anticipated visual and sonic accord of the "star-spangled banner" that is registered as a political crisis for the poem's speaker:

> Oh! how shall I speak of my proud country's shame
> Of the stains on her glory, how give them their name?
> How say that her banner in mockery waves—
> Her star-spangled banner—o'er millions of slaves? (17–20)

Continuing a mode of critique by writers such as William Wells Brown and James Monroe Whitfield, Watkins Harper sardonically invokes the image made popular by Francis Scott Key.[35] Rather than a declarative statement, she fabricates the intended disjunction between the symbol's visuality against its aurality by producing a contrast in timbre by having the lines close with a question mark. Tongue in cheek with her allusion to the "star-spangled banner," Watkins Harper plays with both irony and subversion. As Douglass had done with his "What to the Slave Is the Fourth of July?" speech, Watkins Harper questions the relationship between black bodies and U.S. civic polities and, more generally, between these bodies and the definitions of freedom and liberty.

More than simply revealing the irony of the star-spangled banner as a national anthem, Watkins Harper uses the reference to articulate a theory about U.S. national history and democracy. Figuratively materializing history as a tactile phenomenon, "glory" not only is understood as an ethereal sentiment of nationalism but figuratively assumes a physicality as a "banner" itself. For Watkins Harper, the abrogated "glory" of the nation's banner illuminates the ways in which the nation's claim of the oft-assumed teleological relationship between history and democracy has been collapsed by a superimposition of the present onto the past, thereby making them correlative, rather than sequential, entities. The nation is contravening history or, more specifically, nationalism is vitiating the teleology of historical progress. Watkins Harper views the Fugitive Slave Law as a betrayal of older principles and—as Whitman will later do in "A Boston Ballad"—manipulates history by having the present abrogate the past to telescope her own specific critique of the failures of U.S. democracy that make the idea of the human realizable only through the category of the citizen.[36]

But if Watkins Harper is able to manage a critique of the nation, she can do so only because it is ostensibly rendered through another tongue. In "Eliza Harris," Watkins Harper's creation of a second, accepted figure to articulate this critique is prefigured as an act of ventriloquism. The poem itself functions as a discourse on American inequality. It is the narrator who is experiencing the crisis of conscience, compelled to question the nation. Rather than think of this as a moment when the subversive intentionality of the poem is diminished because Watkins Harper fails to give Eliza control of the narrative position, we should think of Watkins Harper's creation of an interlocutor within the poem as part of her political strategy to endow the antislavery cause with a reverb effect. This kind of interlocution differs from Whitman's strategies of embodiment and ventriloquism that, as I argue in the next chapter, proceed on different grounds to elevate the voice of authority over, rather than through, the individual subjects of *Leaves of Grass*. If the symbolism of Eliza's escape failed in whatever degree to register an aural resonance, Watkins Harper ensured that its political import was unambiguously articulated by the narrator.

This is a moment when Watkins Harper demonstrates a kind of representation that illuminates my earlier reference to "speaking in tongues" as a form of black political praxis that transposes an ecclesiastical phenomenon for a more recognizably political one. If it is disappointing that Watkins Harper does not have Eliza speak to the other subjects within the poem or address the reader directly, it is because the poem encapsulates a larger debate about political representation in the mid-nineteenth century United States that is exemplified here through her depiction of voice and the aural. Mindful of Peterson's assessment that contemporary accounts of Watkins Harper and other black women threatened to "decorporealize" them, I want to suggest a different way to think about the corporeal in relation to the question of democracy as it unfolds in this particular poem.[37] The poem not only functions as an exposé on the Fugitive Slave Law but serves as an occasion to rethink the meanings of representative democracy and direct democracy within the wider U.S. cultural mythology about equality. Given the continual violence perpetuated upon black bodies, the threat of decorporealization was far from trivial. Watkins Harper's poem might be thought of as an poetic illustration of political discourse when she models an instance of representative democracy whereby Eliza's (and by extension, Watkins Harper's) voice is rendered through a proxy.

However, to garner the poem's full sensory affect and political effect, it should not be understood as a pure example of Bahktin's notion of heteroglossia but rather as an example of what I have been calling a polyphonic discourse system.

The stereo effect of "Eliza Harris" is amplified by numerous other nonlinguistic sounds that are not language per se but must somehow be registered. The cacophony of the "strange discord" produced by a slave's chains works in opposition to the internal cadence created by the couplet's rhyme as a way for Watkins Harper to accentuate the dissonance of slavery (44). Like Fred Moten's reading of Aunt Hester's shrieks from the opening chapter of Douglass's *Narrative*, my reading here underscores that the sound produced by the slave's chains should not simply be thought of as noise but rather as political articulations, figured neither decidedly as speech nor as writing, whose social meanings demand to be translated.[38] As a latent *ur*-music, whose rhythms and arrhythms churn out sounds from the low continuous drone to the clamor, the sound of slavery in "Eliza Harris" is meant to contrast with the melody of "The Star-Spangled Banner." If the "banner" of slavery could be said to blanket "Liberty's plain," then the sound of slavery inundated its acoustic channels (44).

Although Watkins Harper rarely specifies blacks or blackness in her poems, they linger in the shadows of her verse as a specter of democracy. In her estimation, slavery and blacks were central to the conceptual and material formations of the idea of the citizen in the United States, and, like Douglass, Melville, and Whitman, she summoned national mythologies of the past to contemplate the future of democracy. As Maggie Sale notes, the use of rhetoric "in the service of people other than those for whom it was originally intended" inevitably changes the very meaning of that rhetoric altogether.[39] In an 1857 speech that condemned the Fugitive Slave Law and Dred Scott decision by exploiting the iconography of Bunker Hill in a manner similar to Douglass's "What To the Slave Is the Fourth of July?" diatribe, Watkins Harper hinted that the travails of a recently escaped slave within the pale of Bunker Hill was more than nominally ironic; it was a violation of the spirit of 1776.[40] Whitman articulated such a critique in one of the original poems of *Leaves of Grass*; in "A Boston Ballad" slavery is viewed as a cancer to the body and soul of the nation.

Watkins Harper's invocation and deployment of national idioms from the founding mythology sought not only to overlay the symbolism and authority of their sanctioned meanings onto black America but also to test the very boundaries of such concepts as "freedom," "rights," and "citizenship." Even when the terms or languages that she deploys are not facsimiles of the original phrases, the underlying concepts remain uncannily resonant. Indeed, returning to the epigraph to this chapter, Wheatley's recognition that blacks sometimes make use of figures of speech indicates as much about the ways in which African Americans are able to create a coded language system as it divulges the social structures that too often disallow them from having a public voice; self-creation and metaphor, then, might be thought of as something endemic to the condition of being black in the United States, a subject position that illustrates the acute differential between the theory of representation and the politics of *res ipsa loquitur* in the national fantasy of democracy.

Although Watkins Harper, Douglass, and Brown were among the most widely known, they were only three of the many African American intellectuals who accentuated the differential between the nation's professed ideals and their corporate materialities as a mode of social critique. James Monroe Whitfield, for example, modified a common refrain from popular songbooks in the eponymous poem in his *America and Other Poems* (1853):

> AMERICA, it is to thee,
>> Thou boasted land of liberty,—
>> It is to thee I raise my song,
>> Thou land of blood, and crime, and wrong. (1–4)[41]

Echoing and ultimately parodying Samuel Francis Smith's "America" (1831), popularly known as "My Country, 'Tis of Thee," Whitfield illuminates the contrast between the America of the free celebrated in the song and the America of slavery at the heart of his poem.[42] At times adopting a tone similar to Douglass's angrily mocking 1852 speech, Whitfield alludes to a familiar song and turns it into a critique of the United States. The poem's opening visceral lines lull the reader with a degree of familiarity and anticipation only to have that familiarity immediately undercut.

My sense of Whitfield's manipulation of sound and allusion draws from Wai Chee Dimock's suggestive proposition of a "dialogical historical" approach to reading how literature travels, although, admittedly, the distance and time traveled here may be on a much smaller scale than she imagines. Her theory of resonance as an "echo chamber" where "meanings are produced over and over again, attaching themselves to, overlapping with, and sometimes coming into conflict with previous ones" is precisely the kind of maneuver we see these African American poets practicing in varying degrees.[43]

The abolitionist songster Joshua McCarter Simpson used these particularly recombinant forms of double voicing to articulate his antislavery message. Simpson believed in the power of music as a mode of reformation and transformation, singing his first poem in public in 1842 and writing more than fifty other pieces that were collected and published under the title *The Emancipation Car, being an Original Composition of Anti-Slavery Ballads, composed exclusively for the Under Ground Rail Road* in 1874. Many of his poems appropriated popular songs by taking their instrumental musical components and adding new words. In his self-published and little-known pamphlet *Original Anti-Slavery Song, by Joshua M'C Simpson, a Colored Man* (1852), he offered an explicit rationale for an understanding of sound and aurality that I have been theorizing as the remix. Some readers or listeners, he wrote in the preface, "will have serious objections to the 'Airs' to which my poetry is set," but "my object in my selection of tunes, is to kill the degrading influence of those comic Negro Songs, which are too common among our people, and change the flow of these sweet melodies into more appropriate and useful channels."[44] As Lindon Barrett reminds us, the singing voice "stands as a primary means of undermining and revising the unacceptable cultural imperatives of dominant *signing voices*," by which he means the privileging of the written text as an index of one's claims to belonging in a national or human community.[45]

No composition is more representative of Simpson's own oeuvre—or more emblematic of the social practices whereby African Americans manipulated aurality as an avenue into political discourse—than his poem "The First of August in Jamaica" (1852). Like Ann Plato's "To the First of August" (1841) and Whitfield's "Stanzas for the First of August" (1853), Simpson's poem celebrated the abolition of slavery in Jamaica as a wishful harbinger of things to come in the United States:

> Hail thou sweet and welcome day,
> > Let the angels join the lay,
> > And help us swell the anthems high.
> Tune all your golden harps once more,
> And strike to notes ne'er struck before. (1–5)

As Simpson's poem continues, it assumes a circum-Caribbean perspective with the wish "May Hayti gladly catch the gale, / And Portorico tell the tale" of black liberation (23–24). The poem, along with the others mentioned, is an indication of African Americans' awareness of their own position within the hemisphere as well as an understanding of the transnational undercurrents of liberatory social movements.

But Simpson's poem differs in significant turns from both Plato and Whitfield with its particular emphasis on music. Whereas the poems by Plato and Whitfield have a latent concern with tone, Simpson's poem manipulates aurality to create a different soundscape. The words that Simpson writes are dedicated to liberation in Jamaica, but the poem itself is set to the musical accompaniment of "Hail Columbia" (1789), a song originally composed for the inauguration of George Washington and used throughout the nineteenth century as the unofficial U.S. national anthem. Without its own chorus or refrain, Simpson's composition might appear more like a poem than a song. But Simpson's piece works precisely by importing the chorus of the popular anthem at the level of the subconscious so that it floats between the registers of his words in "Stanzas for the First of August" and the music of "Hail Columbia." Indeed, the lyrics of "Hail Columbia," written in 1798 by Joseph Hopkinson, aptly suit Simpson's composition:

> Firm, united let us be,
> Rallying round our liberty,
> As a band of brothers joined,
> Peace and safety we shall find.

Simpson's own composition correlates the contemporary antislavery movement in the United States with others in the Caribbean and associates them all with the unfinished business of the American Revolution. Yet, in another sense, Simpson's composition divests "Hail Columbia" of its strict nationalist impulses to perhaps signify a truly hemispheric revolution in the Americas.

Charlotte Forten made similar use of this aural double voicing in her "Parody on 'Red, White and Blue.'" In addition to Watkins Harper's "Freedom's Battle," Forten's "Red, White and Blue" poem was performed at Nell's 1858 antislavery program that gathered at Faneuil Hall. Sung by the Northern vocalists Elijah Smith, James Henry, B. F. Roberts, and Amanda E. Scott, "Red, White and Blue" used the air "Columbia, Gem of the Ocean" (1843), which itself was a rewrite of "Britannia, Pride of the Ocean" (ca. 1750). In describing Forten's creation of antiphonal and antipathetic voices, Eldrid Herrington notes that "Forten's 'revision' is the provisionality carried by a parodic voice that is hopeful, expectant, and lacerating; it snaps back on the voice it stems from."[46] As Simpson had done with his use of "Hail Columbia" for "Stanzas for the First of August," Forten used "Columbia, Gem of the Ocean" to redub "Red, White and Blue" to protest the Dred Scott decision.

■ SONGS FOR THE PEOPLE

Although concerns with the fundamental aspects of resonance and aurality are intrinsic to nearly all of nineteenth-century American verse, what amounts to Watkins Harper's theory of aesthetics is articulated in a later 1871 volume of poetry and two additional subsequent titles: "Songs for the People" (1894) and "Home, Sweet Home" (1895). In two poems, "The Freedom Bell" (1871) and "Fifteenth Amendment" (1871), Watkins Harper invokes the image of the bell to amplify the sonic impulses of her verse. "The Freedom Bell," in particular, correlates an aural resonance with a visual resonance by making use of both instrumentality and iconography. The meaning of the poem outlines the hope that someday "the freedom bell" will ring (21), "Proclaiming all the nation free" (22). Words like "tones" (2), "song" (20), and "melody" (28) emanate from the poem. Comprising seven quatrains, the fourth is the central transitional stanza that marks the tonal shift within the poem from the early sorrow songs of "shrieks and groans" (9) to the later harmonies of the "Freeman's joyful song" (24).

In "The Freedom Bell," the moment of apotheosis is engendered by the bondman merely *hearing* the bell in the first stanza to the freeman *singing* in the seventh, signaling a mode of participatory engagement with the musical languages of democracy that promises to reconfigure the chords of the national composition altogether. By correlating the freedom bell of her verse with the iconography of the Liberty Bell, Watkins Harper accentuates the bell's function as a visual emblem and musical instrument. Watkins Harper reiterates this parallel at the textual level with the line "Proclaiming all the nation free," which modifies the inscription from Leviticus—"Proclaim Liberty throughout all the land unto all the inhabitants thereof"—on the actual Liberty Bell. The visual resonance of this correlation is significant not only because of its association with the War of Independence but because, especially after 1837, the Liberty Bell was increasingly used as an antislavery symbol.[47]

As in "The Freedom Bell," Watkins Harper calls upon the image of the bell again to herald a new national sensibility in "Fifteenth Amendment." Endowed with the "sweetest chimes," these bells are set to act as the accompaniment to "songs of joyful triumph" (9, 12). The specific concern of African Americans and the question of the nation, however, are not borne out until the fourth stanza:

> Shake off the dust, O rising race!
>   Crowned as a brother and a man;
> Justice to-day asserts her claim,
>   And from thy brow fades out the ban. (13–16)

The line "Crowned as a brother and a man" is clearly a reference to the widely circulated image with the phrase "Am I Not a Man and a Brother?" circling a kneeling black man in chains, originally produced by the Society for Effecting the Abolition of the Slave Trade. Watkins Harper formulates an almost antiphonal response to that organization's understanding of blackness, with its token of "an African in chains in a supplicant posture," by crafting a sense of ascendancy when she punctuates the line "O rising race!" with an exclamation. Furthermore, Watkins Harper implies that the answer to the Society's underlying query of whether blacks could become part of the national family will be eventually resolved when the distribution of civil liberties is not continually circumvented. However, even more important, Watkins Harper remixes the official slogan of the Society in her poem by reversing the order of "brother" and "man." Stylistically, her revision alters the meter of the poem while also altering its thematic by prioritizing brotherhood (and perhaps by extension the familial) over manhood.

In a poem ostensibly about the recent passage of the constitutional amendment granting black men the right to vote in 1870, Watkins Harper includes only the slightest reference to the act through a possible allusion to the ballot: "With freedom's chrism upon thy head, / Her precious ensign in thy hand" (20–21). Although it does not share the same degree of play with tonality, her poem "Words of the Hour" (1871) includes a direct reference to suffrage as part of the program of Radical Reconstruction. Taken together, "The Freedom Bell" and "Fifteenth Amendment" are contemplations on two of the most fundamental predicaments of U.S. blacks in the nineteenth century.

Emblematic of what Frances Smith Foster has deemed her pragmatic poetry, "Home, Sweet Home" (1895) exemplifies the strategies that Watkins Harper exploited to manipulate prosody in fashioning a poetics of freedom.[48] The poem discloses Watkins Harper's belief in the power of music to remix democratic national anthems. It describes two factions of the Civil War on a battlefield who, after hearing the melody of "Home, Sweet Home," realize that they indeed do belong to the same national family. Arising from the camps of "Dixie's land" is the song of "freedom's banner"—a "banner" that has already been associated with the North in the preceding stanza (14, 19):

> In one grand but gentle chorus,
> Floating to the starry dome,
> Came the words that brought them nearer,
> Words that told of "Home, Sweet Home."
> For a while, all strife forgotten,
> They were only brothers then,
> Joining in the sweet old chorus,
> Not as soldiers, but as men. (29–36)

The song in the poem that compels the soldiers to desist momentarily is a reference to Henry Rowley Bishop's 1821 opera, to which John Howard Payne added lyrics two years later.[49] The popular song acts not simply as the theme music within the poem but also as its subtextual shadow. In the poem, "a tender strain of music" melts away "the hearts of strong men," signaling a change in the soldiers and prefiguring the larger transformation of the body politic (23, 25).

"Songs for the People" maintains the necessity of broadening the body politic by underscoring a more expansive vision of civic humanism. Whereas African Americans—or the specters of them at least—loom over a good deal of Watkins Harper's poetry, the principal subjects of "Songs for the People" are the old and young. Additionally, the poem has a keen antiwar sentiment, an impulse echoed later in "'Do Not Cheer, Men Are Dying,' Said Capt. Phillips, in the Spanish-American War" (1900):

> Let me make songs for the people,
> Songs for the old and young;
> Songs to stir like a battle-cry
> Wherever they are sung. (1–4)

Watkins Harper's use of simile in the opening stanza, which compares her poetic project to a "battle-cry," inverts the overtones of war and violence throughout the poem's six remaining stanzas. These are to be songs "Not for the clashing of sabres, / Nor carnage nor for strife" (5–6) but "Music to soothe all its sorrow, / Till war and crime shall cease" (25–26). These are not to be songs of the nation but rather anthems of a new civic humanism. Watkins Harper's repetition of variants on the phrase "Let me make the songs…" resembles a refrain, and, in a poem about music, the referentiality of the phrase oscillates between the narrator and reader to approximate a chorus.

By contextualizing Watkins Harper with a cadre of other mid-century writers, I have tried to illuminate the importance of music as a way to think about the formal aspects of African American poetics as well as to illustrate the ways that poetry was used as political discourse. The monumental shift in U.S. poetry ushered in by Whitman has had the effect of occluding the deep engagement with questions regarding equality and representation by Watkins Harper and others such as the Fireside poets for being too conventional. However, if there is a way to limn the radical impulses of Watkins Harper, to acknowledge the instances in which she manifested a "runaway tongue," we should begin by considering the ways that she took one of the most conventional poetic forms to make a claim for a reconstituted U.S. civic humanism.

4 Black and Tan Fantasy

Walt Whitman, African Americans,
and Sounding the Nation

Whitman viewed the spoken idiom of Negro Americans as a
source for a native grand opera. Its flexibility, its musicality, its
rhythms, freewheeling diction and metaphors, as projected in
Negro American folklore, were absorbed by the creators of our
19th century literature even when the majority of blacks were still
enslaved.[1]   RALPH ELLISON

Whereas Joshua McCarter Simpson and other nineteenth-century African
American writers used poetry to conceptualize blackness as a hemispheric sensibility of the New World, Walt Whitman used poetry to conceptualize the United
States itself as instantiating a new-world globality, and nowhere is this more evident than in his deployment of the catalogs. Throughout the various editions
of *Leaves of Grass*, Whitman's signature use of the catalogs becomes a way to
imagine the world in America and America as the world by enumerating various
national bodies. "Salut au Monde" (1856) is only one of many examples in which
the American identity of Whitman's speaker is imagined as the simultaneous
incarnation of transnational subjectivities:

> I see the cities of the earth, and make myself a
>   part of them,
> I am a real Londoner, Parisian, Viennese,
> I am a habitan of St. Petersburg, Berlin, Con-
>   stantinople,
> I am of Adelaide, Sidney, Melbourne,
> I am of Manchester, Bristol, Edinburgh, Limerick,
> I am of Madrid, Cadiz, Barcelona, Oporto, Lyons,
>   Brussels, Berne, Frankfort, Stuttgart, Turin,
>   Florence,
> I belong in Moscow, Cracow, Warsaw—north-
> ward in Christiana or Stockholm—or in
> some street in Iceland;
> I descend upon all those cities, and rise from them
> again.[2]

Bodies are everywhere in *Leaves of Grass*, so much so that the incorporative
process that he fashions is often identified as a form of "embodiment" as much as

the term "body politic" is associated with Whitman's poetry, even though it was a phrase that he never used in print. Harold Aspiz examines Whitman's preoccupation with bodies as a way to investigate the poet's understanding of science and medicine.[3] Karen Sánchez-Eppler, for example, argues that Whitman seeks to reconcile the fraught difficulties of slavery in an American democracy by both expressing the particularity of the bodily experience and idealizing an undifferentiated oneness through a "poetics of merger and embodiment."[4] By limning homosexuality as a latent impulse throughout Leaves of Grass, Michael Moon uses the trope of "fluidity" as a way to theorize Whitman's practices of corporeality.[5] Beyond certain corporeal thematics in the poems themselves, the body has been used to understand the form and shape of Leaves of Grass itself.

But what happens to our understanding of Whitman and his cultural project if we turn to the question of sound by thinking about the aural resonances of the words, lines, and passages of his poems? In the section quoted earlier from "Salut au Monde," although the lines are arrhythmic, they do have a sense of melody created by Whitman's use of approximate anaphora. And, importantly, the sound of the catalogs approaches a kind of white noise, one where the democratizing taxonomy of the litanies is converted in the reader's ear and manifested as a consistent hum or monotonous drone.

By accentuating the prosodic elements of his poetry, we are better able to recognize what the nation sounds like when Whitman is arranging the compositions. In holding to the word "composition" over "melody" I want underscore the former's sonic approximation as a near homology of "constitution," mindful of Moon's argument that the founding political document of the Constitution and the early editions of Leaves of Grass are both texts that foreground their revisionist impulses.[6] In resisting the word "melody," I am cognizant of Whitman's aversion to overproduced and calculated melodies over what he considered natural rhythms.[7] The sounds produced by Leaves of Grass are as important as those emanating from within the poems. Thinking through the nuances, inflections, tenor, idiosyncrasies, and cadences of Whitman's poetry might disclose the sounds of a particular rhetoric that is attempting to constitute itself as a national idiom. Disclosing how Whitman sounds the nation—what he calls in a later essay its "autochthonic song"—is especially important for delineating competing sounds that may be said to interrupt the tenor of these songs or otherwise threaten to create cacophony in them.[8]

Music—both its conception and its performance—was important to Whitman's understanding of America and the arc of his poems. Whitman was variously influenced by popular and classical music, as Eric Lott has noted about the poet's fascination with minstrelsy and as Justin Kaplan has noted on his passion for the opera.[9] Even the most cursory glance at Leaves of Grass reveals a number of poems that announce themselves as songs: "Song of Myself," "Song of the Open Road," "Song of the Broad-Axe," "Song for Occupations," and "Song of the Banner at Daybreak" are but a few. Ralph Ellison reminds us of Whitman's enchantment with black dialect, which Whitman saw as the basis for an organic native American culture. Writing in the *Primer* notebook, Whitman notes that black speech might inform a "future theory of the modification of all the words of the English language, for musical purposes, for a grand native opera in America."[10]

Whitman's preoccupation with the audible—as the most basic unit of the sonic field upon which the poems and songs are built—shapes his poetics to amplify the central ideas of *Leaves of Grass*. While it might be tenuous to argue that all the editions of *Leaves of Grass* have a perceptible composition that governs their sonic productions and their social meanings, the poems themselves can be understood as palimpsests of sometimes complementary, sometimes competing sounds that makes them examples of what could be called "soundscapes."[11] In riffing on Arjun Appadurai's theorization of the global flow of culture and capital, I am, admittedly, narrowing the precincts under consideration from the global to the national as a way to prefigure both the spatial dimensionality of Whitman's poems as shapes and their aural resonances as the transcription of words and sounds. Put slightly differently, focusing on the sounds of *Leaves of Grass* better allows us to assess their tactility as political discourse as well as their aesthetic registers as poetry. By working through questions that are latent to the sonic infrastructure of *Leaves of Grass*, I seek to investigate the sustainability of the egalitarian impulse of Whitman's democratic project when black bodies are understood to enter the national composition through examinations of "A Boston Ballad" (1855) and "Ethiopia Saluting the Colors" (1872).[12]

■ I HEAR VOICES

Before turning to the question of sound in Whitman's poems that feature black subjects, I would like to revisit two of the most identifiable features of *Leaves of Grass* that have been conventionally understood by critics to delineate Whitman as the "democratic bard"—the invention of the counterpoint "you" subject position and the practices of interlocution that simultaneously unfold as an aggregate chorus.

The invention of Whitman's "you" is wanted, perhaps even structurally needed, to engender the rhetorical underpinnings of his poetic and political project. This "you" is everywhere in *Leaves of Grass*. Alan Trachtenberg has argued that the full promise of *Leaves of Grass*, one where the political theory of democracy is translated to poetry, is not possible without the transcendent subject that Whitman calls "you."[13] In this respect, the "you" subject of Whitman's poems might be more important to *Leaves of Grass* than the "I" subject. By instantiating the "you" subject, Whitman sought to fabricate a conversation between two speakers.

While the positioning of the "you" subject attempts to engender a contrapuntal exchange within *Leaves of Grass*, the pronouncement of a shared corporeality forecloses this communication from emerging as dialogue, pushing it instead closer to the realm of the soliloquy. In the very opening lines of "Song of Myself," Whitman writes:

> I celebrate myself,
> And what I assume you shall assume,
> For every atom belonging to me as good belongs to you. (*LG* 1855, 1)[14]

The would-be exchanges between the "I" and "you" at these moments are reconstituted as a kind of echo that is produced by the nominative self of the poems, the "I" subject.[15] Thus, rather than being an example of an antiphony between "I" and "you," the voice of the shared corporeal entity "I" collapses into self-referentiality, one where the duet is distilled to the solo.[16] In other words, the spatial arrangement of the contrapuntal exchange between the "I" and "you" of *Leaves of Grass*, figured as a romanticized social pairing, a philosophical dialectic, or duet, is presented as a vocal unison that is the synchronic or perhaps even the redoubled articulation of the same voice.

In contrast to the solo singing enacted by the ontologically recursive vocalizations of Whitman's corporealized "I," *Leaves of Grass* is also marked by other moments where the speaker-subject materializes only as a mode of projection and form of amplification. At a later moment in "Song of Myself" Whitman writes:

> Through me many long dumb voices,
> Voices of the interminable generations of slaves,
> Voices of prostitutes and deformed persons,
> Voices of the diseased and despairing, and of thieves and dwarfs,
> Voices of cycles of preparation and accretion,
>
> ...
>
> Through me forbidden voices,
> Voices of sexes and lusts.... voices veiled, and I remove the veil,
> Voices indecent by me clarified and transfigured. (*LG* 1855, 29)

In the most immediate sense, this aspect of Whitman's poetics illustrates Spivak's concept of *vertreten* as a political form of representation that is a "speaking for" someone. This version of *vertreten* is illustrated in later lines from "Song of Myself: —"It is you talking as much as myself.... I act as the tongue of you, / It was tied in your mouth.... in mine it begins to be loosened" (*LG* 1855, 53). Here the poet seeks to diminish his own voice and have it supplemented by that of others. These voices come together as a suite, as a democratic chorus of shared voices. If we think about Whitman's aesthetic practices of interlocution here as a form of choral ventriloquism, the multiplicity of sounds and voices anticipates a model of the United States as an orchestra articulated early in the twentieth century by the philosopher Horace Kallen.[17] If there are moments in *Leaves of Grass* where the relationship between the "I" and "you" subjects projects two bodies through one voice as a kind of unison, then this form of a choral ventriloquism sings multiple voices at once, ostensibly producing a kind of symphony.

■ BALLAD FOR AMERICA

"I hope," the speaker of Whitman's "Boston Ballad" proclaims, that "the fifes / will play Yankee Doodle" (*LG* 1855, 89). But the speaker's desire to hear "Yankee Doodle"—a national anthem, of sorts—is eclipsed by the august silence of the procession. Although the poem's aural resonance is seemingly overshadowed by its visual stagings, I want to suggest that this attenuation is integral to the poem's mechanics. There are two primary sources of sound in the poem. The first is the regulated, formal cadence of the military phalanx of the "President's marshal." The "federal foot," methodical and synchronized, is slowly drawn out, creating a steady and extended rhythm—evinced by the word "dragoons," whose very auditory phonetics extend the sound out and out. The second source of sound in the poem is the constant hum produced by the "Yankee phantoms" themselves (*LG* 1855, 89). Their vocalizations, not figured as articulated words and speech but nonetheless audibly registered, are generated by the "chattering of bare gums" (*LG* 1855, 89). This lull—which lingers throughout the unfolding of the poem's movements—is the sonic equivalent of the poem's visual order. Their complaints, which cannot emerge as words and speech, are underscored by the poem's maneuvers in the visual field that renders the black body at the center of the procession apparitional.

By fabricating a near silence and invisibility, the poem's structural design attempts to divorce the issue of chattel slavery from the procession through Boston. The discourse about the Fugitive Slave Law raging at midcentury is another "unspeakable thing unspoken." In "A Boston Ballad" the specificity of chattel slavery is vacated from the precincts of the poem in order to constitute it as an archetypal lamentation and a ballad for America. What follows, then, is an attempt to perceive the meaning of these unspoken things barely audible on the lower frequencies.

In "A Boston Ballad," Whitman interpolates the aura of the American Revolution to fortify the theme of the poem—a theme that ostensibly is caught in the latent history of the 1850s.[18] The poem opens with "the President's marshal," "government cannon," and "federal foot and dragoons," all apparently trying to make their way through a crowded populace in Boston. The significance of the town itself as the locale for the poem's procession assuredly would not have been lost on the reader, who would have recalled the centrality of Boston to the cultural memory of the United States. The invocation of the radicalism of the colonial era is produced not only by the Revolutionary "phantoms" but by the speaker's admission of his "love to look on the stars and stripes" and his hope that the "fifes will play Yankee Doodle."

The subject and meaning of the poem are initially vague, however. Whitman seemingly refuses to divulge that the poem was about anything beyond the mere reassemblage of colonial spirits. It is only in the seventh stanza when the speaker asks, "What troubles you, Yankee phantoms? What is all this / chattering of bare gums?" Their presence in the parade is meant to suggest that the ideals of the Revolutionary War have been betrayed. However, the protestations of the Yankee phantoms are characterized as feeble and near silent gestures. In the same stanza, the speaker inquires, "Does the ague convulse your limbs? Do you mistake your / crutches for firelocks, and level them?" (*LG* 1855, 89). Whitman's circuitous strategy for imparting the meaning of the poem is coordinated through a series of delays, the most perceptible of which is the absence of the figure that has caused the apparent rupture of democratic ideals in Boston.

Whitman takes great care in "A Boston Ballad" to occlude the presence of the runaway slave who is the catalyst for the gathering depicted in the poem. It should be less than surprising that Whitman himself would consign his African American to the veiled recesses of the poem at the very moment when the latter is actually at the center of the procession through Boston and the key to unfolding the meaning of the poem. Whitman's maneuver in the poem is characteristic of a nation that had formulated an intricate labyrinth of denying the presence of African Americans, especially in regards to political representation, while simultaneously being economically dependent upon their very existence and culturally indebted to them. Perhaps it is all the more ironic that in a poem where the spirits of 1776 are invoked, the African American too is made a phantom, an invisible man of sorts. In fact, the runaway slave never makes an appearance in the poem. Instead of having the African American paraded through the poem, Whitman has his speaker imply that some other presence is more direly needed by asking, "But there is one thing that belongs here.... Shall I tell you / what it is, gentlemen of Boston?" (*LG* 1855, 89).

It is only in the thirteenth stanza that the reader finally learns that the poem is colored by the issue of slavery that engulfed the United States in 1854. While Whitman circumvents the centrality of slavery in his poem, the spectators who observed the actual Boston procession were duly aware of its significance. As Albert J. Von Frank has written, the case of the runaway slave Anthony Burns ignited a wide range of responses from different Bostonians.[19] For Whitman's speaker, the procession of the runaway slave escorted by federal marshals would be best accompanied by the song "Yankee Doodle." Although originally used by the British to disparage American colonials as simpletons, "Yankee Doodle" was embraced after important battles at Lexington, Concord, and Bunker Hill as an anthem of American populist will and fortitude.

But the desire of Whitman's speaker to hear "Yankee Doodle" also reveals the Anthony Burns case as an occasion to illuminate the soundscape as a palimpsest of overlapping and competing cultural forms. Whitman's "Boston

Ballad" needs to be understood for how it stages political debate through art and culture, figured here as the distinction between the embedded anthem and the contextual minstrel song. Among the observers who congregated in Boston as Burns was being conducted through the streets were a group of militiamen who crooned the minstrel song "Carry Me Back to Old Virginny." With its romanticization of plantation life, "Carry Me Back to Old Virginny" depicts slavery as a benevolent institution, one where blacks were happy to be born and die. Thus, while both songs invoke the past, Whitman's summoning of "Yankee Doodle," in a poem where he has deliberately faded the principal black subject, disallows chattel slavery from being understood as a constitutional crisis of U.S. democracy as much as "Carry Me Back to Old Virginny" fabricates a nostalgia to obliterate the violence that the Fugitive Slave Law was doing to black subjects.

Instead, Whitman rehistoricizes "A Boston Ballad" as a crisis of nation formation for American colonials attempting to break away from the British crown:

> I will whisper it to the Mayor .... he shall send a committee to England,
> They shall get a grant from the Parliament, and go with a cart to the royal vault,
> Dig out King George's coffin .... unwrap him quick from the graveclothes ....
>   box up his bones for a journey:
> Find a swift Yankee clipper .... here is freight for you blackbellied clipper,
> Up with your anchor! shake out your sails! .... steer straight towards Boston bay.
>   (*LG* 1855, 89–90)

Whitman's depiction of the king's bones being exhumed from their royal English grave and transported to the cradle of American democracy seeks to proclaim the reestablishment of the British monarchy on the other side of the Atlantic. The image of the king being transported *back* to the United States should not be lost because it suggests that the country, with this recent infraction of Revolutionary ideals, is reverting to a pre-1776 relationship with England.

Yet still further, in the context of mobility and enslavement, King George's bones traverse the Atlantic on their way to Boston with the effect of putting the reader to mind of both the imminent return of the runaway slave Anthony Burns and the incalculable number of Africans being transported to the New World. The subtextual constellation of the poem's structure, then, remaps its spatial cartography to intersect the vertical axis of the U.S. north/south trajectory with the horizontal axis of the east/west movement of the Middle Passage, revealing the global matrix of racialized chattel slavery. Hence, the reference to the "blackbellied clipper" now makes it evident that the vessel upon which King George should be transplanted to Boston is a slave ship whose interior would have been colored black with African bodies. With the arrival of King George's bones, Whitman's speaker announces that the true "centerpiece" of the procession is now present for proper viewing by the assemblage. Whitman's critique of chattel slavery here is as circuitous as King George's itinerary to the United States.

Whitman's unwillingness to indict the African American as a criminal for violating the Fugitive Slave Law is accomplished by the poet's very refusal to reveal him at all in the poem and instead substitute King George as a replacement. He implies that it is not the runaway slave who is criminal but rather the nation at large for succumbing to the dictates of the slaveholding states and their sympathizers. Yet in typical Whitman fashion, he is reluctant to forthrightly offend the sensibilities of slaveholders. It is here that he performs the most delicate and perplexing of surgeries. Instead of attributing the assumed infractions of Revolutionary ideals to the country's slaveholding constituency, Whitman submits that the violations were due rather to a regressive form of subservience to the British monarchy. As Jay Grossman notes, Whitman used the Anthony Burns case and the enforcement of the Fugitive Slave Law as occasions to bemoan a citizenry who had not sufficiently recognized or condemned this encroachment upon the idea of popular will by the federal government.[20]

One of the hallmarks of Whitman's cultural nationalism was his propensity to identify "America" and "democracy" uniformly as synonyms as he wrote in *Democratic Vistas* (1870).[21] Consequently, when he detects an element of society that he feels is nondemocratic (or even antidemocratic), his inclination is to see it as something outside the boundaries of the United States. This strategy is deployed in "A Boston Ballad" with astonishing effect as he disassociates chattel slavery with the slaveholding states and then designates the institution both as something that is aligned with the British monarchy and as something that is anachronistic.

In a strategy comparable to the one employed in "A Boston Ballad," Whitman invoked the American Revolution of 1776 to accentuate the seemingly similar political conditions of the present moment with the past in "Europe, The 72nd and 73rd Years of These States." Whereas "A Boston Ballad" describes the ideals of 1776 as being compromised, they are sustained and regenerated in "Europe, The 72nd and 73rd Years of These States"—"Not a grave of the murdered for freedom but grows seed / for freedom.... in its turn to bear seed, / Which the winds carry afar and re-sow, and the rains and / the snows nourish" (*LG* 1855, 134). Not only is a continuum between 1776 and 1848 established, the poem also implies that Europe will soon take its cues from the United States; in essence, that it is indeed the political off-spring of the United States. Unlike "A Boston Ballad" which evinces a fear that the United States might be figuratively enfolded back into the British empire—to, in essence, revert to being a mere colony again—"Europe, The 72nd and 73rd Years of These States" intimates that the natural and proper dissemination of "organic compacts" would be filtered through the United States. In a circuitous enactment of re-temporalization, Europe is depicted as leaping forth into futurity. Whitman imagined that the principles and ethos of democracy would emanate onto a global stage.

Upon closer reading, "A Boston Ballad" is perhaps much less scathing of the institution of slavery than initially appears—again, another indication of Whitman's political strategy of consensus that is displayed in his poetry.[22] Although Whitman was less vehement than Ralph Waldo Emerson in his condemnation of the Fugitive Slave Law, his arrival in "A Boston Ballad" was far from the dreary conclusions reached in Melville's "Benito Cereno." Perhaps for Whitman it was the forced return of a runaway slave by federal mandate that impinged upon democratic inclinations rather than the institution of slavery itself. However distasteful Whitman himself may have thought it, he felt little impetus to condemn the institution during this especially intense period at mid-decade in his prose works.

The meaning of the multiple ways in which the specter of the African American is obfuscated gains new meaning. It becomes evident that it is neither slavery nor the forced return of the escapee that has piqued the speaker's chagrin. Rather for Whitman, the real threat to American democratic affinities was the diminishment of popular sovereignty. Whitman associates this kind of oppression with the autocracies typified by those like King George's reign. As still a further indication that the nation was moving backward politically, he intimated that North America would revert to being a colony of England with the line "You have got your revenge old buster!... The crown is / come to its own and more than its own" (*LG* 1855, 90). It is in this fashion that Whitman's ostensible critique of slavery is sufficiently diluted to reveal itself properly as a lamentation regarding the whittling of popular will in the United States.

■ PRIMARY COLORS

Whereas the Fugitive Slave Law could only remain a shadow concern in "A Boston Ballad," it was conspicuous in Whitman's essay "The Eighteenth Presidency!" In this piece, Whitman uses the upcoming presidential election between James Buchanan and Millard Fillmore as an occasion to offer a theory of the nation. Although it remained unpublished during his lifetime, "The Eighteenth Presidency!" is as important for revealing Whitman's views on the Fugitive Slave Law as it is for intimating his idea of the "organic compact" as a political theory of liberal democracy.

Whitman opens the first section of "The Eighteenth Presidency!" by outlining his definition of the nation and its citizens. He notes that the United States had essentially inverted the former, more antiquated, "programme of the classes of a nation," where kings, nobility, and the gentry were the identity of the nation. By contrast, in the United States "all laboring persons... are in fact, and to all intents and purposes, the American nation, the people."[23] Despite tallying slave owners in answering the query "First, Who Are the Nation?" Whitman elected not to include millions of slaves in his informal census. Whitman's decision not to include slaves—and, by extension, millions of blacks—pushes the teleology of the original logic of the Three-fifths Compromise to its furthest extreme, one where blacks are nearly vanished altogether.

Whitman had expressed similar sentiments about laborers as quintessential Americans earlier but with particular emphasis on the white working class.[24] In his Free-Soil editorials for the *Brooklyn Eagle*, Whitman returned again and again to the sanctity of the white working class. In a September 1847 article entitled "American Workingmen, versus Slavery," Whitman criticizes the extension of slavery as a threat to *"the grand body of the white workingmen, the millions of mechanics, farmers, and operatives of our country."* Slavery, Whitman continues, benefited a "few thousand rich, 'polished,' and aristocratic owners of slaves at the South," promising to put working-class whites on a par with black slaves.[25]

Whitman's condemnation of the Fugitive Slave Law was based on his Free-Soil beliefs and his impression concerning the proper equilibrium between the state and its citizens. His vision of one hellish slave state begetting another, where plantations thoroughly eclipsed free laborers, prompted his initial affiliation with the Free-Soil Party. But the Fugitive Slave Law did not sanction the expansion of slavery; it maintained, however, that the laws of one state could not be neglected in another: "As to what is called the Fugitive Slave Law, insolently put over the people by their Congress and President, it contravenes the whole of the organic compacts, and is at all times to be defied in all parts of These States, South or North, by speech, by pen, and, if need be, by the bullet and sword" ("Eighteenth," 2132–33). Here, Whitman's tenor nearly approximates that of the abolitionists. Indeed, moments later, in a direct plea to the young men of the Southern states, Whitman asks if all should not be abolitionists. He makes an appeal for each man to voice his opposition to slavery "on account of the whites" and to see it "abolished for their sake" ("Eighteenth," 2133). Further still, Whitman concludes this section with a conventional invocation of the founding fathers: "Do you know that Washington, Jefferson, Madison, and all the great Presidents and primal warriors and sages were declared abolitionists?" ("Eighteenth," 2133). In a quintessentially Whitmanian fashion, he employs abolitionist rhetoric but not actually in the service of abolitionism itself.

While he continually worried that slavery discounted white workers, Whitman felt that Congress had endangered the nation's "organic compacts" when they passed the Fugitive Slave Law, interfering with individual state legislation. He maintained that once a state organized itself, the federal government should withdraw, only re-entering for certain duties specified by the Constitution. Whitman insinuated that the federal government infringed upon the free states by making them culpable to the laws of slaveholding states. This was reiterated by Emerson who, thinking of its ethical consequences, regretted that the "new Bill made it operative, required me to hunt slaves, and it found citizens in Massachusetts willing to act as judges and captors."[26] But, whereas Emerson's aversion to the Fugitive Slave Law was based primarily on what he saw as an ethical violation, Whitman saw it primarily as a violation of the procedural underpinnings of the "organic compact." Whitman proposed instead that these matters should be adjusted by the "good faith" of the states—"Good faith is irresistible among men,

and friendship is; which lawyers can not understand, thinking nothing but com-
pulsion will do" ("Eighteenth," 2132).

Whitman's views on the Fugitive Slave Law are conspicuous especially when
viewed in relation to the "runaway slave" passage of "Song of Myself" from only
the year before, a passage that is often invoked by critics as a sign of his sympathy
for blacks:

> The runaway slave came to my house and stopped outside,
> I heard his motions crackling the twigs of the woodpile,
> Through the swung half-door of the kitchen I saw him limpsey and weak,
> And went where he sat on a log, and led him in and assured him,
> And brought him water and filled a tub for his sweated body and bruised feet,
> And gave him a room that entered from my own, and gave him some coarse clean
>   clothes,
> And remember perfectly well his revolving eyes and his awkwardness,
> And remember putting plasters on the galls of his neck and ankles;
> He staid with me a week before he was recuperated and passed north,
> I had him sit next me at table .... my firelock leaned in the corner. (*LG* 1855, 19)

As Wai Chee Dimock notes, "The runaway slave is not a *particular* slave, he is
any slave, for the poet would have done as much for anyone bearing that generic
identity."[27] Desiring the well-being of his guest, the speaker bathes and dresses his
wounds, giving "him a room that entered from [his] own." Although Whitman's
poetic project calls for an abrogation of conventional divisions and binary rela-
tionships, the intimacy of the speaker's kindness is circumscribed by the juridical
impulses of the U.S. definitions of the citizen and noncitizen that govern how
this particular relationship will follow the mandates of the state. What Whitman
wants instead is a kind of intimate America, to use a phrase by Peter Coviello,
subsumed in his notion of the "organic compact."[28]

Although he mentions the term in a letter to Ralph Waldo Emerson in August
of 1856, the "organic compact" was more fully formulated in "The Eighteenth
Presidency!" Here Whitman wrote that that the platforms for the presidency were
"simply the organic compacts" of the states, the Declaration of Independence,
Constitution, acts of Congress, "and the now well-understood and morally established rights of man, wherever the sun shines, the rain falls, and the grass grows"
("Eighteenth," 2130). Whitman's description of the "organic compact" here signaled a more expansive theory of relation not simply between the states themselves that comprise the U.S. but between the States and its founding documents
(Declaration and Constitution), intermediaries (Congress), and meta-narratives
("rights of man"). The phrase "organic compact" was emerging for Whitman as
a concept to describe a social, as well as a political, cohesion. Although he was
principally outlining his theory of the Union in "The Eighteenth Presidency!,"
no small quality of the poet emerges here with the reference to images of nature,
ending, as it does, with the signature image and metaphor of grass itself.

Whitman would further illustrate the idea of "organic compacts" in his poetry. Encouraging the reader to "remember the organic compact of These / States!" in "Poems of Remembrances for A Girl or A Boy of These States," Whitman uses language that echoed "The Eighteenth Presidency!"—"Remember what was promulged by the founders, / ratified by The States, signed in black and / white by the Commissioners, read by Washington at the head of the army!" (*LG* 1856, 42). In the 1856 edition he refers to the United States as a "compact organism" in "Poem of One in Many." As a veritable turn on the U.S. national motto "E Pluribus Unum," Whitman's use of the term "compact organism" here accentuates it as something more than simply a theory of political relation but rather as a sociality of cohesion. And for Whitman, this sociality of cohesion—or what he called "fusion"—was best illuminated through metaphors of nature and the body rather than accounts of political processes per se. In the stanza immediately following the one where he mentions "compact organism," Whitman describes this form of cohesion.

> To hold men together by paper and seal, or by
>   compulsion, is no account,
> That only hold together which is living
>   principles, as the hold of the limbs of the
>   body, or the fibres of plants. (*LG 1856*, 188)

One of the most identifiable characteristics of Whitman's idea of the "compact organism" here in "Poem of One in Many" is that it privileges a social cohesion that is not promulgated or maintained by contract or force. The metaphors of the body and plants are deployed to underscore "compact organism" as a living operation. While it seems as if this living quality of the "compact organism" might threaten to make it unduly contingent or too bound (and determined) by the present moment, the concept is, in fact, undergirded by a host of governing ideas which direct how it will unfold.

Taken together, the numerous iterations of the "organic compact" throughout Whitman's works—from poetry to letters to essays—need to be understood as a fundamental concept intrinsic to his vision of America and his cultural logic of cohesion. The "organic compact" is not simply a mode of sociality particular to America but also Whitman's theory of poetics. His vision of America and poetry is informed by the organizing principle of the "organic compact" that operates as both a philosophical concept and formal principle to seemingly engender a sense of equilibrium—an equilibrium that is often registered as social equivalency. Given the multiple permutations of the phrase "organic compact" which were repeated again and again between 1856 and 1860, it is not altogether surprising that Whitman saw slavery as an issue that could compromise the cohesion of America.

In Whitman's poetry, the "organic compacts" often emerges as the process where various identities, locales, and histories mere into one identity through his manipulation of numberless dialectics and catalogs. Whitman's dialectics take two positions or categories that have been rendered antipodal and makes them the ontological complement of one another, producing, in effect, multiple localized "organic compacts" of binary units. For example, Whitman's famous lines—"Do I contradict myself? / Very well then…. I contradict myself;"—act as the quicksilver announcement of scores of seeming opposites in *Leaves of Grass* which are placed in ever closer propinquity with one another—"I am of old and young, of the foolish as much as the wise"; "I am the poet of the body, / And I am the poet of the soul"; "I help myself to the material and immaterial"; "The call of the slave is one with the master's call . . and the master salutes the slave" (*LG* 1855, 74; 78; 96; 123). Whitman's centripetal maneuvers of contraction shorten the circumference between the center and its periphery yielding a series of dialectics that produce no ostensible antinomies.

Almost in contradistinction to the strategies of contraction that create multiple "organic compacts" comprised as binary units, *Leaves of Grass* is inundated with catalogues. In his early defense of the catalogues against the charge of formlessness, Buell argues that Whitman structures his catalogues in such a way to move beyond merely capturing the plenitude of the nation with a latent sensory capacity.[29] But what seems equally important to Buell's notation of Whitman's patterns is the putative positive political charge that he ascribes to the catalogs, a reading that is representative of much of the critical assessment of the catalogs. Suggestion that "catalogue poetry" approximates a form of "political action," Buell describes Whitman's catalogue rhetoric" as particularly "democratic" technique where the "prosodic equalitarianism" of each line guarantees that every "line or image is of equal weight in the ensemble."[30] The "prosodic equalitarianism" that Buell finds in the catalogs might be thought of as white noise, a seemingly unending sonic field where differences and nuances exist but are flattened and compressed within a finite frequency range to give the sensation of approximate sameness.

Whitman's poetic theory of "organic compacts" not only reverberated the concept of the "social contract," most often associated with John Locke and other Enlightenment philosophers, but extended it, pushing it to its conceptual limits where an American social order could be maintained without the surrendering of any rights. Whereas Whitman's other colloquialisms translate an equality of condition among persons who are more types than individuals, his notion of the "organic compact" sought to evince the naturalization of social contracts to such an extent that they appear organic or rather, more precisely, do not appear at all. He considered "organic compacts" material objects as much as processes, a phenomenon in transference and equilibrium that could guarantee equality. Whitman's conceptualization depends upon the double nature of "organic compacts": "organic compacts" as *natural* material objects and "organic compacts" as a process of *naturalization*. I would add that whatever degree of formlessness

Whitman's catalogues display, they are prefigured by a certain logic. Although there are no ostensible hierarchies or rankings in the catalogues, the repetition of key American archetypes—the farmer, mechanic, sailor, for example—divulge an idealized subject for Whitman.

While the catalogues are seemingly the most conspicuous aspect of the unbound nature of Whitman's poetry, they also offer perhaps the most profound example of the "organic compact" as a theory of poetics. To read Whitman's catalogues as simply an illustration of how things are continually "expanding and always / expanding, / Outward and outward and forever outward" is to fail recognize how they manipulate aurality to create a sonic relationship that allows for the fluid oscillation between the here and there (*LG* 1855, 112). The repetition of words—often the opening words of new lines—creates a sense of reverberation, an echo that anchors the speaker in his present locality at the same moment that he is gravitating elsewhere and thus represent a complicated interplay between expansion and contraction.

For example, in poems like "'Song of Myself'" and "'A Song for Occupations,'" with catalogues that often appear not simply as interminable but, not infrequently, as non-sequiturs, Whitman's poetics perform a dual operation. On the one hand, the ever-expanding catalogues are figured as litanies that abrogate conventional stanzaic formation—as if traditional poetic formulas themselves could not "contain the multitudes." On the other hand, while the aural resonances of the catalogues, generated by the repetition of key phrases and words, seem to move with the trajectory of these lines outward, they nonetheless fabricate a sense of stasis, less of permanence than of constancy, through a kind of sedimentation.

If the dialectics and catalogues persist as examples of Whitman's vision of "America" and the "great Idea" of "organic compacts," then perhaps the place where a new American subjectivity becomes most realizable are the words themselves. In this respect, the most democratic aspect of Whitman's poetics is not its all-encompassing vision but rather Whitman's inclusion of other languages.[31] As much as his catalogues and syntactic constructions help to produce a new vernacular, his inclusion of words like "libertad," "Americanos," and "camerado," reflect this fusion of cultures, changing the idioms and rhythms of Whitman's poetry, if not the national language altogether. These new idioms are further announced by Whitman's neologisms. Significantly, these words index an important, if not necessary, modification on the "organic compact" as a form of fusion. By destabilizing the primacy of English as the national language of America, Whitman intimates that the United States will itself be fused by the influences of other cultures and peoples. "Camerado" might be thought of as the anticipated or ideal subject position produced by the "organic compact." But, as a neologism, "camerado" is an example of a seeming fusion, one where the resonance and timbre of its aurality sound as if they come from elsewhere but are also immediately and intimately recognizable.

■ "ETHIOPIA SHALL STRETCH FORTH HER HANDS . . ."

It is a commonplace in Whitman scholarship to note that his departure from conventional verse forms was an attempt to develop a poetics that was distinctly new, a new literary form that was marked by the occasion of the United States being a new kind of nation the world had never before seen.[32] Perhaps the most conspicuous aspect of "Ethiopia Saluting the Colors" (1872), then, is how it feigns an approximation of the earlier poetic conventions Whitman found staid and what his adoption here of these conventions suggests about the poem's relationship to other pieces in *Leaves of Grass*.[33] Composed almost as five tercets, "Ethiopia Saluting the Colors" is one of a handful of Whitman poems with a discernible rhyme and meter. The tercets display a pattern whereby lines 2 and 3 end-rhyme, with the first featuring an internal rhyme that accentuates the poem's overall tonality.

> WHO are you, dusky woman, so ancient, hardly human,
> With your wooly-white and turban'd head, and bare
> > bony feet?
> Why, rising by the roadside here, do you the colors
> > greet?
>
> ('Tis while our army lines Carolina's sand and pines,
> Forth from thy hovel door, thou, Ethiopia, com'st to me,
> As, under doughty Sherman, I march toward the sea.)
>
> *Me, master, years a hundred, since from my parents sun-*
> > *der'd,*
> *A little child, they caught me as the savage beast is caught;*
> *Then hither me, across the sea, the cruel slaver brought.*
>
> No further does she say, but lingering all day,
> Her high-borne turban'd head she wags, and rolls her
> > darkling eye,
> And curtseys to the regiments, the guidons moving by.
>
> What is it, fateful woman—so blear, hardly human?
> Why wag your head, with turban bound—yellow, red
> > and green?
> Are the things so strange and marvelous, you see or
> > have seen? (*LG* 1872, 412–13)

Phonetically, the lines sound as if they are approximate, but the prosody of the lines is slightly off; the lines approach heptameter but frequently deviate. The visual outline of the poem itself suggests that something is askew, as if the form of the line threatens to compromise the particular sonic impulse of the poem's rhyme and rhythm.

Carrying the parenthetical statement "A Reminisce of 1864," "Ethiopia Saluting the Colors" is an anomaly among Whitman's Civil War poetry because it is the only one that explicitly illustrates the centrality of slavery and race to the fate of the country. It describes a brief encounter with a soldier and an old black woman during William T. Sherman's March to the Sea campaign in 1864. The solider is confused as to why the woman would salute the flag and is perplexed by not being able to ascertain whether she herself can appreciate the symbolism of the Stars and Stripes or the meaning of Union soldiers. Whitman began writing the poem in the summer of 1867 and featured it in the "Bathed in War's Perfume" cluster of the fifth edition of *Leaves of Grass*.

Like "Ethiopia Saluting the Colors," the Lucifer passages from "The Sleepers" is important because it is one of only two poems where Whitman's black subjects have a voice. Ed Folsom notes that the passive voice of the dusky woman in "Ethiopia Saluting the Colors" contrasts with the "powerful expression of agency" of Lucifer, who "speaks a full subjectivity out of his enslavement, and his 'I,' displacing Whitman's narrator's 'I,' is clear and strong."[34] Following the "red squaw" section of "The Sleepers" where the Native American woman is conspicuously silent, Lucifer is comparatively vocal:

> Now Lucifer was not dead.... or if he was I am his sorrowful terrible heir;
> I have been wronged....I am oppressed....I hate him that oppresses me,
> I will either destroy him, or he shall release me. (*LG* 1855, 43)

Citing the original 1855 version of the Lucifer passage, Betsy Erkkilä has noted that the "passage links the logic of slave revolt with the revolutionary origins of the American republic."[35] Erkkilä's reading of the initial iteration of the Lucifer passage from "The Sleepers" underscores how Whitman conceptualized a robust form of democratic egalitarianism by invoking the tenor of the right of revolution articulated by Thomas Paine and others—a strategy that African American intellectuals including David Walker, Frederick Douglass, William Cooper Nell, Martin R. Delany, and William Wells Brown all used before the Civil War. Lucifer's presence makes less sense after the Civil War as a cry against slavery. After the first two postwar editions of *Leaves of Grass*, he disappears, as does his strident voice, which had been redoubled by its having been intertwined with the poem's speaker, leaving Ethiopia as perhaps the most visible—and audible—black subject in the later editions of *Leaves*.[36]

One of the most striking features of the visual encodings of "Ethiopia Saluting the Colors" is how it demarcates national subjectivities through the visual optics of clothing and attire. The most conspicuous of these is the dusky woman's turban that is meant to differentiate and orientalize her as an exotic. Accentuated by the contrast of the colors upon the white palette of hair, the yellow, red, and green tones are meant to evince her affinity with Ethiopia. Her insignia as a foreign national is set against the designation of the guidon of the military uniform. The placement of these colors upon her head is significant because her head is sym- bolized as a site of consciousness as much as of cognition. From the soldier's per- spective, the dusky woman can neither comprehend the scene proceeding before her eyes nor understand the symbolism of the flag.

As conspicuous as the visual encodings of "Ethiopia Saluting the Colors" remain, the aural dynamics of the poem as a soundscape are even more pro- nounced. Contesting the accord produced by the poem's rhyme sequence, the interior monologues of the soldier and the dusky woman exist as self-contained speeches that cannot come together in dialogue. Indeed, underscored by their placement directly in the middle of the poem, the dusky woman's words are ren- dered in dialect. Rendered as such, with no constructed interlocutor, the dusky woman's speech remains intelligible. Indeed, although her dialect is seemingly removed from the recognized national language, artistically her words have a greater poetic quality against the more narrative form of the soldier's words. If Whitman thought of black dialect as the basis for a "grand native opera," there is little suggestion here in "Ethiopia Saluting the Colors" of how blacks might shape American culture. If black dialect was going to foment into a "grand native opera," it seems like it would have to wait until after the turn of the century.

Forty-five years after "Ethiopia Saluting the Colors" found its way into the 1871–72 edition of *Leaves of Grass*, it was made anew by Henry Thacker Burleigh. Born in 1866, Burleigh was a classical composer who trained with Antonín Dvořák while at the National Conservatory of Music in New York City. A bari- tone, he was one of the earliest African Americans to attend the conservatory, and was later appointed soloist at Saint George's Episcopal Church, a position that he held for more than fifty years. In the 1890s, he began publishing his arrangements of art songs, and by the end of the decade, he was composing his own songs.[37] An art song is a vocal music composition, traditionally written for one singer accompanied by a piano or orchestra. More specifically, art songs are typically intended to be performed as part of a recital or similar relatively formal occasion and usually are not part of a staged work. Importantly, art songs are settings of lyric poetry. By integrating poet, composer, singer, and accompanist into one moment, the art song strives to perfect the interplay between music and literature that places equal weight on tone as much as the word.

Beyond his acclaim for arranging art songs, Burleigh was also praised as the first to make formal orchestral arrangements for dozens of Negro spirituals, spirituals by anonymous African Americans that might be thought of as consti- tuting the "grand native opera" that Whitman so desired and that James Weldon Johnson announced as one of the only distinctly American products to spring from its soil.[38] In the same note that Whitman speaks of the need for a "theory of the modification of the English language, for musical purposes, for a grand native opera in America," he writes that black dialect has furnished an entirely new vocabulary as well as new modes of pronunciation.[39]

As a social text, Burleigh's composition is significant because it revises two earlier artworks—one literary, the other musical—that depicted one of the most decisive historical events that rescripted black subjectivity in the United States. Burleigh's "Ethiopia Saluting the Colors" is marked by its militaristic accompaniment, underscored by his weaving strands of the Civil War tune "Marching through Georgia" (1865) (figure 4.1).[40] With a tempo of 116, the music is fully a march (an element that is also supported by the bass clef accompaniment) and fast for the vocal line, especially at the section which begins "As under doughty Sherman." There are a number of accidentals, which, in conjunction with the forte volume, distinguishes this brief line from the rest.

No.1 in C minor
116339

No.2 in D minor
116157

DEDICATED TO AND SUNG BY MR. HERBERT WITHERSPOON

ETHIOPIA SALUTING THE COLORS

SONG

The Poem by

WALT WHITMAN

The Music by

H.T. BURLEIGH

Price 75 cents

COPYRIGHT MCMXV
BY G RICORDI & CO,INC.
116157.

An orchestral accompaniment can be had on hire from the publishers

G. RICORDI & CO.,
14 EAST 43RD STREET
NEW YORK

AND AT
LONDON, PARIS, LEIPZIG,
ROME, PALERMO, NAPLES,
BUENOS-AYRES AND MILAN.

Figure 4.1 Continued

Figure 4.1 Harry Thacker Burleigh, "Ethiopia Saluting the Colors" sheet music, c1915. Performing Arts Reading Room, Library of Congress.

Thematically, Henry Clay Work's "Marching through Georgia" is similar to Whitman's poem in that in refers to Sherman's March to the Sea campaign. But where Whitman's poem is identified by a sense of morose confusion, Work's piece is ebullient and bright. Burleigh quotes "Marching through Georgia" to signal a brighter, new day for African Americans, and in this sense, his musical composition undercuts the dreary pessimism of the words and images of Whitman's poem.[41] Unlike a number of anthems and fanfares in the Western tradition in major keys, this version is written in C minor.[42] Burleigh's performance of "Ethiopia Saluting the Colors," in this sense, remade Whitman's poem as much as it did Work's song, illustrating my wider claims about the remix aesthetic in African American cultural production regarding the practices and politics of reinterpretation.

Burleigh's decision to make an art song of "Ethiopia Saluting the Colors" not only allowed him to rework an image of a black woman as being outside the national body politic but perhaps also signaled a moment of identification with an emerging black diasporic consciousness.[43] Although "Ethiopian" was used indiscriminately throughout the nineteenth century to describe generically various peoples of African descent, after the Battle of Adowa in 1896, "Ethiopia" and "Ethiop" gained greater specificity and significance in the African American imagination. In the same year as the Battle of Adowa, Paul Laurence Dunbar published *Lyrics of a Lowly Life* (1896), which included his own poem "Ode to Ethiopia." The African American preoccupation with Ethiopia would continue through the mid-1930s with Haile Selassie's campaign against Italian fascism. Beginning in 1911 as the music editor for the New York branch of the Milan-based G. Ricordi and Company, Burleigh had to spend summers in Italy, where he may have been increasingly politicized in the wake of the assaults on Ethiopia.

In addition to Whitman's, Burleigh composed art songs from both white and black poets to stylize a palpably high art form. Burleigh arranged Robert Burns's "I Love My Jean" (1787) in 1914, a poem written in Scottish dialect that approximates ballad stanzas, and Adela Florence Nicholson's "Five Songs" in 1919. But, importantly, Burleigh composed arrangements for James Weldon Johnson's "Young Warrior" (1917) and Langston Hughes's "Lovely Dark and Lonely One" (1935). While Johnson's poem makes use of the antiquated symbol of the sword, his poem, like Claude McKay's "If I Must Die" (1919), was not immediately interpreted as a commentary on race but rather used as an anthem in one of the world wars.[44]

In transforming Whitman's poem specifically into an art song, Burleigh also undercut Whitman's desire for *Leaves of Grass* to be a grand native opera by which Whitman probably meant something more organic, vernacular, and polyvocal than something strictly formal and highbrow.[45] But if Burleigh's version could be said to undercut Whitman's vision of America's "grand native opera" as an organic national aesthetic, then it could also be said to literalize the political underpinnings of Whitman's poetics of a shared corporeality, as if in essence Whitman's tongue had been further loosened, finding home in yet another body.

PART TWO

Visuality and the Optical Illusions of National Belonging

5   Framing the Margins

Geometries of Space and American Genre Painting

After strolling through the streets of Brooklyn in the early days of the new year of 1851, Walt Whitman found himself reminiscing about two particular images. He had just returned from viewing the exhibits at the Brooklyn Art Union, where he had offered a few opening remarks, and, as usual, America was on his mind. He wrote his impressions of the exhibit and of the paintings by the venerable William Sidney Mount and the younger Walter Libbey, in the February 1, 1851, issue of the *New York Evening Post*:

> I returned, the other day, after looking at Mount's last work—I think his best—of a Long Island negro, the winner of a goose at a raffle; and though it certainly is a fine and spirited thing, if I were to choose between the two, the one to hang up in my room for my own gratification, I should take the boy with his flute. This, too, to my notion, has a character of Americanism about it. Abroad, a similar subject would show the boy as handsome, perhaps, but he would be a young boor, and nothing more. The stamp of class is, in this way, upon all the fine scenes of the European painters, where the subjects are of a proper kind; while in this boy of Walter Libbey's, there is nothing to prevent his becoming a President, or even the editor of a leading newspaper.[1]

Libbey's boy embodied a national ethos—an ethos that, in Whitman's estimation, exemplified the absence of the reified class structures he believed endemic to European societies and one where a newspaper editor was the ostensible equal of a president. Whitman, tongue-in-cheek and with no small gleam of subdued laughter to boot, perhaps saw a bit of himself in the young boy, especially as he himself had been a newspaper editor and, thus, in his mind's eye, Libbey's painting symbolized a figurative continuum of boys to men as a particular index of the nation. To be sure, when he spoke of a certain undeniable "character of Americanism," Whitman was referring to the archetype of a boy playing a flute, which had a kind of national iconicity. And although the "Children of Adam" poems of *Leaves of Grass* were still several years away, Whitman's assessment of Libbey's painting intimates the sensory, if not erotic, pleasures of viewing the boy.

Whitman thought the painting by Mount, *The Lucky Throw* (1851), was "a fine and splendid thing," but he also estimated that while the black subject might forever approximate a national identity, he certainly would not embody it to the degree that Libbey's boy could. He conceded that the black subject in *The Lucky Throw* bore some evidence of an American character but stopped slightly short of the enthusiastic praise he bestowed on Libbey's work: "Mount's negro may be said to have a character of Americanism, too, but I must be pardoned for saying, that I never could, and never will admire the exemplifying of our national attributes with Ethiopian minstrelsy, or Yankee Hill characters upon the stage, as the best and highest we can do in that way."[2] Whitman's characterization of the black subject as an "Ethiopian minstrel" was probably informed by his taking in more than one minstrel show or two in his day.[3]

Whitman's review of the paintings by Mount and Libbey divulges how the image of blacks split his understanding of political representation by disaggregating the body politic and the national body. In this sense, blacks might invariably be part of the body politic, everywhere present and impossible to circumvent, but they could not be understood as a national body per se—only a specter of it.[4] Whitman's assessment is symptomatic of the larger dilemmas of representation latent within U.S. politics, a dilemma that he explored through various uses of metonymy and synecdoche in his poetry but that are expressed here in his Brooklyn Art Union review through the pretext of art and beauty and the subtext of spatialization. In Whitman's reading, there is a certain unease with black bodies, even the simulacra of them, when they are too close for comfort or too close to home, as it were. More specifically, it is precisely through his comments on personal space that Whitman articulates an understanding of aesthetics as pleasure, sensation, and "gratification."

Whitman's assessment of Libbey's painting illustrates the relationship between space and race as a central problematic concerning the aliened status of African Americans and the predicament of that alienation as they inform and maintain political representation in the United States. Space is not simply the area in between one coordinate and another or the empty zone between two points; rather, if we graph space, if we visualize it through such concepts and realities as "contested spaces," "occupied areas," and "border zones," for example, then an understanding of space as a differentiated and differentiating domain becomes increasingly perceptible. If, as Gaston Bachelard has argued, space has a certain phenomenology that informs how it is experienced, then there was perhaps no one more conscious, often painfully so, of the ways in which U.S. space—from the plantation house to the slave quarters, city landscapes to pastoral farms, public thoroughfares to secret passageways—dictated the sensory and political forms of national being than African Americans.[5] By graphing areas, we are able to interrogate how space is used ideologically to delimit zones, domains, and spheres that undergird our notions of subjectivity through a mode of analysis that I am calling the "social logic of spatial forms."

Many of Mount's paintings, like a host of other works by American genre painters, need to be understood through the social logic of spatial forms; for if the claims of their democratic pretensions lie primarily in the depictions of everyday life, it is essential that we examine how and through what means those scenes of everyday life are being depicted. Such an interpretative mode of analysis implies that reading space through an attendant set of correlated ideas such as areas, coordinates, and precincts provides a critical lens for decoding the ways in which the body politic and its margins are demarcated in nineteenth-century visual culture. Recognizing, for example, that blacks often share the same physical precincts with whites but all too often do not occupy the same social domain underscores the idea of approximation (temporally, physically, and politically), as a form of spatialization.

In turning to Whitman's assessment of Mount, I seek to not only underscore his importance as arguably the preeminent nineteenth-century American genre painter but also prefigure the significance of race, space, and blackness to his political aesthetic and other subsequent painters who followed in his wake.[6] Important recent work has been done on race and representation in nineteenth-century American and African American painting by Martin A. Berger, Michael D. Harris, Guy McElroy, and Gwendolyn DuBois Shaw; my analyses in this chapter seeks to contribute to this discussion of race and representation by examining architectonic elements of scenes in American genre painting to interrogate how social belonging is coded through spatial configuration.[7]

The spectrum of the images under consideration in this chapter is for the most part divided into representations of the private realms of social interaction and the civic arenas of politics. Some of the illustrations of private realms depict African Americans in primarily white domains, such as Mount's *Rustic Dance after a Sleigh Ride* (1830); others, such as Eastman Johnson's *Negro Life at the South* (1959), depict African Americans in spaces that are more discretely their own. Representations of civic arenas of political discourse include Richard Caton Woodville's *War News from Mexico* (1848), Mount's *California News* (1850), and Thomas Waterman Wood's *A Bit of History* (1866). By analyzing the spatial forms in works by Mount, Woodville, Johnson, Winslow Homer, and others, I argue that the compositional logic of American genre painting strategically organized zones in terms of centers and margins in various settings, such as parlors, barns, and post offices, as a means to illustrate the forms of democratic belonging in the United States.

■ HOMEFRONTS; OR, THE POLITICS OF INTERIORITY

Perhaps no other painting is more emblematic of how the private realm of social interaction is politicized than Mount's *Rustic Dance after a Sleigh Ride* (figure 5.1). First displayed in the National Academy of Design in 1830, Mount's painting was prompted by a desire for familiar scenes of everyday life in his immediate environment of rural New York.[8] Given the popularity of the image, which earned Mount associate status in the academy in 1831 and full membership status only a year later, Michael D. Harris surmises that Mount's painting may have contributed to the acceptable "formulae of the form" for subsequent American genre painting whereby black subjects are placed at the margins.[9] In the painting, Mount offers a scene of refinement, marked by the central coupling of a gentleman courting

Figure 5.1 William Sidney Mount. *Rustic Dance after a Sleigh Ride.* 1830. Oil on canvas. 22 x 27¼". M. and M. Karolik Collection. Museum of Fine Arts.

a woman. Although it is unclear whether they are the couple of honor or simply the first to begin dancing, they are clearly meant to be a precursor for other such unions, as indicated by the three other pairings where men appear to be whispering into the ears of women. Here, Mount separates the subjects of the painting; the tentative couples of men and women have all gravitated toward the right half of the painting, while the cohort of single men dominate the left half. Mount's manipulation of space demarcates a social registry of those in the parlor.

Although the painting has one primary visual plane that moves horizontally, Mount delineates coteries of social belonging by manipulating space to convey his idea of proper association. When one considers the African American presence in *Rustic Dance after a Sleigh Ride*, the entire geometric matrix of the painting changes. In a sense, the black presence in the painting is a reminder of what Foucault has called the "fantasmatic" quality of space; a reminder that space is not homogeneous and empty.[10] The three African Americans, for example, are positioned on the left and perhaps serve to further distance and socially differentiate the single white men on the left from the couples on the right. Rather than having two sides, three triangulated zones become more apparent: the group of men and women that begins in the background of the painting, slanting downward diagonally to the right foreground; the centerpiece triangle that is accentuated by the illuminated floor before the main couple; and the triangle to the left formed by the three African Americans, which essentially contains the cadre of single men. The African Americans here, far from being the foci of the painting, are relegated to the margins of the painting but central to the action depicted in the scene. Their musical instruments indicate that their attendance in the parlor is merely a by-product of their service to the guests. While they too occupy the same physical area of merriment, the African Americans are nonetheless isolated from the other leisured bodies at the very moment that they themselves are connected to each other through the superscript of class.

Many of Mount's other paintings employ similar manipulations of space and shadow zones to delimit social groups. Five years after *Rustic Dance after a Sleigh Ride*, Mount finished *The Breakdown* in 1835. In another scene of relaxation, Mount depicts a small gathering of men who are entertained by a ragged dancer. Whereas Mount emphasized the gentry in *Rustic Dance after a Sleigh Ride*, the subjects of *The Breakdown* are noticeably more modest. The dancer appears to be slightly destitute; his shabby jacket is torn, and he seems to be using his drinking cup as some type of stage prop. It may be that the ad hoc entertainer has just returned from another enterprise of labor himself; his hat, jug, and ax all rest on the floor. The entertainer here is differentiated less by his proximity to his audience (which is close) than by his attire. Instead, Mount reserved his spacing techniques for the sole black man who is separated from the group in the far corner of the room's entrance.

Unlike in *Rustic Dance after a Sleigh Ride*, his relationship to the other figures in the painting is not self-evident. Also known as *Bar-room Scene*, *The Breakdown* continued Mount's depiction of music and dance as veritable themes within his oeuvre and as cultural mediums that could put blacks and whites in seemingly closer social proximity with one another. However while the representation of music increasingly becomes a recurring motif in Mount's works, functioning often as a latent *ur*-text, the architectonic elements of many of these paintings pull their meaning in a different direction altogether. In *The Breakdown*, the black subject watches the dancer from his vantage in the alcove but at a distance that separates him from the others. Here, then, is an example of how Mount synchronizes the subjects to the rhythm of the dancer but simultaneously disallows them from *seeing* each other as part of the same contingent, if not contiguous, sociality. In one sense, it might be said that the black male figure is on the precipice of this sociality; he stands symbolically at the very door. But the presence of the shadow in the alcove is a powerful and graphic reminder of the spectrality of blackness that I have been discussing throughout this book. In this instance, Mount's painting evinces a particular manipulation of space that activates its architectonic features, to bifurcate social positions primarily through racial codings.

Mount deployed similar techniques of spatialization in *The Dance of the Haymakers* (1845) and *The Power of Music* (1847), where the African American subjects, albeit in the foreground, are removed from the scene of action and

Figure 5.2 William Sidney Mount. *The Dance of the Haymakers.* 1845. Oil on canvas, 25 x 30". Collection. The Museums at Stony Brook.

inclusion by a physical boundary. These paintings of private spaces create the impression that however close African Americans are to the vicinity of whites, they will be precluded from the inner sanctum of social belonging. Although the African American subjects of both *The Dance of the Haymakers* (figure 5.2) and *The Power of Music* (figure 5.3) are foregrounded, they nonetheless remain quite outside the realms of social interaction that are occurring in the interiorized spaces of the barns. Both works depend upon constructing a delineated frame within the paintings themselves that highlights the stages of social interaction. In both works, these stages are off center and to the left. Given the similarities of their techniques and themes, *The Dance of the Haymakers* and *The Power of Music* should be thought of as companion pieces that depict similar scenes at different periods. In her authoritative analyses of the paintings, Elizabeth Johns notes that *The Power of Music* garnered the greatest response, in part because of how it configured its particular organization of the black male and space, concluding that it is the more powerful and challenging of the two.[11]

However, I would like to suggest that *The Dance of the Haymakers* is more complicated than *The Power of Music*—and this complexity is more fully borne out when one considers how its spatial architecture informs the social logic of the painting. The men in *The Power of Music* are not only attentive but also contemplative and ethereally detached from one another; it is a depiction of isolation

Figure 5.3 William Sidney Mount. *The Power of Music*. 1847. Oil on canvas, 17 x 21".
Collection. The Museums at Stony Brook, Long Island.

that is underscored by the segregation of the sole black subject. The subjects in
The Dance of the Haymakers, by contrast, are jovial, celebratory, interactive.
Although both works feature stages that occupy two-thirds (or slightly less) of
the total area of the paintings, the triangulated zones in Mount's *The Dance of the
Haymakers* are used to demarcate different coteries of belonging. If, as Barbara
Novak has pointed out, Mount's major concerns here were "essentially architectonic," then his manipulations of particular spatial geometries were used to
translate the social meanings of gender and race.[12] By manipulating shading and
the positions of the painting's subjects, Mount created a diagonal line that moves
across the upper left corner down to the bottom right corner. This line delineates
the two zones of the painting that trace the interior space of the loft where the
two girls are posted, through the center of action where the two men are dancing, down to the young African American boy with the crude drumsticks. As
much as this transverse line links and codifies the painting's gendered and racial
subjects as such, it also delimits the men upon the makeshift stage as a particular
demographic.

All four of these Mount paintings put into high relief the efficacy of Laclau's
notion of the "constitutive outside" to visual art and American genre painting

specifically. In these paintings, the radical otherness which might otherwise circumscribe the boundaries of a given hegemony (or what I have been calling throughout this study "sociality") and, in whose very threat to that system, continually pushes toward a more fulfilled democratic potentiality is diminished and lessened by the seemingly neutralized black subjects, who, far from embodying a kind of antagonism, are apparently on cue, if not in queue, with the existing hegemony.[13] The black figures in these paintings are not strict examples of Laclau's "constitutive outside" but they remain perceptibly outside of the boundaries of belonging.

However elegant Mount's depictions of African Americans were, they were for the most part, notwithstanding the series of paintings of black musicians, studies in the everyday life of white folks.[14] Although one contemporary critic called Mount the painter of "Ethiopian portraits," something that he himself noted in a letter to William Schaus, few of these paintings depict blacks in privatized spaces of their own.[15] By "privatized," I mean to destabilize the paradigmatic deployments of the public/private sphere dialectic as well as call attention to the resonance of the specific political economies that the term invokes, especially when we consider the strategies that African Americans exploited to gain a sense of their own possessive individualism. Depictions of African Americans in the privatized spaces of their interior lives in nineteenth-century U.S. visual culture are rare, which, among other reasons, makes Christian Friedrich Mayr's *Kitchen Ball at White Sulphur Springs, Virginia* (1838) (figure 5.4) exceptional.

Mayr presents a different image of the "Negro ball," certainly unlike the one described in William Wells Brown's *Clotel*. In this painting, a coterie of well-dressed men and women gather to dance for a celebration accompanied by musicians playing flute, fiddle, and cello. The primary light source, a simple four-candle chandelier, further accentuates the couple in white, who were most likely recently married. In the Mount paintings discussed earlier, shadows are used to designate the parameters of social (and perhaps political) boundaries as an ostensibly putative negative charge; the shadow is used here in Mayr's painting to signal the recuperative pleasures (and possible socialities) of black belonging that emanate in the still of the night. Mayr's manipulation of space is delineated but not geometrically subdivided in the same ways as Mount's *Rustic Dance*, as if to demonstrate that this is a space where the lines of association and belonging are indeed blurred. If this is a scene of refinement, it is also one that is delicate, in the sense that the painting contains reminders that this social setting is both irregular and provisional. The first indication is the space itself that is in the kitchen—a veritable prescribed work zone for African Americans, especially women—and not the parlor, which is more readily understood as a space of leisure. Perhaps more important, the lit candles, in addition to the setting's overall dimness, suggests that this is a late night affair, probably after the end of the workday. As Richard Powell has argued, the "painting's distinctiveness separated it from the

Figure 5.4 Christian Friedrich Mayr. *Kitchen Ball at White Sulphur Springs, Virginia.* 1838. Oil on canvas, 24 x 29 ½". North Carolina Museum of Art.

majority of paintings and portraits of its day, giving its African American subjects and their candlelit setting an almost phantasmagoric quality."[16]

Whereas Mayr created an image of black interior life that was exceptional, if not atypical, Eastman Johnson's *Negro Life at the South* (1859) (figure 5.5) was interpreted as the more representative depiction of the inside life of black America. The critic of Horace Greeley's *New York Tribune* considered it as telling as a chapter from Theodore Weld's *Slavery As It Is* (1839). In a similar manner to how Mount's reputation grew because of his paintings of black subjects, so too did Johnson's after *Negro Life at the South* was unveiled at the National Academy of Design—with other paintings such as *The Freedom Ring* (1860), *A Ride for Liberty—The Fugitive* (ca. 1862), and *Fiddling His Way* (1866) following suit. And like Mount's popular images of blacks, Johnson's *Negro Life at the South* gained a wider viewership beyond exhibition halls when Rintoul and Rockwood made a photograph of it that was published by George W. Nichols. Johnson's most famous paintings, along with his others featuring black subjects, were all produced in the immediate years before and after the Civil War, a fact that Patricia Hills suggests signals his commitment to the humanitarian question of black freedom but his ambivalence about the subsequent national question of black citizenship.[17]

Figure 5.5 Eastman Johnson. *Negro Life at the South.* 1859. Oil on canvas, 36 x 45 ¼".
The Robert L. Stuart Collection. The New-York Historical Society.

The *Tribune* critic's commentary about Johnson's painting having "a story within a story" prefigures my larger concerns with how the geometries of space are manipulated in *Negro Life at the South* to evince the private lives of black folks at the same moment that this seeming privacy is theatrically exposed.[18] A couple is placed to the left, and directly above them on the second floor is an older woman resting a child on the moss-laden roof outside her window. To the right of the fireplace, an older man strums the banjo while an adolescent boy listens, and closer to the right foreground, a woman extends her arms to a young dancing boy while a somewhat older girl sits reclined next to them. Still farther to the right, a white woman enters a portal with perhaps her black handmaid in tow slightly behind her. The scene feels as if it is staged with clusters of activity, none of which, however, can be said to be the apparent focal point.

Although Johnson may have endeavored to depict African American life in the more generic setting of a putative South, it was continually associated specifically with the rural, agrarian states of Virginia and Kentucky. Commencing with the initial exhibition, the urban background of *Negro Life at the South* had been routinely obfuscated. Some of this obfuscation, as John Davis details, must be attributed to the popular minstrel song "Carry Me Back to Old Virginia," for which a reproduction of Johnson's painting was used as the cover, as well as to the subtitle "Old Kentucky Home," which was added to the painting when it was brought to auction in 1867.[19] As Elizabeth Johns argues the "second title pushed the institution of slavery away from the Eastern seaboard, indeed, the nation's capitol, where legislators from New England as well as the South had so long countenanced it, and into the backwoods, where other citizens could be represented as having been its perpetrators."[20] This symbolism was not lost on African American intellectuals like Frederick Douglass and William Wells Brown, who, as I observe in part I of this book, were keen to note the ubiquity of slavery in the nation's capital and underscored Washington, D.C. as a symbolic location that was evenly positioned between the North and the South.

The most immediate aspect of the scene is the dilapidated structure itself, apparently made of wood and attached to the rear of a brick house. Describing the scene as if it were "arranged behind a theater proscenium," Davis notes that Johnson essentially tore down a wall to reveal slavery as it was in Washington, D.C. and hence offer a necessary representation of it in an urban space to counter or supplement the more commonplace images of slavery as only rural and agrarian.[21] The exposed beams reveal that there once was a roof, the absence of which undercuts the possibility of a black interiority. Johnson used the immediate vicinity of his family's home in Washington, D.C. as the setting, where, as in other urban environments, it was not uncommon to have slave quarters in very close proximity, if not attached, to their master's home. The painting is divided into upper and lower halves by the line produced by the roof. But this line is not completely horizontal; it is slightly askew and, along with White's use of shading and light, generates the painting's sense of dimension.

This asymmetrical plane undergirds the spatial equation of Johnson's work, which directs the viewer's perception of the painting, creating the sensation that one is moving farther and farther into the interior recesses of black life. The sensory design of the painting, therefore, subverts the processes of perception by subsuming the question of whether it is possible to know the souls of black folk, indicated by the white woman, who, like the viewer, is on site to get an inside look at how the other half lives. This is where, I think, the specific geometries of space in *Negro Life at the South* differ from other articulations of the interiority of black life, such as Winslow Homer's later *Visit from the Old Mistress* (1876).

Homer's own *Uncle Ned's Home* (1875) is seemingly a response to Johnson's famous earlier pre-Civil War painting. Given the popularity and wide circulation of Johnson's *Negro Life at the South*, it is more than probable that Homer knew the painting or at least its image well. Although his techniques were very different from Mount's, Homer's oeuvre has been likened to Mount's with its depictions of common everyday life. And, like Mount, Homer's oeuvre is marked by a subset of rich and complex depictions of African Americans, including *The Bright Side* (1865), *The Cotton Pickers* (1876), *Dressing for Carnival* (1877), and *The Gulf Stream* (1899). The relationship of this subset to his overall production, from his Civil War sketches for *Harper's* to his later watercolors of seascapes, complicates the representational capacity of blackness as a metaphor, either metonymic or synecdochic, that could stand as the body of the national citizen.

Homer completed *Uncle Ned's Home* when the allure of Radical Reconstruction was under serious duress, and the painting's treatment of space reflects the ambiguous place of African Americans at this particular moment. Homer's painting made use of many of the customary props—including a dilapidated structure, playful pets, and young children—in staging the African Americans of *Uncle Ned's Home*. The sense not only of disrepair and decay but of depression is illustrated by the bowed arc of the roof pushing the impulse of the painting downward. Furthermore, the political aesthetic of Johnson's painting produced by his deployment of spatialization is nowhere present in Homer's work. There is little manipulation of dimension here. Among a host of black caricatures in the national imaginary, the Uncle Ned figure was especially ubiquitous in nineteenth-century American culture and a counterpart to the unduly pious Uncle Tom stereotype. As evidenced by such works as John Rogers's *Uncle Ned's School* (1866), the enthusiasm for the Uncle Ned character had begun more than three decades before Homer's painting with the eponymous minstrel song "Uncle Ned" by Stephen Collins Foster, who also popularized "My Old Kentucky Home" (1850).

The most conspicuous revision of the stock Uncle Ned figure in Homer's painting is that the customary banjo has been replaced with a bucket, perhaps a suggestion for black America that labor must replace leisure. The image of the black male playing the banjo would not be rehabilitated until Henry Ossawa Tanner finished *The Banjo Lesson* near the end of the century in 1893. Rather than rhapsodizing about a stairway to heaven (as Foster's song evinces), the visceral quality of *Uncle Ned's Home* implies that life has not been a crystal stair. The full resonance of the symbolism of the bucket would later be articulated by Booker T. Washington in his 1895 Atlanta compromise speech where he implored white Americans to cast down their buckets in the sea of America's black population right before them in their very midst.

Importantly, the modes of visuality in Homer's painting proceed on very different grounds than in Johnson's work. If the viewer is meant to read the scene through the eyes of the young boy on the right, then his expression, which appears startled if not puzzled, translates the vexed position of African Americans. But the foremost signal of the obfuscated field of vision is the three children who are peering into the structure itself. What they see is not made known to the viewer, a suggestion that the viewer will not be made privy to the inside life of black America. What is "displayed" here is opacity rather than interiority, reified by the absence of a discernible intermediary through whom this scene might be translated. If works like Homer's *The Bright Side* and *At the Cabin Door* (1865–66) present African Americans at the portal of a new relationship to the national landscape, then this window seems opaque and sufficiently darkened as to prevent a clear view of a new vision of black citizenship.

Figure 5.6 Edwin White. *Thoughts of Liberia, Emancipation.* 1861. Oil on canvas, 17 x 21".
The Robert L. Stuart Collection. The New-York Historical Society.

While Johnson's *Negro Life at the South* furnishes an ostensible inside vision
of black American life, and Homer's *Uncle Ned's Home* leaves one suspended at
the front door, Edwin White's painting *Thoughts of Liberia, Emancipation* (1861)
(figure 5.6) heightens the sense of black interiority by presenting a subject in isolation. The sparse, almost nondescript room is devoid of action. As in Johnson's
Negro Life at the South, the space is dilapidated, but this is no communal area,
and the sense of interiority is marked by the structure itself that, far from opening onto the outside world, is enclosed without the presence of windows or even
a door slightly ajar. White's manipulation of space here to compose a sense of
black interiority—both physical and psychological—is intensified by obliging the
viewer to focus on the painting's sole action of a man in deep concentration reading a paper. In Barbara Gloseclose's reading of the painting, she suggests that the
shadows of the room "look as though they might breed a melancholy phantasmagoria of the escape and warmth and community that Liberia, not the newspaper,
represented to African-Americans."[22]
    The painting's activity is more cerebral than anything else; furthermore, it
is an activity that correlates the action of the black man reading with the act of

viewing by the painting's observer. Although the subject himself is stationary, the painting nonetheless has a subsumed sense of purposeful movement, engendered by the interplay of the image and the textual which puts its blackness in motion, as it were, by compelling the viewer to come to terms with what is depicted visually and what is articulated through words. The titular reference to thoughts of Liberia figuratively transposes the subject to Africa. But the poster on the door marked "HAYTI" places him in the Caribbean. One way to read the painting, then, is to consider how its visual mechanic conceptualizes U.S. black subjectivity by framing it within the coordinates of the New World hemisphere and the black Atlantic.

Such an emphasis on White's understanding of space puts his painting in conversation with African American intellectuals who debated the relationship between blackness and U.S. citizenship. Martin R. Delany, James Monroe Whitfield, James Theodore Holly, and other African Americans all weighed in on the possibility of black emigration, a proposal that gained increasing prominence after the American Colonization Society helped establish Liberia in 1822, which literalized a variation of a transnational blackness with the creation of "Americo-Liberians." Colonization, in its most benevolent if not paternalistic guise, sought to "repatriate" black Americans to Africa and allow them to spread the gospel with the residual benefit of also alleviating the race problem in the United States by removing its black population altogether, leaving in its place an ostensible *herrenvolk* democracy of whites.[23] The specter of St. Domingue/Haiti lingered in the U.S. imagination for decades in the nineteenth century, and even those writers who admired Toussaint L'Ouverture, like John Greenleaf Whittier and Wendell Philips, nearly all represented the Haitian Revolution (1791–1804) less as an exercise of liberation than as an instance of wanton violence. This sentiment was also allegorized in episodes of U.S. fiction such as Stowe's "San Domingo Hour" and Melville's "Benito Cereno."

If the writing on the wall served to transmit a vision of the Haitian Revolution into the mind's eye of the viewer in White's painting *Thoughts of Liberia*, then the title itself is meant to act as a superscript to counterbalance it, to contest the revolutionary actions of blacks with benevolent emancipatory acts by white Americans. The hermeneutical imperative of White's painting is actually concerned with conveying two possibilities for white America: support the sanctioned nation-state of Liberia where democratic self-governance might eventually materialize in Africa under U.S. sponsorship, or remain paranoid that U.S. blacks might indeed someday revolt. Whereas Stowe's novel presented a romanticized vision of life inside Aunt Chloe and Uncle Tom's cabin, a home proper, complete with copies of biblical scriptures and a portrait of George Washington on the wall, White's painting of an inside view of black life without the authenticating documents of either the Bible or the image of George Washington threatens to position his black subject as being outside of the national landscape.

■ STEP INTO A WORLD: REPRESENTATIONS OF BLACKS IN THE PUBLIC SPHERE

In the wake of Benedict Anderson's *Imagined Communities* (1983), it has become commonplace to associate the emergence of nationalism with the historical rise newspapers, and nineteenth-century genre painting is replete with scenes of periodical reading. Richard Caton Woodville's *Politics in an Oyster House* (1848), for example, presents two men of genteel deportment engrossed in an animated conversation, a newspaper dangling from the hands of one of the men, and Mount's painting *The* Herald *in the Country or Politics of 1852* (1853) features another pair of men who discuss the key issues of the day. There are also a number of works, like White's painting and Homer's *Sunday Morning in Virginia* (1877), that depict African Americans reading.[24]

While it remains speculation whether the male subject in White's *Thoughts of Liberia* is specifically reading a black periodical, the painting itself is a reminder of the sheer proliferation of newspapers in the nineteenth-century United States, which saw the emergence of periodicals such as the *Christian Review*, the *Southern Illustrated News*, and *La Patria*, as well as more well-known titles like the *New York Tribune*. Furthermore, while *Frederick Douglass' Paper* was probably the most well-known African American periodical, *New York Freedom's Journal* began its circulation in 1827, followed by the *Rights of All*, the *Weekly Advocate*, and the *Colored American*. These papers are evidence not only of the competing discourses within the national narrative but also, especially when we consider the relationship of African Americans to the letters of the republic, of the strategies and efforts of creating counterpublics.

In the works discussed earlier where music is meant to serve as the lingua franca, African Americans are situated outside the frames of national belonging, even if, as with the young boy in Mount's painting *The Dance of the Haymakers*, they are synchronized with the country music of the national idiom. In this section, I pay particular attention scenes of reading newspapers, for it is this object that makes these scenes "public" in particular and not just social.[25] For example, James Henry Cafferty's *Baltimore News Vendor* exchanged the *Baltimore Patriot*, a pro-slavery democratic paper, of the original Thomas Waterman Wood painting for the *Baltimore American* in his 1860 version. And one of the few nineteenth-century African American painters, Edwin Bannister, completed his painting *Newspaper Boy* in 1869. Few works from the nineteenth-century United States illustrate scenes of reading and the constitution of social space more starkly than Richard Caton Woodville's painting *War News from Mexico* (1848) (figure 5.7).

Completed while he was actually in Düsseldorf, Woodville's *War News from Mexico* intimates that any portrayal of the United States and Mexico must be registered in global terms. The Mexican-American War, which ended with the United States assuming approximately one-half of what was then Mexico from

Figure 5.7 Richard Caton Woodville. *War News from Mexico.* 1848. Oil on canvas, 27 x 24 ¾". The National Gallery.

Texas to California by the time the Treaty of Guadalupe Hildago was signed in 1848, in some ways transformed the sentiment of Manifest Destiny into an electrified national impulse and also extended the debate about slavery into new territories. The wide distribution of reports about the war was enabled by the numerous penny press newspapers.

War News from Mexico depicts a conjoined assembly who are gathered around an excited man reading a newspaper. Set at the "American Hotel," the figures are gathered on the outside porch of the building rather than in the interior spaces of a lobby or sitting room, as if this zone is constitutively open to any and all passersby. The democratic sensibility of the painting is engendered, as Bryan Wolf notes, by the translation of the pediment and pillars of the hotel as classical into a vernacular idiom of the "clapboard classical."[26] In the painting, the reading of the paper not only constitutes the central action of the painting but also figuratively circumscribes the field of national belonging. A moment ago I used the word "porch" to describe the platform upon which the conjoined assembly is congregating; I invoke this word to intimate the geometries of form that contort, rearrange, and define social space in the painting. Here, I also mean to emphasize its resonance as an index of verticality. Those on the porch occupy one plane and could be said to thereby make up a particular stratum. This constituency is delimited by those within reading sight or earshot of the newspaper's announcements. It is noteworthy that a man whispers into the ear of the elder man next to him to share the details of the news. If Habermasian definitions of the public sphere depend upon speech communities that make use of systems of language, then the interlocutor is indeed one of the most important figures of the painting, for he saves the older man from falling out of the loop as it were, prevents him from being out of sync with national time.[27]

The social logic of the painting's spatial format is underlined by Woodville's use of light and color. The assembly is gathered on the porch where it is decidedly more luminous; this light creates a transverse zone that begins in the upper left region of the painting and terminates in the lower right quadrant, where the painting's two black subjects are positioned. Symbolically dressed in the primary colors of the nation in red, white, and blue, and close in proximity, they are clearly at the borders. Woodville's painting suggests perhaps that they too are Americans, or can become so, if only allowed to take the steps up the porch and enter the municipality it signifies. The corridor produced by Woodville's manipulation of light, importantly, also contains a sign announcing the direction of the local post office and a seated man wearing Scottish plaid. Woodville's political aesthetic, however, reconstellates the meaning of the illuminated plaid by situating its wearer within the boundaries of belonging marked by his placement on the porch. The figurative distance, which might otherwise be signified by the plaid, is diminished and does not reify him as an unincorporable foreign national. In a painting where the ideogram of plurality is literally lost in space, the man in plaid signifies the ways in which national identity consolidates whiteness and blurs and erases ethnicity.

The transverse zone of light which illuminates the plaid-wearing man, the two men wearing top hats (one reading, one listening), and the black pair at the bottom right of the painting is graphically delimited as a kind of coming community. If the plaid of the man seated at the left is meant to suggest the negotiations of ethnicity, whiteness, and political sensibility, then so too is the attire of the African Americans which has received no commentary by critics of the painting. Together, they are adorned in the national colors of red, white, and blue; but the condition of their relation to United States is borne out in another register when one considers Woodville's use of light, colors, and shadows. Resting gently on the young girl's neck, slightly below her head that is veiled in shadows in ways that her body with its white attire is not, sits a necklace in colors of red, black, and green. In particular, red and green were already associated with the national colors of African countries, such as Ethiopia's 1798 flag. In this manner, Woodville's painting not only thematically stages a consideration of blacks to the United States but to Africa as well. Compositionally, then, the creation of these triangle zones is as important as the more apparent numerous rectangular forms.[28]

Ultimately, however, the social logic of the painting is determined by its formal approach to architecture. The wood beams that uphold the awning, upon which the hotel's marquee rests, create a frame within a frame or a shadow box. Woodville manipulates dimensionality here by reframing the margins to guide the viewer to the central focus of the painting by narrowing the borders that constitute the ostensible domain of immediate spectatorship coded as reading. Peering out of a window, lurking in the shadows, is an older woman wearing a bonnet. Although she is on the same plane as the men, she, like the two African Americans, is graphically segregated from them by the wood beams of the structure that partition the domain of sociality. And while the woman and another man are separated by a gate and are outside of the immediate range of the newspaper reading, they nonetheless share the same latitudinal plane as the other white men.

The location of the two African Americans illuminates how the outside porch is tied to the idea not only of elevation but of hierarchy. They are withheld from the precincts of the de facto town meeting that is delineated in the painting as the space that immediately falls under the canopy with its commanding and prescriptive letters of the republic. The hotel may be a social space, but in the nineteenth-century United States, the hotel, like the post office, was also a heightened political space—as Stowe illustrates in *Uncle Tom's Cabin* with George Harris's passionate speech about liberty and democracy to his former employer. Furthermore, Woodville's hotel is symbolically coded with a specific idiom from the national lexicon. Painted on the marquee of the "American Hotel" is the phrase "E pluribus unum." But the phrase is abrogated, conspicuously missing its central word "pluribus," which, given the trajectory produced by its arc, cannot be contained within the frame of the painting. Far from producing an effect similar to Whitman's catalogs, the painting—with its truncated ideograph—vitiates the romanticized rhetoric of the United States containing the multitudes.

Like *War News from Mexico*, Mount's painting *California News* (1850) depicts a group bound together by their proximity to a man reading a newspaper. Gathered in the post office, a group congregates around a man reading the *New York Daily Tribune*, with a sole black subject lingering in the corner. In this scene, the position of translator is reserved for the young woman perhaps a sign that she falls, or soon will, within the pale of a public sphere constituted through print. Critics have long taken notice that the painting above the door is a miniature of his brother Shepard Mount's *Pigs* and that the publisher of the *New York Daily*

Figure 5.8 Thomas Waterman Wood. *A Bit of History: The Contraband*. 1866. Oil on canvas, 28 ¼ x 20 ¼". The Metropolitan Museum of Art.

Tribune, Robert McElreth, commissioned *California News*, possibly after seeing one of Woodville's paintings at the Art Union.[29] One of the most noticeable features of the painting is the number of documents that are strewn about the scene. The ubiquitous documents, both written and ideographic, are fundamental to the painting's meaning. The *Tribune* featured in this painting was one of the most strident antislavery organs among the New York presses, whereas the paper in Mount's painting *The* Herald *in the Country* was noticeably pro-slavery.

Figure 5.9 Thomas Waterman Wood. *A Bit of History: The Recruit.* 1866. Oil on canvas, 28 ¼ x 20 ¼". The Metropolitan Museum of Art.

Documents are visible on both the left and right edges of the painting. An advertisement for the sale of a farm is positioned at the left; a notice for passage to California is on the right. It is through these documents that Mount's painting manifests its subsumed impulse of movement that makes his use of space akin to my earlier discussion of White's *Thoughts of Liberia*. The movement is not

Figure 5.10 Thomas Waterman Wood. *A Bit of History: The Veteran.* 1866. Oil on canvas, 28 ¼ x 20 ¼". The Metropolitan Museum of Art.

transatlantic as in White's painting but continental and articulates a latent concern with Manifest Destiny.

The trope of the intersection between blacks, public spaces, and documents recurs in Thomas Waterman Wood's *A Bit of History: The Contraband, the Soldier, and the Veteran* (figures 5.8–5.10), finished in 1866. All three paintings make use of various props, including drums, chairs, notifications, and flags. In the work, an African American male is arranged in three different configurations of national being. In the first painting, the subject has newly arrived at the provost marshal office to volunteer for the Union forces. In the second, he has undergone his first transformation and now wears Union military issue complete with a rifle. In the final painting, he stands at attention with the aid of crutches because his left leg has been amputated.

Wood's series employs a particular engagement with visuality to articulate a sense of social space. In the first painting, the subject's knapsack functions to script him as "contraband." His tipped hat is clearly meant to be a salutation, a symbolic greeting of a new day for the United States and especially black America. The preoccupation with visuality is illustrated by the subject's gaze which has him staring out to a horizon beyond what can be immediately recognized or ascertained by the viewer. But this peering out beyond the immediate domain of the marshall office serves to transpose the viewer and the recruiter, making them one and the same. Wood's manipulation of space here creates a zone of perception that obliges the viewer to impulsively respond to the contraband's greeting, if not to intuitively nod one's head in a reciprocal gesture of acknowledgment by creating a kind of communicative procedure that expands the precinct of associative belonging—it might be thought of as one of the examples of greeting that Iris Young has theorized as necessary to the rehabilitative form of deliberative democracy that she calls communicative democracy.[30] The first painting activates the visual hermeneutics of the entire series that instantiates recognition as a nationalizing operation. The first painting of the series implicitly asks the viewer if she or he is going to follow the contraband through the various stages of his national identity.

In the next painting, the conspicuous placement of the flag and the volunteer's contemplative gaze serve to intensify the higher ideals of freedom and liberty. With the bend in his left knee overstated and his body tilting slightly forward, as if he is striding toward the materialization of these ideals. What remains most obvious in the third painting is that he now faces the opposite direction and is propped up by crutches because the left leg that had formerly leaned toward freedom and liberty is now amputated. Absent too is the drum found in the first and second panels; there would be no drum cadence here. The hollow expression of confusion on the volunteer's face conveys his uncertain future as a subject in the newly restored nation, an uncertainty that is exaggerated by the general blurring and effacement of the interior wall that no longer features the public documents that had formerly symbolized the possibility of his inclusion into the body politic. If acts of reading conventionally associate progress as the movement from left to right, then the last panel, with its repositioned subject who stares in the opposite direction, dislodges African Americans from a U.S. national time. The concretization of his contradictory affiliation with the state, not only with standard time but with the accoutrements of the nation, is exemplified by the remnants of his knapsack—the very symbol that formerly designated his position as "contraband"—which is now used as a scarf on his head underneath his uniform cap.

■ IN THE SHADOWS OF THE STATE

In the widest sense, this chapter has returned to questions of race and representation in works by some of the most well-known and important American genre painters. In doing so, I have argued that the formal compositional qualities of these paintings produce a frame within a frame or shadow box device that mobilizes the shadow figure to encode and render legible their social positions within a pictorial schema of national belonging. Resisting a facile taxonomy that the shadow is putatively negative or positive, I have insisted that its meaning—the conditions which make it figurative and not simply apparitional—is made emanate through the architectonic features of different physical structures ranging from markedly private spaces like the parlor to decidedly public places like the post office. In a more critical if not speculative sense, my readings where black figures intersect with their white counterparts suggest that depictions of these black bodies, whether at the center or the margins or anywhere between, work to frame the paintings' scenes; the black presence, in a word, functions to delimit boundaries. In the chapters that follow, I continue this interrogation of blackness and the visual optics of political aesthetics in ekphrastic illustrations of two different non-state institutional spaces: the slave ship and the museum.

6

The Spectacle of Disorder
Race, Decoration, and the Social Logic of Space

> Out there,
> in darkness,   .
> stuck in the Middle Passage
> of time.   THE LAST POETS

> [Ships] were mobile elements that stood for the shifting spaces in
> between the fixed places that they connected. Accordingly they need
> to be thought of as cultural and political units rather than abstract
> embodiments of the triangular trade. They were something more—a
> means to conduct political dissent and possibly a distinct mode
> of cultural production.... Ships also refer us back to the middle
> passage, to the half-remembered micro-politics of the slave trade
> and its relationship to both industrialisation and modernisation.[1]
>   PAUL GILROY

In the early moments of *Moby-Dick*, after he has made the acquaintance of his
new comrade Queequeg, Ishmael thinks to himself that the tattooed harpooner
sitting before him has an expression on his face that contains a profound sentiment: " 'It's a mutual, joint-stock world, in all meridians. We cannibals must help
these Christians."[2] When the *Pequod* is dashed into oblivion at the novel's end,
Ishmael is able to avoid drowning because Queequeg's coffin keeps him afloat.
Notwithstanding its prophetic quality, Queequeg's would-be rumination about
the "joint-stock world" prefigures two of the most recurrent understandings of
the ship as an emblem of modernity in the contemporary criticism of *Moby-Dick,*
one being that the *Pequod* is a heterotopia, the other being that it is a node on a
constellation that comprises a world system.

Both of these positions are more fully illuminated when we consider the competing visions of the *Pequod* as a particular kind of space. The first understanding
of the *Pequod* intimates that it is a Foucauldian heterotopia, an area that contains
the multitudes or, as Cesare Casarino defines it, "a special type of space from
which one can make new and different sense of all other spaces."[3] This image of
the *Pequod* as a heterotopia is illustrated in the chapter "Midnight, Forecastle"
as the crew—variously composed of a French sailor, a Maltese sailor, a Sicilian
sailor, and a Tahitian sailor, among many others—join in chorus to the rhythm
of the young Pip's tambourine. Sterling Stuckey has underscored the retentions
of African culture that belie an ostensibly totalizing social death of black subjectivity and locates in this very subjectivity a poetics capable of unfolding a

liberatory politics through culture itself.[4] This illustration is also reminiscent of Paul Gilroy's theorization of the ship as an alternative modality to the social formations of the nation-state.

The other view of the *Pequod*, as a ship of a totalitarian or imperial state is rendered powerfully throughout the novel as the wanton obsession of Ahab's monomaniacal pursuit.[5] In one of the central chapters that comprise the final episodes, however, Melville's imagination depends as much on the language of spatial architecture as it prefigures psychoanalysis: "For as the one ship that held them all; though it was put together of all contrasting things—oak, and maple, and pine wood; iron, and pitch, and hemp—yet all these ran into each other in the one concrete hull, which shot on its way, both balanced and directed by the long central keel;...all directed to that fatal goal which Ahab their one lord and keel did point to."[6]

With chapters like "The Cabin Table" and "The Quarter-Deck," *Moby-Dick* reflects the significance of space and spatialization in Melville's works. From the vast expanse of the South Seas in *Typee* (1846) to the office crevices in "Bartleby" (1853), from a love triangle where things become a little too close for comfort in *Pierre* (1852) to the regulated zones of production in the second half of "The Paradise of Bachelors and the Tartarus of Maids" (1855) thinking through the meanings of space in Melville's oeuvre is a necessary consideration for the author who once wrote, "You must have plenty of sea-room to tell the truth in."[7] In no Melville work is space more important than in "Benito Cereno."

Melville's story about a revolt gone awry aboard the *San Dominick* and the subsequent efforts to reestablish law and order has been the subject of a considerable amount of recent criticism. In much of the subsequent criticism following Eric J. Sundquist's *To Wake the Nations* (1993), many of the readings of "Benito Cereno" have decidedly taken a turn to the historiographical impulses of Melville's story with keen attention to the relationship of the Fugitive Slave Law and the global economies of new-world slavery to the mid-nineteenth-century United States as well as to the histories of the Haitian Revolution. Other criticism has focused on Melville's story as a metaliterary allegory about the vicissitudes of reading.[8] Still others have explored the latent issues of performativity that undergird the story from Eric Lott's understanding of the minstrel show subtext to Jennifer Jordan Baker's recovery of the high (formal) artistry of an operatic Babo.[9] But in much of the criticism it seems as if the ship itself has been lost at sea.

The relationship of historical events to the underpinnings of "Benito Cereno" and, more generally, the place of the ship in Melville's imagination is an important consideration, but interrogating the objets d'art of the *San Dominick* promises to reroute our understanding of the story altogether. What are the ways that we can begin to examine the slave ship as a distinct cultural artifact? How can we begin to approach the slave ship as a physical unit and not simply as an emblem of modernity but rather as a material entity with a certain composition and substance? What readings of "Benito Cereno" urgently need is a line of critical inquiry that analyzes the political codings of the objets d'art in Melville's tale. By turning to what W.J.T. Mitchell has called the "special objects" and "visual scenes" embedded in literature, we are able to analyze the ekphrastic moments in the story that underwrite its ideological purposes.[10] The evidence of the *San Dominick* as a damaged space is everywhere with things strewn about here and there.[11] It is, in a word, unsightly and hardly looks like what would be expected from a well-maintained ship. But if the *San Dominick* does not look well-maintained in the eyes of the American captain Delano, it is because the ship has been rearranged with "special objects" in ways that confuses the idiomatic expression "shipshape" and violates the underlying spatial economics of the term's meaning.

It might be said that the space of the *San Dominick* has been curated by the insurgent Africans. Taking Philip Fisher's observation that the *San Dominick* feels "like a museum of objects no longer in use" as well as Nancy Bentley's understanding of the museum trope in U.S. literature as cues, I want to examine how the story's preoccupation with the arrangement and rearrangement of outsider art is a metaphor for regulating social polities.[12] To analogize a slave ship to a kind of museum space might seem specious but it is precisely the use of these would-be pieces of art—objets d'art that remain as mere things in Delano's eyes but are later registered as unduly sublime—that Babo and his compatriots arrange a counter-symbolic order that evinces their own fraught status as being stuck between freedom and enslavement. The meanings of these reconfigured objects challenge what Rancière calls the "distribution of the sensible," the implicit law governing modes of perception that circumscribe the fields of what is visible and audible. My central claim here is that we should attend to the ways that the effort by Babo and his compatriots to push these objects outside of the realm of art proper parallels, and is itself constitutive of, the ways that they attempted to exceed the agential limits imposed upon them by the authority of slavery.

The *San Dominick* is a contested space of multiple Žižekian symbolic orders— the American, the Spanish, and the African—unorthodoxly overlaid with and continually protruding into each other, stalling the national symbolic from consolidating as a specific fixed singularity. In "Benito Cereno" nearly every image or icon is re-scripted as a sign of sub- or extra-nationality. Objects such as the Spanish flag, Aranda's bones, and the chalk caption scrawled on the forward side of the ship, constitute a provisional counter-symbolic order that leans toward a new black subjectivity. In this sense, the objects by Babo and the other African leaders of the revolt in varying degrees create (as much as they themselves are created into) museum pieces and public art that are meant less to monumentalize the past as they are a sign of a coming community.

In the opening lines of the story, the *San Dominick* is described as having been devastated by an epidemic of lawlessness. Law and order, in the political sense, is a governing concern throughout "Benito Cereno." But the story is also preoccupied with a subsumed question about the aesthetics of law and order, with how one reads "Benito Cereno" given its architecture, its outline, and its spatial organization. By underlining the issue of organization and, equally important, decoration, this chapter seeks to foreground how space is mobilized to regulate forms of subjectivity, something that the semantic term "slaver" belies and the graphic representations of the slave ships can only nominally approximate. These spaces need to be read not simply as areas, as in domains, but as designations with specific coordinates, operations, and, as it turns out, political repercussions. More specifically, by deconstructing the particular precincts of the ship (such as the stern, cuddy, and bow), as well as the parts of the story that constitute the text of Melville's work, we are better able to decipher how space works to organize both the tale's textual formatting and its ideological codes. Analyzing the visual field of how these objets d'art are arranged promises to reveal what Michael Chaney, writing in different context, has called "the unspeakable and unseeable trace of a subjectivity not yet become."[13] In attending to the social registers that disallow the crude African pieces from being concretized completely as mere things or readily identified objets d'art, constituted and exhibited simultaneously as museum pieces and public art, I seek to uncover the ways that Babo and his compatriots (re)imagined art to articulate their claims for a reconstituted subjectivity.

■ LOST IN SPACE: STATELESSNESS AND THE MIDDLE PASSAGE

As the tale begins, the *Bachelor's Delight* is resting in the St. Maria harbor off of the coast of Chile when one Captain Amasa Delano, from Duxbury, Massachusetts, is informed that a strange sail is veering into the bay. Dropping a whaleboat, Delano decides that he will venture out to assist the ship. With heavy fog rolling in and out like vapors, Delano initially thinks to himself that the ship resembles a "white-washed monastery" with "Black Friars" pacing to and fro.[14] The vessel is not only seemingly off course but in disrepair as well, and Delano later notices that the ship is in fact a slaver. The *San Dominick* apparently was one of those "Spanish merchantmen of the first class" that moved "from one colonial port to another" (354).

The ships in "Benito Cereno" are planked, sea-bound versions of joint-stock companies and a veritable example of what Fredric Jameson has noted as being the early forms of a global network that enabled the formation of imperial capital-ism.[15] Given the fact that the *San Dominick* was holding 150 slaves in addition to other commodities, Cereno's "transatlantic emigrant ship" symbolically evinces the compatibility of slavery and the protoforms of capitalism or at least reveals how the slave ship becomes the site where these two world system overlap (366). But unlike the *Pequod*, which is ostensibly a floating factory that produces goods from whales, the *Bachelor's Delight* and *San Dominick* are more identifiable components of a global mercantilist economy. As he tries to discreetly gauge the condition of Delano's ship, Cereno learns that the *Bachelor's Delight* was most recently in port at Canton, where its crew collected teas and silks. Because it was a major center for international trade bordered by the South China Sea, which Melville's readers would have been more aware of because of his earlier sea romances, the reference to Canton reveals one coordinate within a world system that linked various regional economies and, collaterally extended, peoples, cultures, and ideas.

In Cereno's initial story to Delano, the *San Dominick* began its most recent expedition in Buenos Aires bound for Lima on the opposite side of South America. To get there, the *San Dominick* tried to travel around Cape Horn; it was here apparently that the crew were hit with heavy gales and then the fever and scurvy. But as his testimony in the deposition makes clear, they were already on the western side of South America, actually beginning their voyage in Valparaiso bound for Callao. In the aftermath of the second insurrection, both the *Bachelor's Delight* and the *San Dominick* make their way first to Conception and then to Lima, "where, before the vice-regal courts, the whole affair, from the beginning, underwent investigation" (637). Perhaps Melville wanted to underscore the irony of Cereno indeed arriving at his initial destination, albeit as only a shadow of his former self, but it seems unusual that the deposition and trial had to occur in Lima when both Chile and Peru remained colonies until 1818 and 1821, respectively. Ultimately, however, the references to Buenos Aires, Conception, Valparaiso, Lima, and Callao outline a constellation within the larger cartographic map of the Spanish empire and thereby evince a different world-historical formation engendered by imperialism. Both of these world systems, the global mercantilist and the imperialistic, mapped the globe and created specific destinations and particular locations such that even when off course, one could hope to find one's way back onto the grid. That is, one might be lost at sea but not have to be lost in space.

But this is exactly where the black subjects of the *San Dominick* were—lost in space. In the moments when the ship drifted farther and farther northwest off of the coast of Chile, farther into the Pacific Ocean, the enslaved blacks of the *San Dominick* must have thought they were reliving their first voyage through the Atlantic Ocean ad nauseam and ad infinitum. The distinction being drawn here, then, between being lost at sea and lost in space, is that in the former condition one might very well be able to still imagine a given location as a possible destination whereas in the latter condition the spatial equation between a present "here" and its conceptual complement of a future "there" is dissolved, producing a sensation, if not psychology, that one might forever be in transit. As Hortense Spillers has famously written, "Those African persons in 'Middle Passage' were literally suspended in the 'oceanic'... removed from the indigenous land and culture, and not yet 'American' either, these captive persons, without names that their captors would recognize, were in movement across the Atlantic, but they were also nowhere at all."[16] Here in Melville's tale is a Middle Passage that pushes beyond its conventionally understood triangulated zone—rather than being part of the Atlantic world, this story is set off of the Pacific coast, illustrating the global trajectory of slavery. In desperate need of provisions, the black subjects aboard the *San Dominick* were not only out of place but also out of time—not in the sense that it denotes the normativizing temporality of history but quite literally out of time in the quantitatively mathematical sense of the word.

If blacks stuck in the Middle Passage were suspended in a liminality between a here and there, simultaneously somewhere and nowhere, they were also subjected to practices that threatened to reconfigure their identities altogether. The Middle Passage was part and parcel of the processes that attempted to obliterate the specificity of their being Ashantee or Igbo or Fulani, among other distinctions, and classify them into systems of social formation that organized racial definitions and categories. Furthermore, a latent preoccupation of the Middle Passage was concerned with transforming black "subjects" into "objects" so that those very "objects" could be placed on the auction block for purchase, trade, or exchange like any other commodity. The Middle Passage was a particular form of commodification, one that nautical mile by nautical mile attempted to reconfigure the African into someone—and all too often, into something—else. A fundamental component of the Middle Passage was always about transubstantiating black bodies into commodities and, tellingly, also the means of production. Captured black bodies were entered into a process of commodification that subjected blackness to the dictates of a certain global political economy, and the revolt, therefore, disrupted not only the charted itinerary of the *San Dominick* but also the ship's relation to a global economic circuit. The *San Dominick* emblematizes this contestation of space, one that underlines the machinations of fraught subjectivities and one in which identities are in transit as it were.

■ STATELINESS ABOARD THE *SAN DOMINICK*

Cereno becomes the very embodiment of Melville's duality in the narrative of the interplay between statelessness and stateliness. Although he is not quite stateless, the conspicuous quality of Cereno's appearance is interpreted by Delano as a sign of his ostentatious stateliness. When he finally makes his way through the throng of people, Delano finds himself captivated by the sheer extravagance of Cereno's attire. The loose jacket of dark velvet, the high-crowned sombrero, and the silver sword all place Cereno in a culture of decadence, marking him, as Nicola Nixon has argued, a kind of dandy.[17] Delano thinks it peculiar that Cereno is not dressed in less ostentatious attire but then recalls that Chileans had not yet adopted "the plain coat and once plebeian pantaloons" and still "adhered to their provincial costume, picturesque as any in the world" (360). Delano's confusion here fails to translate the coded message of Cereno's appearance in the sense that Roland Barthes has suggested that every image has a rhetoric; instead Delano is calmly reassured by what he assumes to be simply the non-coded image of a quintessentially decadent Spanish captain.[18] And the comeliness of Cereno's appearance is punctuated by, what Delano thinks to be, his daily grooming habits. But Cereno's dress is accentuated to the point where he becomes a caricature. Given the dire condition of the *San Dominick*, he becomes a spectacle as he parades about the ship, making Delano feel as if he were being subjected to a surreal carnival and prompting him to think that Cereno was merely "masquerading as an oceanic grandee" (364). Cereno's appearance puts Delano in mind that there is something singularly incongruent with his look, that his attire does not match the setting and is but another illustration of the failed order of things aboard the *San Dominick*.

Delano's own *Bachelor's Delight* becomes the unstated example of what a ship should look like, of how a vessel should be organized. When he first sees the *San Dominick*, Delano had been resting in the harbors of St. Maria with valuable cargo. Although the contents of the *Bachelor's Delight* remain unknown until Babo later prompts Cereno to learn the specifics, one of the principal differences between the ships is the status and quality of their inventories. The *Bachelor's Delight*'s is contained and well accounted; the *San Dominick*'s, while open to public view, is in disarray.

Making his way to offer assistance to Benito Cereno and his crew, Delano is taken aback by the poor condition of the ship, causing him to remark to himself that the *San Dominick* is nothing but a "spectacle of disorder" (459). The most conspicuous sign of this disorganization is the sheer number of black subjects strewn about the ship in the oddest places. A random oakum picker here, a puzzling man who ties knots there, and a random coterie of strange hatchet polishers all seem arbitrarily placed to Delano, who, even though he does not command a slave ship himself, surmises that something must be out of order.

Melville's description of the "spectacle of disorder" aboard the *San Dominick* is accentuated by his particular use of the languages of race and space. In a free moment away from Cereno, Delano decides that he will engage one of the white sailors to gain his perspective on the events that have debilitated the *San Dominick*. Descending the poop, he makes his way through the "Ghetto" of blacks to approach the sailor (459). Melville's use of the word "Ghetto," still primarily associated with the quarter of Italian cities to which Jews were restricted, did more than associate the ship with the later more idiomatic connotations of the word that would become increasingly prominent at the end of the nineteenth century; the word also associated the *San Dominick* with a certain configuration and topography, spatializing the ship as if it were a city on a map with distinct quarters, domains, and precincts. Rather than being a ship where space is properly configured, one where the ship's superstructure is governed by a subsumed mode of hierarchical stratification, space is flattened on the primary deck of the *San Dominick*, evincing the overall feeling that there is not enough distinction from the top to the bottom, that there is not enough vertical delineation of space.

Delano concludes that the *San Dominick*'s condition is a result not only of ill-trained sailors but also of improper organization, and his thoughts equally imply that the ship has been mismanaged. In ways that we now readily associate with Foucault's reading of Jeremy Bentham's notion of the panopticon, Delano surmises that the numerous anomalies he witnesses aboard the *San Dominick* are due in large part to "the absence of those subordinate deck-officers to whom, along with higher duties, is entrusted what may be styled the police department of a populous ship" (358).[19] Such a body might have been especially useful in one of the most vivid moments of "Benito Cereno" where a young white boy is assaulted by a young black one, forcing some blood to trickle from his head: " 'I should think Don Benito,' he now said, glancing towards the oakum-picker who had sought to interfere with the boys, 'that you would find it advantageous to keep all of your blacks employed, especially the younger ones, no matter at what useless task, and no matter what happens to the ship' " (361). Although he is startled by this act of violence, one that no less goes unpunished, Delano offers a curious suggestion to the Spanish captain that is as much about space as it is about regulation. Rather than suggesting to Cereno that the Africans be remanded to the bowel of ship, for example, or otherwise punished, he proposes instead that they be "employed," fastened into place at a workstation intent upon one task. Useless tasks, therefore, were less about work per se than one of the means through which a monitorial system could better regulate social space by ordering and enforcing positions in whose ritualistic performance Philip Fisher locates aspects akin to a police state.[20]

An early signal of Delano's interventionist practices of realigning the space of the *San Dominick* occurs when one of his small boats brings the first round of provisions.[21] As the *Rover* approaches, the black subjects are anxious for some relief. Melville's language underlines this sense of desperation by depicting the scene as being in need of control and containment, with the *San Dominick*'s black subjects "hung over the bulwarks in disorderly raptures" (464). Delano reestablishes the necessary law and order—"with good-natured authority he bade the blacks stand back; to enforce his words making use of a half-mirthful, half-menacing gesture. Instantly the blacks paused, just where they were, each negro and negress exactly as the word had found them" (464). After the oakum pickers quell the hatchet polishers, both blacks and whites join in hoisting the casks of water "singing at the tackle," a fleeting moment that echoes the "Midnight, Forecastle" scene in *Moby-Dick*. This reconfigured spatiality of equality is produced not by the authoritarian impulses of a strict ideology of law and order but rather by a kind of "republican impartiality": "The casks being on deck, Captain Delano was handed a number of jars and cups by one of the steward's aides, who, in the name of Don Benito, entreated him to do as he had proposed: dole out the water. He compiled, with republican impartiality as to this republican element, which always seeks one level, serving the oldest white no better than the youngest black" (465). Delano's act of "republican impartiality" here reverberates with what Melville elsewhere calls "ruthless democracy." While in the midst of finishing *Moby-Dick*, Melville wrote a letter to Hawthorne, articulating his notion of a "ruthless democracy on all sides," a sentiment summarized by the declaration that "a thief in jail is as honorable a personage as Gen. George Washington."[22]

This sense of disorganization afflicts not only the open, public areas of the ship but even the private corridors and zones of the *San Dominick*. The oft-discussed "play of the barber" scene has been analyzed as an example of tautology and as a theatrical performance, both of which complicate the dynamics of power and authority on board the ship, but this subversion is keenly prefigured through Melville's description of the cuddy as a particular space that suffers from a lack of compositional unity.[23] Part of the cuddy had formerly been officers' quarters, but after the *San Dominick*'s difficulties, the hall fell into a kind of "picturesque disarray, of odd appurtenances" (466). Melville then moves to an extended description of these odd appurtenances, from a claw-footed table to a torn hammock, from cane settees to a black mahogany pedestal. Portentously, there are also a misshapen armchair and a flag locker. Not only are things in disarray, they simply do not match, making the cuddy feel as if it were poorly decorated. Like Melville's story "The Paradise of Bachelors and the Tartarus of Maids," where a more pronounced cognitive similitude yokes two seemingly disparate places together, the incongruity of the objects strewn about the cuddy is intensified by a similitude that makes "the country and ocean seem cousins-german" (466). When Delano walks into the room with Cereno, his senses are assaulted by the unkempt nature of the room as much as they are by the collapse of the conventional borders of space itself:

> "This seems a sort of dormitory, sitting-room, sail-loft, chapel, armory, and private closet all together, Don Benito," added Captain Delano, looking around.
>
> "Yes, Señor; events have not been favorable to much order in my arrangements." (466)

The violation of space that Delano registers here is one produced by the dissolution of the demarcated perimeters that act as the borders that would properly contain and align areas. The cuddy is, in essence, all mixed up, with one quarter being improperly superimposed on another and another. This obfuscating of the would-be separate domains of the *San Dominick* acts as a precursor to convey the dangers of failing to maintain proper assignments, positions, and ultimately roles—a confused setting that quite literally sets the stage for the "play of the barber" scene.

As they all retire to the cuddy so that Cereno can be shaved, Delano finds himself amused by the "African love of bright colors" as Babo casually selects a bunting of many hues to use as an apron for the Spanish captain (467). Delano is brought to mind that blacks, by their very disposition, are somehow especially suited for the positions of valets and personal servants, and the tone of the entire passage associates Delano as a quasi ethnographer intent on decoding the cultural practices of the Spanish and the African. Delano can only see a jovial and happy servant who is all too pleased to groom his master. But Babo is actually in control here; he sets the stage, chooses the props, and directs the script in a fascinating panorama.[24] It is ironic that in order to complete the revolution, the black subjects must revert to a previous condition—that they don the masks that Paul Laurence Dunbar later speaks of—to effectuate the materialization of their escape. Delano finds himself nominally disturbed that Cereno is apparently so nonchalant about the use of national symbols: "'The castle and the lion,' exclaimed Captain Delano—'why, Don Benito, this is the flag of Spain you use here. It's well it's only I, and not the King, that sees this,' he added, with a smile, 'but'—turning towards the black—'it's all one, I suppose, so the colors be gay'; which playful remark did not fail to somewhat tickle the negro" (468).

Babo, "that hive of subtlety," is unduly aware of the symbolic importance of this particular accoutrement (644). Gaining its resonance through metonymy, the flag becomes the sign that associates a vessel to a discernible, landed territory while floating upon the high seas. With a locker full of other flags and a random assortment of other material laying around, Babo's selection of the Spanish flag attempts to resignify its meaning as a particular symbol. Rather than remaining an icon of the Spanish empire, Babo's manipulation of the flag figuratively brings the subaltern underside of imperialism to the fore. Already removed from the mast, the flag placed on Cereno intimates that far from being figuratively tethered to the empire, the Spanish captain was in danger of being cut off altogether.

■ ICONS OF NATIONALISM

By having Delano harp on the distressed condition of the ship as an indication of the faded grandeur of an overly decadent Spanish empire, Melville continually underscores the absent or missing stateliness of the *San Dominick*. This absence of stateliness is initially prefigured, however, as a kind of statelessness, as if the ship were somehow devoid of national affiliation: "To Captain Delano's surprise, the stranger, viewed through the glass, showed no colors; though to do so upon entering a haven...was the custom among peaceful seamen of all nations" (353). How utterly stateless the *San Dominick* is, Delano has little clue. The opening lines of the tale are replete with observation after observation regarding the poor look of the ship, from the frayed ropes and moldy forecastle to the torn sails and the moss-covered balustrades, all giving Delano the impression that the *San Dominick* had been reduced to a mere shadow of its former glory, which, "like super-annuated Italian palaces, still, under a decline of masters, preserved signs of [its] former state" (354).

If the country and ocean are depicted as cousins-german in "Benito Cereno," then the correlative of the ship and house has an even greater resonance in the story. Ships might be microcosms of society, complete with their own set of laws, but given their intricate architecture with numerous rooms, cabins, and quarters, they also were a kind of floating house. For enslaved Africans, it must have seemed more like a prison house. Houses and ships, as Melville notes, both made particular use of privacy: "Both house and ship, the one by its walls and blinds, the other by its high bulwarks like ramparts, hoard from view their interiors till the last moment" (355). The notion of a veiled interiority is exemplified in "Benito Cereno" whenever Delano attempts to go past the figurative anterior room of Cereno's story, to strike through the mask, so to speak, and learn more specifics about the San Dominick's inside narrative. Even though the signs are in plain view, the public life of these things has an interior meaning that Delano cannot translate. One of the most important of these signs is the shieldlike stern-piece of Castile and Leon, which is more than merely an emblem or decoration.

Examining the things, objects, and writings that adorn the exterior of the San Dominick is fundamentally necessary to decode both the aesthetic and the political intricacies of Melville's story; for as Edith Wharton will later articulate, decoration occurs "by means of those structural features which are part of the organism of every house, inside as well as out."[25] In another degree, what I am calling attention to by underscoring these particular objects is their spectacularity, both in the sense that they are staged as quasi-museum pieces on the ship and as a variation of Guy Debord's claim that the spectacle obfuscates the ways in which commodities have supplanted the relations between people.[26] Here, aboard the San Dominick, is an instance instead where the spectacularity of these images insistently reveals these very relations before they are reified racially through the iconography of "master" and "slave" and illuminates the shifts in modernity between the violent and confounding histories of colonial slavery and early capitalism.

The stern-piece is situated directly below the farthest extremity of the cuddy, where one of the most dramatic scenes of "Benito Cereno" unfolds in spectacular degrees. Its placement—both on the ship and in the narrative—is far from random. As the cuddy extends out and forms an overhang, from certain angles its image would be clouded in shadows, becoming clear only as Delano closes in on the San Dominick. Its placement intensifies the boding impression of "shadows present, foreshadowing deeper shadows to come" (353). Looking at the rear of the ship at the end of the story, it becomes manifestly evident that the stern-piece is, more critically, meant to offer a different mode of visuality that competes with the shaving scene that unfolded immediately above it. While the "play of the barber" scene has the effect of being animated and dramatized in a certain way, the stern-piece is not a static, inert image. Rather, the image carries within it a subsumed imperative that prefigures how the action of the story will develop and culminate and, by the end of the story, is an image that is set into motion and brought to life. Interrogating the properties of the form of the stern-piece, including its imagery and its placement, reveals the complicated interplay between Melville's manipulation of the visual and the textual in his story—an interplay that is illuminated by an analysis of the story's use of visual culture and an outsider art that is quite literally raw.

Although Delano reads the stern-piece allegorically, as a sign of the deterioration of the Spanish empire, it also needs to be read literally, as an engagement with its prima facie meanings that later exposes its recursive function within the story to legitimate a specific social formation. Delano first sees it while riding in his small whaleboat as he approaches the *San Dominick*: "But the principle relic of faded grandeur was the ample oval of the stern-piece, intricately carved with the arms of Castile and Leon, medallioned about by groups of mythological or symbolic devices; uppermost and central to which was a dark satyr in a mask, holding his foot on the prostrate neck of a writhing figure, likewise masked" (354). The figures in the image are meant to be not only abstract but, in their masks, anonymous and concealed. With one figure in submission, the act of subjugation is already an accepted phenomenon here in the stern-piece. Although it is introduced in the opening pages, its seemingly innocuous presence lurks in the shadows and, ultimately, guides the entire narrative plot. Throughout "Benito Cereno," the stern-piece functions as both pre-text and subtext. More than simply corresponding ex post facto to a plot that will ensue, the description of the stern-piece essentially dictates the action to follow. But to make the plot correspond to the image intricately carved on the stern-piece—to make it not merely pictorial but didactic—the plot can only achieve closure with a complementary image.

Cereno has just bid good-bye to Captain Delano, and, at the crucial moment, he jumps overboard only to have a "sooty avalanche" of Africans follow (635). Delano thinks that the Spanish captain is after him and that Cereno's ever trustworthy slaves are his allies. Finally, Delano realizes that Babo is trying to kill Don Benito: "At this juncture, the left hand of Captain Delano, on one side, again clutched the half-reclined Don Benito, heedless that he was in a speechless faint, while his right foot, on the other side ground, the prostrate negro; and his right arm pressed for added speed on the after oar, his eye bent forward, encouraging his men to their utmost" (635). The moment of revelation depends upon a transliteration of the fictions of representation into the materialities of actualization, where the good American captain transforms this imitation of life into a very real world, replete with its own scenes of subjection and acts of imperial domination. Delano's actions transform the static image of the stern-piece by animating it, by moving it from the second dimension into the third. Bringing this image to life, putting it in motion, as it were, Melville deconstructs and then inverts the aesthetic functionality of the image as a simulacrum by interpolating the real into the imaginary.[27]

Furthermore, the stern-piece determines how the text's numerous examples of tautology—those moments and episodes where things both are and are not, such as Babo being both a "master" and a "slave"—are put into relief. By animating the final image, the story confirms that Cereno was little more than a "paper" captain and that, indeed, a slave is nothing but a slave (361). As the scene unfolds, there is a curious substitution. The prostrate figure is Babo, but the position that should ostensibly be occupied by Cereno is held instead by Delano. The stern-piece of the *San Dominick* not only evinces the consolidation of whiteness as a kind of racial confederation but also illuminates Delano as a symbol of U.S. imperialism, where his authoritarian inclinations over both the African and the Spanish are simultaneously veiled and coded as white hegemony. Rather than refurbishing the fading grandeur of the Spanish empire, Delano's actions mark the beginnings of an imperial U.S. nationalism.

As much as Delano's actions bring the image of the stern-piece to life, they also serve as the delayed reaction to the initial revolt. Promising his officers that the *San Dominick* had gold and silver worth more than a thousand doubloons, Delano assures his men that if they took her, "no small part should be theirs" (636). This is no "Revolutionary Atlantic" where sailors and slaves come to represent a community bound by the planks of ships.[28] Far from "leaguing in against" whiteness by running with the black insurrectionists, the sailors of both ships come together as one ("November," 462). Killing or maiming the black subjects in recovering the ship was much less desired than reclaiming the ship and its blacks subjects as property per se outright:

> They were almost overborne, when, rallying themselves into a squad as one man, with a huzza, they sprang inboard, where entangled, they involuntarily separated again. For a few breaths' space, there was a vague, muffled, inner sound, as of submerged sword-fish rushing hither and thither through shoals of black-fish. Soon, in a reunited band, and joined by the Spanish seamen, the whites came to surface…in five minutes more, the ship was won. (637)

Melville's language, which has been so precise in maintaining the differences between Cereno and Delano as being the distinction of national cultures, invokes whiteness as the quotidian register through which the Americans and Spanish locate their coalition politics. And, more critically, this is the one moment, however fleeting, that the Spanish are translated as the social equal to the Americans. The national affiliations of the Americans and the Spanish temporarily dissipate only to be reconfigured within a racialized dialectic that illuminates the black and white polarity that has lingered under the surface of the story throughout the text.

■ AFTERWARD AND AFTERWORDS; OR, THE DIVIDED TEXT OF "BENITO CERENO"

The story of "Benito Cereno" is contained by the functionality of the stern-piece as an objet d'art and its subsequent embodied animation; everything else is seemingly outside of the story, including the first revolt and the trial itself, thus making "Benito Cereno" very much a divided text. Given the literal placement of the stern-piece on the ship, the plot essentially concludes where the tale itself began: at the rear. What initially seems, therefore, to be a linear plot progression is, in actuality, much more akin to a circuit. That is, "Benito Cereno" as a text can attain closure only with the appended documents that function as the stern-piece to the very text itself. Furthermore, when one considers that the stern is not merely at the rear of ship but, in nautical parlance, a term that implies pursuit and chase, it becomes unduly apparent that the stern-piece, although a dilapidated adornment, structurally undergirds the entire tale by framing the "living spectacle" that is about to occur on the ship, not on that of the enfeebled Cereno but the good American Delano (355). These contrapuntal images evince that "Benito Cereno" needs to be approached from the stern and that the text of Melville's story can be made intelligible only by approaching it from the rear, in this case, the appended legal documents.

The story begins after the revolt, and the reader becomes privy to the prior actions only after the *San Dominick* is recovered, and even then only by the scanty selective "legal documents" provided by the narrator. "Benito Cereno" is essentially a sequel to a prehistory that the reader is ultimately denied. Thinking about space within the story and the text, the revolt is both off-site and out of sight. The ordeals of the *San Dominick* are made to seem all the more distant and, perhaps, less imminent by the fractured nature of the text itself, which, like Douglass's story *The Heroic Slave*, refuses to illustrate the action of black insurrections. Yet whereas Douglass abbreviates Washington's actions aboard the *Creole* by having them finitely compressed in the linear sequence of his story, Melville excises the revolution of Babo and his counterparts and, in essence, makes "Benito Cereno" a sequel to an earlier event. The reader gains some insight into how the revolt occurred through the legal documents but nothing from the Africans' testimony conveys late-eighteenth or nineteenth-century liberation discourse like Douglass's *Heroic Slave* or Brown's *Clotel*. It is these documents positioned as postscript that act as a corrective to essentially revisit and, in the end, clarify previous ambiguities. Moreover, they not only act as an explicatory legend included as a subsequent addendum—not dissimilar to Stowe's *Key to Uncle Tom's Cabin* (1854)—but they get realigned in the reader's imagination as a cognitive map to retrospectively allow one to understand what happened on the *San Dominick*.[29] Within the space of "Benito Cereno," Melville destabilizes linearity by inverting the sequence of present and past in his text.[30]

Ultimately, the framed court depositions bring closure to the text of "Benito Cereno." Ironically, however, Cereno's deposition, like his silences in the narrative, is riddled with omissions.[31] With the shadow of Babo still cast, Cereno is nearly incapable of speaking. Before the deposition hearings, Cereno furnishes his account, much to the disbelief of those who hear it. In the eyes of the tribunal, Cereno's story smacks of paranoid phantasm, and it is only after the "subsequent depositions of the surviving sailors" that the court "rested its capital sentences upon statements which, had they lacked confirmation, it would have deemed it but duty to reject" (637). Near the deposition's end, the court increasingly relies upon the testimony of the Africans themselves, yet within the deposition itself, they are never quoted. That is, there is a keen manipulation of spacing voice within the deposition itself. Cereno's knowledge of the

mutiny is substantiated only because "the negroes afterwards told the deponent" and his account verifiable "because the negroes have said it" (641). Many
of the black subjects, however, remain silent after their recapture, an aspect
that one critic has identified as "evidence of a consciousness that privileges the
efficacy of deeds over words."[32] The acts of appropriation that incorporate the
words of the enslaved black subjects literally extend the forms and meanings
of court-ordered representation. It is all the more ironic here because Cereno
now shapes the words of the very individuals who previously held him and his
voice hostage.

■ FLESH AND BONES: CORPOREALITY AND THE COMING COMMUNITY

The outline of "Benito Cereno" as a divided text draws attention to the very vicissitudes of reading. Read as the incongruities of interpretation between Captain
Delano and Benito Cereno, the text seems preoccupied with reestablishing the
law and order of U.S. political logic. Read through the vantage point of Babo,
the text seems latently concerned with the rerouting and rerooting of black
subjectivity.[33] For example, at the end of the text, the "legal identity" of Babo
is confirmed by the testimony of sailors because Cereno is incapable of speaking. The aspects of Babo's subjectivity that extend beyond this legal identity are
made little known to the reader by the court documents themselves, save that he
was "a small negro of Senegal, but some years among the Spaniards, aged about
thirty" (638). Condensed in the testimonies, the court documents are presented
as the most accurate source of the true sentiments of Babo and the other enslaved
subjects. Given the abbreviated form of the documents, frequently announced
underneath the rubric that "the negroes have said it" and the fact that they have
been selected by none other than Delano himself, locating the subjectivities of
the captured slaves by reconstructing their voices calls attention to the very fault
lines of representation in the text. But to do so is also an act of recuperating the
traces of agency, which have been pushed into the recesses of the spectral, to better theorize the correlation between agency and the idea of freedom in the black
imagination during the age of global slavery.

Although the insurgent slaves have set their course for Senegal in particular,
their actions have coalesced them into an interstitial coalition, indeed a coming
community.[34] I invoke Giorgio Agamben here, most notably his idea of "whatever
singularity" as an "inessential commonality, a solidarity that in no way concerns
an essence" to underscore the processes of collectivities that bind the African
slaves as a coalitional bloc in a temporally or spatially delimited moment. As
Sterling Stuckey has argued, slave ships "were the first real incubators of slave
unity across cultural lines."[35] Babo, Atufal, and Francesco are reminders of the
terminal points within the circuits of slavery—something that is further illuminated by the names of the other black subjects of the *San Dominick* that are

revealed in the deposition. The names of the four oakum pickers (Muri, Nacta, Yola, Ghofan) and those of the six hatchet polishers (Martiniqui, Yan, Lecbe, Mapenda, Yambaio, Akim) are set in contrast to José and Francesco, who have been under Spanish rule for some time longer than the rest. In fact, José is described as being fluent in Spanish, and Francesco, "a mulatto and fine singer," was a native of Buenos Aires (638). The Ashanti hatchet polishers, apparently, were recently captured, being described in the deposition as "all raw" (638). Although they remain nameless throughout the text, the enslaved women are earlier associated with the Ashanti, putting Delano in mind that some of them might have been made into "capital soldiers" (472). In particular, their singing is a form of communication that Delano cannot translate and constitutes a form of nonspeech communication that indicates their efforts to circumscribe themselves as a coming community. This community was marked not only by Babo but by the various roles that the other black subjects played within this system, such as the four older caulkers who were assigned to keep "domestic order" (640). As much as Senegal might have been an imaginary homeland for all the racialized subjects aboard the *San Dominick*, their insurrection instantiated blackness as a kind of transnational politics.

The deposition's early declaration that the "negroes revolted suddenly" is counterbalanced by a later statement that Alexandro Aranda was killed to ensure the liberty of the ship's slave population (638). Death might not guarantee freedom, but the killing of Aranda belies the Hegelian formulation of the master/slave dialectic in very stark terms. More specifically, however, Babo and his counterparts are compatriots in name only, in possession of a conditional liberation with nowhere to go in the New World: "They told the deponent to come up, and that they would not kill him; which having done, the negro Babo asked him whether there were in those seas any negro countries were they might be carried, and he answered them. No; that the negro Babo afterwards told him to carry them to Senegal, or to the neighboring islands of St. Nicholas" (638).

This is where Melville's setting of 1799 is crucial; for had he set the story after 1804, the newly independent country of Haiti might have been suggested. As it is, with the ship in serious disrepair and without water, Babo and his counterparts would indeed need the assistance of Saint Nicholas, the patron saint of sailors, if they were going to take control of their new itinerary and reverse the routes of the Middle Passage. The document that is drawn up and "signed by the deponent and the sailors who could write, as also by the negro Babo, for himself and all the blacks," becomes a receipt for the change in their itinerary from a one-way to round-trip sojourn (639). It also approximates a social contract, protecting certain privileges and rights among those within the closed system aboard the *San Dominick*.[36] Babo's statement urging that they push on toward Senegal intimates that only a return to a black nation-state could reverse the "malign machinations" of the Middle Passage that attempted to transubstantiate Africans bodies into something less than human (643).

The story concludes with two competing images of the body being torn asunder: Babo's head and Aranda's bones. In the moments before Delano and his men work to recover the ship, these objects are examples of Frank Ankersmit's notion of representation as the "intermediate limbo between what is already and what is not yet reality."[37] The severed head of Babo has been commonly understood as the excessive, but expected, corporeal punishment of the leader of an insurrection. Placed on a pole, his head "met unabashed, the gaze of whites" (644). In her reading of DuBois, Spillers notes "the importance of the *specular* and the *spectacular*" in his conceptualization of racial subjectivity.[38] Surely Babo's head functions as a device of the spectacular, as something that one's eyes are impulsively and compulsively drawn to. But the description of his head leaves the reader feeling as if Babo could still see, as if he is still specular, as if he were still staring into the whites of their eyes demanding recognition. Even when Babo is severed, Melville gives him a sense of near agency, as if Babo were staring back at his onlookers in defiant reconfirmation of his actions. Babo's head—"whose brain, not body, had schemed and led the revolt"—echoes another curious Melville depiction of heads (643). Earlier in the story, as Babo finishes grooming Cereno, the American captain thinks to himself that "the negro seemed a Nubian sculptor finishing off a white statue-head" (469). In *Moby-Dick*, as they share quarters together at the Spouter-Inn, Ishmael thinks to himself that with his head freshly shaven, Queequeg's appearance reminds Ishmael of "General Washington's head, as seen in the popular busts of him."[39]

At the close of "Benito Cereno," what remains is a violent inversion of the "Nubian sculptor" and the "white statue-head." Babo's head becomes a bust of sorts, truncated and damaged to be sure and its function as an icon of imperialism is palpably discernible. Babo's head is not an icon of black transnationalism. On public display, his severed head allows the constituents of Lima to reconfirm the illegitimacy of the efforts of the captured slaves. Babo's head signifies not only the containment of an insurgent black transnationalism but an emerging racial order that arranges race and nation through the commingled world systems of slavery and colonialism. In view of Babo's refusal to have his testimony otherwise transcribed, the head contests the meanings of the phrase *res ipsa loquitur*, as part of the public sphere legal discourse on the claims of representation, by undermining its impulses as a self-evidentiary mechanism. As a violent act of separation that materializes a literary device, Babo's severed head pushes synecdoche to its outer boundaries at the very moment that the solubility of synecdoche is disclosed as a function of representation for both culture and politics. But, I want to emphasize that only recognizing or privileging the countersignatory moment, to borrow Derrida's concept, of the trial (if not the earlier moment of U.S. intervention aboard the *San Dominick*) threatens to disallow us from recognizing Aranda's bones and the chalk-lettering produced as the manifestation of a political aesthetic attempting to articulate a claim for a new black sociality. Both of these instances illustrate how art furnishes a source of autonomy and opposition to the status quo.[40] The efforts of Babo and his counterparts, who conceptualize and foment for a new political horizon through art, are akin to what Rancière identifies as "dissensus" or political processes that resist the "sensible order" and established horizons of what is visible and audible.[41] To read Babo's head in this way, then, is an attempt to recover and interpret the meanings of the "virtual discourses" of his silence.[42]

The second closing image of the text is Aranda's skeleton. There is an exhaustive history of debate about the alleged cannibalism of the black subjects, but Aranda's bones serve a different function in the story as a metonym for the mass carnage of Africans decimated during the Middle Passage. Although the black subjects were vindictive in destroying the conditions of their bondage, the fact remains that they were initially enslaved and that violence had thus been done to them. As Sterling Stuckey and Joshua Leslie argue, "The slaves' shaving down of Aranda's body is a symbolic reflection of a white historical act."[43] Spillers's distinction between "body" and "flesh" helps to illustrate Babo's reconfiguration of the Middle Passage. In Spillers's estimation, the central distinction "between captive and liberated subject-positions" recognizes that "before the 'body' there is the 'flesh,' that zero degree of social conceptualization that does not escape concealment under the brush of discourse, of the reflexes of iconography."[44]

As the San Dominick's figurehead, Aranda's remains are symbolically important not only as body and flesh in Spillers's construction but also specifically as a corpus of bones, which remain unmarked and unidentifiable to Delano until the battle. Although the reader has premonitions that these bones may indeed belong to Aranda early in the narrative, placing the skeleton as the ship's figurehead unnames Aranda as owner and symbolically situates the carcass as guiding the return to Africa. Substituting the figurehead of Christopher Columbus, the placement of Aranda's bones on the bow indicates that the Africans plan to take a reverse route. Reduced to the spectral, Aranda's bones thus become a parallel representation of the bones of millions of Africans trapped at the bottom of the Atlantic Ocean. These bones outline a figurative network, a subterranean constellation, which reroutes the itineraries of black subjectivity through the dream of an imagined community. Divested of its corporeal attachments, Aranda's bones are reconfigured as an icon of black transnationalism.

By so doing, Babo and his counterparts attempted to figuratively put flesh on these bones and raise the dead—a sentiment that is intimated in the text with the reference to Ezekiel's Dry Valley of Bones. Given the pervasive machinations of violence perpetrated upon their bodies, reconnecting the flesh and bone has been a central preoccupation of modern black thought and culture. DuBois opens *The Souls of Black Folk* (1903), for example, by inquiring of his readers if he needed to "add that I who speak here am bone of bone and the flesh of the flesh of them that live within the Veil."[45] Likewise, the African American spiritual "Dry Bones" imagines the reconstitution of the black subject from the ground up, from the toe to the head.[46]

It is in this resignification of iconicity—an iconicity that gains its fullest purchase as a symbol for the anonymous dead—where Babo inverts the processes that have too often made blacks phantoms of the state. As Sundquist notes, Babo's power is exercised "through his uncanny manipulation of the revolt's linguistic and visual *narrative*."[47] Babo is an embodiment of the signifying monkey, one who, in Gates's definition, is a "trope for repetition and revision, indeed our trope of chiasmus itself, repeating and reversing as he does in one deft discursive act."[48] It is consequential that the signifying monkey is said to appear at the crossroads because the Middle Passage is thought of as one such crossroads—a nexus where the cultures of the Americas, Europe, and Africa meet. Babo's attempt at reversing the traditional route of the Middle Passage, then, renders new meaning to the chalk-scripted words "*Seguid vuestro jefe*" (355).

The words "follow your leader" become an unduly freighted symbolic phrase throughout the text—not the least of which is the near taunting of the reader to either follow the narrator or follow the author. But my insistence here on maintaining "*Seguid vuestro jefe*" is an attempt to recover the closest thing to a vernacular statement articulated by the ship's black subjects: "Rudely painted or chalked, as in a sailor freak, along the forward side of a sort of pedestal below the canvas, was the sentence, '*Seguid vuestro jefe*,' (follow your leader); while upon the tarnished head-boards, near by, appeared, in stately capitals, once gilt, the ship's name, 'SAN DOMINICK,' each letter streakingly corroded with tricklings of copper-spike rust" (355).

The visual depiction here accentuates how the differential in art is used as an index of the state of affairs. The faded gilded letters proclaiming the ship's identification are put into stark relief by the "sailor freak" writing of the phrase "*Seguid vuestro jefe*," as if the latter words were graffiti upon a stately edifice. The words are placed below the canvas that conceals Aranda's bones, as if they were a label denoting a work of art about to be uncovered for public display. The words are even expressed in the deposition, as if they were a quote: "The negro Babo, coming close, said words to this effect: 'Keep faith with the blacks from here to Senegal, or you shall in spirit, as now in body, follow your leader'" (639). But, more important, "*Seguid vuestro jefe*" signals the permutations of lexicons and codes of languages that black subjects have manipulated to state their claims to the social machinations that governed subjectivity and citizenship. Scrawled on the side of the *San Dominick* as a veritable precursor to outsider art, the phrase "*Seguid vuestro jefe*" challenges its viewers to read the writing on the wall that blacks will no longer remain apparitions of the state, specters of the nation, of this one or any other.

7 The Colored Museum

William "Ethiop" Wilson and the Afric-American Picture Gallery

> Man is the only picture-making animal in the world. He alone of all the inhabitants of the earth has the capacity and passion for pictures.... Poets, prophets, and reformers are all picture-makers, and this ability is the secret of their power and achievements: they see what ought to be by the reflection of what is, and endeavor to remove the contradiction.[1]   FREDERICK DOUGLASS

In the October 5, 1855, issue of *Frederick Douglass' Paper*, the New York correspondent for the periodical, James McCune Smith, included an observation about African Americans and aesthetics. Recalling a recent article in *Putnam's*, Smith noted that blacks were essentially "an *aesthetic* people": "We have an inborn love of art: how much this explains! Poor black humanity, too poor to have marbled halls and pictured galleries of its own, cleaving to the walls and the ceilings and the halls where these things be, would rather be a door in the temples of art, than a rawboned angular struggle with wiry independence!"[2] Smith's statement is charged by a marked degree of disappointment that blacks do not have their own institutional spaces for art—an absence that is exacerbated, in his mind, because blacks are ontologically "an *aesthetic* people." If few nineteenth-century African Americans had a room of one's own to produce art, even fewer had access to the larger spaces within which to display that art or the art of others.

It seems precisely because of the lack of such actual spaces that William J. Wilson must imagine the Afric-American Picture Gallery. Over the course of seven issues, Wilson sketched the imaginary gallery in the pages of Thomas Hamilton's monthly *Anglo-African Magazine* from February through October 1859. In the series, Wilson essentially stylizes the pseudonymic persona he had used for his newspaper writings into a veritable character for his short story. Wilson was an important member of the antebellum black public sphere whose activism included engaging the electoral system in New York by contesting the validity of state officials, challenging the census, and calling for a national convention of African Americans in Philadelphia.[3] Frequently featured in black periodicals, his name was prominently circulated—from an 1837 petition to obtain signatures for the right of suffrage in the *Colored American* to an 1865 appeal to fund a memorial for Abraham Lincoln in the *Christian Recorder*. Wilson's presence was especially heightened in the 1850s by his writing a regular column for

Frederick Douglass' Paper, which also published his short story "Terance Ludlam: Founded on Fact" and, later, editorials for the *Weekly Anglo-African*. Brown included a sketch of him in *The Black Man*, in which he applauded Wilson as "sketch writer of historical scenes and historical characters,—choosing his own subjects, suggested by his own taste or sympathies."[4]

As entrenched as Wilson was in New York's black institutions in education (as a teacher), newspapers (as a correspondent), and politics (as a pamphleteer), he develops the "Ethiop" character to illuminate the necessity of black self-representation in the arts.[5] Wilson describes Ethiop as an art collector who stumbles into a large one-room gallery. The story does not consist solely of descriptions and interpretations of art but also includes episodes that depict Ethiop drawing sketches, conversing with other patrons both black and white that visit the gallery, and traveling to the Black Forest to meet a reclusive artist. The major part of the story, however, focuses on Ethiop's interpretations of paintings as he walks through the gallery and encounters landscapes of Abeokuta, Nigeria and Mount Vernon, Virginia; genre scenes of black conventions; and portraits of Toussaint L'Ouverture and Crispus Attucks. Ethiop, thus, functions as the conceit through which Wilson offers his thoughts on art and culture as well as to evince that the progress of the race will be determined by black participation in the arts.

By focusing on Ethiop's encounter with three different kinds of painting—landscape, genre, and portraiture—this chapter seeks to examine how Wilson illustrates ways of reading art as a means to theorizing a radical black subjectivity. Wilson accentuates this radical black subjectivity by depicting a series of companion pieces such as "Pictures 5 and 6—The Under Ground Railroad," "Picture 12—The Two Portraits that Ought to Be Hung Up," and "Pictures 19 and 20—Preaching and After Preaching" throughout the gallery that invite comparison. Part of how "Afric-American Picture Gallery" works is that it calls upon the reader to view these images comparatively such that, even when the paintings are not curated as companion pieces per se, they are nonetheless meant to be contrasted with other similar types of images as landscape, genre, or portraiture.

"Afric-American Picture Gallery" remains exceptional not only for conceiving a collection of artwork as a kind of museum but also for how it convolutes the practice of simulation as an underlying problematic in African American aesthetics specifically and the very idea of representation in both art and politics more generally.[6] In her acute analysis of the "museum idea" in late nineteenth and early twentieth century American literature, Nancy Bentley argues that the emergence of a sphere of high literary culture occurred under the sign of the modern museum as a means to organize its own cultural perception. Following Bentley, we might foreground the question of what kind of cultural perception Wilson is trying to fashion by arranging the objects in a certain order of display.[7] Wilson's particular description of the arrangement of the works in the gallery, his curatorial efforts if you will, becomes the means through which he articulates a form of black subjectivity that is hemispheric and transnational. The gallery, in this respect, might be said to be an interiorized iteration of a black globality and any discussion about how Wilson is contemplating the meaning of liberty and freedom for U.S. blacks must be framed within this transnational context. As much as the story is about imagining a figurative space where blacks can have their own works presented, the story also becomes a metaliterary site where Wilson's readers are challenged with imagining an African American subjectivity that encompasses and subsumes a black politics that moves beyond the history and borders of the United States.

■ THE WHITES OF THEIR EYES: INTERPRETING ART AND BLACK VISUALITY

In a letter published in the March 11, 1853 issue of *Frederick Douglass' Paper*, Wilson (using his pseudonym) recounts a visit to Plumb's gallery in Manhattan where he found himself surrounded by images of Benjamin Franklin, Thomas Jefferson, Daniel Webster, and Henry Clay as well as Queen Victoria of England and Napoleon Bonaparte but none of historical African American subjects. When he asks the proprietor if he has likenesses of any black subjects from the United States or elsewhere, the proprietor replies that the busts of "great colored men of [the] West Indies" he owns are boxed and bound for the Caribbean because there is no demand for such art—that is, black iconography—in the United States.[8] This experience becomes a moment for Wilson to implore his readers to embrace the arts as practitioners and, importantly, as viewers, patrons, and consumers. Extending his thoughts further in a letter published two weeks later, he concludes that African American art necessitates its own institutional space: "Let a room for readings, or drawings, paintings, or sculpturings, or music, rare collections or inventions, or all of these, be opened in the heart of Gotham; and Ethiop's word for its success."[9] In this way, he offers a remedy to his earlier lamentation of six years before that the proprietor of Plump's gallery had no black subjects on display.

At the same moment, Wilson also implored his readers to recognize the relationship between the production of art and the progress of the race: "Now is the time to begin to cultivate among us both a taste for the arts and sciences themselves, before we become more deeply immersed in the rougher affairs of life. Our present peculiar situation well prepares us for their highest perfection."[10] Wilson's mentioning of their "present peculiar situation" is noted elsewhere with slight variation to signal the anomalous states of social being for African Americans who were suspended in the thirdspace between slavery and freedom. Wilson's idea of the "peculiar situation" of free blacks is therefore part and parcel of a set of terms including the "nominally free" and "alien" variously used by Frederick Douglass, Charles Lenox Remond, and Franes Ellen Watkins Harper to describe the predicament of blackness and the crisis of liberal democracy.[11] If Wilson's suggestion prefigures the later contentious debates between W.E.B. DuBois and

Booker T. Washington on the role of high art versus the practical arts in the Jim Crow era, it also puts into high relief the question about the efficacy of any attempt at black art in the era of chattel slavery for African Americans, free and enslaved alike. Wilson seems to have imagined "Afric-American Picture Gallery" both as a response to his experience at Plumb's and as a fantastic space that could encourage the production of art by "real," that is, actual African Americans and, in this sense, Wilson inverts the process of ekphrasis.

What makes Wilson's "Afric-American Picture Gallery" so rich is that it has so many layers: Wilson envisions art (as a cue for African Americans to produce art themselves); he establishes its arrangement in space to create a (historical) narrative; and he offers ways of interpreting it according to ostensibly black ways of seeing. Still, all of this is narrated, which creates substantial tension between the written word and the visual image; a tension that illuminates the dialectical trope of word and image as a "relay between semiotic, aesthetic, and social differences" according to W.J.T. Mitchell.[12] Wilson stresses the need for art; perhaps less for its own sake per se than as a means to humanize and elevate black people through the visual. But, ultimately, the art—and its spatial arrangement as well as its representation of space—cannot speak for itself. Wilson is representing the interpretation (and arrangement) of the visual, not simply the production of art itself and this hermeneutics of black visuality is put into effect through Wilson's use of Ethiop as a conceit. While Wilson intends for the paintings to act as a prescription for subversive black agency, the fact that Wilson has Ethiop interpret imaginary paintings heightens the quality of the images as a "potent absence or a fictive, figural present" that Mitchell finds endemic to the genre of ekphrasis—a quality, I would add, that similarly identifies the predicament of antebellum free blacks.[13] The fact that Wilson imagines a gallery and has his protagonist engage in ekphrasis itself means Wilson is continually imagining (both artistically and institutionally) that which does not quite exist in these almost-there forms as a way to present alternative ways of seeing for his black readers and, in this manner, intimates that these shared ways of seeing constitute the basis upon which an imagined community might coalesce.

This latent mandate of interpreting art as a way to instantiate and coalesce a radical black community is especially animated in the sixth installment of the story where Ethiop escorts a group of visitors who are visiting the gallery. Unlike an earlier moment in the story where the visitor was white, at least some of the visitors from this group are black. They are variously identified as the "stout lady," the "tall lady," the "lady from abroad," the "old lady," the "Doctor," the "Philosopher," and "two colored gentlemen, in white cravats" (219). The members of the party debate the meaning and significance of a number of paintings including one titled "Condition" where a young destitute African American boy sits on the banks of a river; a group of black farmers in a painting entitled "Farm Life in Western America"; a series of small pictures entitled "City Life" where, among the other images, a young African American girl holds a white doll; and

"Picture 27—The First Convention." While members of the party disagree as to whether the condition of the boy is a result of his nature or environment, they are also at odds as to whether it is appropriate to have the image of the black girl with the white doll in the Afric-American Picture Gallery at all. In ways that prefigure the devastating story of Pecola Breedlove in Toni Morrison's novel *The Bluest Eye* (1970) more than a century later, Wilson's short story uses the debate between the museum visitors to critique the forms of ostensibly black bourgeois sensibilities encapsulated in the designation "City Life" that do damage to the psychological and emotional, if not political, registers of representing the self.

But if there remains little agreement regarding the interpretations for most of the works viewed by the gallery visitors, Wilson depicts a later moment when they reach consensus while viewing "Picture 27—The First Convention" as a way to model the practices of black visuality that coalesce political sensibility. With its cast of black founding fathers, Wilson describes "The First Convention" in a manner to liken the image and scene to those of the white founding fathers depicted in such paintings as John Trumbull's *Declaration of Independence* (1795) and Junius Brutus Stearns's *Washington as a Statesman at the Constitutional Convention* (1856). Pointing to different figures such as James Forten and Hezekiah Grice, the doctor notes with pleasure that "the leading minds of that time, who did most to advance the cause of Afric-America, were outside of the clergy" (246). One of the two African American visitors replies by noting the other faces in the painting including Richard Allen and William Watkins were all respected members of the church.[14] In a wider sense, this episode becomes less about their specific claims regarding the particular religious and secular dimensions of black political action than it is an instance of how Wilson illustrates the hermeneutics of sight and being that he wants to encode as a political mode of black visuality. It is through this African American visitor, in pointing to portraits of Peter Williams, Theodore S. Wright, and others, that Wilson is able to limn a more subversive impulse of black political thought that might otherwise be too easily veiled or hidden in the shadows.[15]

▪ NATIVE SOIL: "LANDSCAPE" PAINTING AND PECULIAR POSITIONALITY

While Wilson dramatizes the debate between the party of visitors as a way to insist upon a comparative (or, at least, binary) understanding of black political subjectivity, he stages this approach in the story primarily by having Ethiop compare and contrast two works in an effort to uncover the more subversive political undertones that could potentially circumscribe a black community as such if only viewed and interpreted properly. If U.S. black subjectivity includes both the conventional and the subversive, the religious and the secular, Wilson is also at pains throughout the story to evince that this subjectivity is both national and diasporic. The "peculiar position" of African Americans, which Wilson mentions in the 1853 letter to Douglass's newspaper and elsewhere, was partly determined by their relationship to the land that made many African Americans feel as if they were aliens on their own "native soil" in the United States. Indeed, this political predicament was so visceral for free blacks in the antebellum North that Wilson employs his descriptions of landscape paintings in the first two installments to allegorize the genealogies of that peculiar position.

With their water imagery that perhaps prefigures a "floating" subjectivity, "Picture 1—The Slave Ship" and "Picture 4—Sunset in Abbeokuta" begin to illustrate the latent presence of transatlantic slavery to U.S. nation formation and also perhaps signal the "floating" condition of African American political subjectivity between slavery and freedom, slave and citizen. "Picture 1—The Slave Ship" is positioned at the very entrance of the gallery and therefore is one of the first images one can encounter when entering the space. As a would-be curator, Wilson intends for the gallery's visitors to have to confront slavery and, in some respects, this obligatory confrontation, this compulsory moment of recognition, is a narrative version of what Fred Wilson and Kara Walker have achieved in their own curatorial efforts in the late twentieth and early twenty-first centuries, respectively.[16] Everything about "Picture 1—The Slave Ship" is dark, including its placement in the gallery, where it hangs near the entrance on the south side in poor light, almost as if it is imbued with Melville's phrase from the opening of "Benito Cereno": "Shadows present, foreshadowing deeper shadows to come."[17] The view depicts the harbor of colonial Jamestown in 1609 and the artist, in Ethiop's estimation, has remained faithful to some of the most important features of landscape painting by accurately illustrating the natural surroundings of the region, "even to every shrub, crag and nook," Ethiop remarks (53).

As the depiction of the slave ship begins to compete with the illustration of the environmental setting as the primary focal point, the image increasingly loses its purchase as a landscape painting. Ethiop's description of the waters as fierce and angry is meant to indicate that nature itself is antagonistic to the illicit commerce of the slave trade, or perhaps that the slave trade has corrupted nature. The most pronounced symbol of the painting's characteristic as allegory, however, is the skiff, which is rendered in starkly gothic terms: "The small boat struck by, and contending with a huge breaker, is so near the shore that you can behold, and startle as you behold, the emaciated and death-like faces of the unfortunate victims, and the hideous countenances of their captors; and high and above all, perched upon the stern, with foot, tail, and horns, and the chief insignia of his office, is his Satanic Majesty, gloating over the whole scene" (53). Rather than a new-world paradise, Ethiop describes early America as a hell, punctuated by the presence of a demon figure. If slavery sought to transform black bodies into commodities, subjects into objects, Wilson conjures the painting here to render how slave traders themselves were transformed and disfigured into something other than human.

But perhaps the most compelling feature of the picture as a failed landscape is not simply its use of allegory or even its accurate illustration of topography but rather its use of point of view and perspective as a contrivance to simulate animation. Ethiop expresses how the Africans are pictured as being so close to the shore that the viewer can almost "behold" them. By emphasizing their faces, Ethiop creates a moment whereby he figuratively rearranges the geometrics of the painting's compositional design to create a reconfigured zone of perspective. This reconfigured zone of ocularity, which places the viewer face-to-face with the slaves, engenders the painting's mode of sensational affect and threatens its claim as a landscape painting per se with its apparent focus on humans and social action. Wilson seems to be suggesting that part of what prevents this image from becoming an example of landscape painting is that, even in a painting where the figures may be relatively small, they are nonetheless prominent and the focus of Ethiop's descriptions.

By contrast, "Picture 4—Sunset in Abeokuta," another painting discussed by Ethiop in the first installment with its depiction of an idyllic African landscape, recasts the debates about the place of blacks in the United States and subtly proposes emigration as an alternative to remaining in the United States. Ethiop notes that it is a fine painting, emphasizing that it graciously shows an African sky abounding with colors nowhere to be found in the United States. He concludes the short entry on the painting with a telling comment: "The last touches of the artist's pencil has [sic] made the glow of the coming evening to softly spread itself over here and there a dusky inhabitant reclining upon the banks of an unrippled lake. The effect is fine, and the whole scene is so charming that one could almost wish to be there" (54). The assessment of the painting as a work of art, however, hinges on the word "charming," as if the scene were bedazzling. This effect is engendered by the composition's use of color to paint the sky, which, even with its "warmth of hue and softness of tint," is ostensibly more resplendent that any rainbow in the United States. The idyllic quality of the painting is rendered by its sense of calmness, such that there is not even a ripple in the lake, and Ethiop understands this to be the quintessential natural state for Africans and perhaps even the ideal state to which blacks in the diaspora should return.

The comment that "the whole scene is so charming that one could almost wish to be there" might be said to be a latent aim of nearly all landscape painting, but Ethiop's words here take on a particular valence concerning the position of blacks in the United States. It is possible that Wilson learned about Abeokuta from Martin R. Delany, whose novel *Blake; or, The Huts of America* was being serialized in the *Anglo-African Magazine* at the same moment that "Afric-American Picture Gallery" was featured. Ethiop's use of the conditional word "could" encapsulates the ambivalence of such a return to Africa for U.S. blacks, even when that world is illustrated in the most alluring light. Abeokuta was an important refugee town in Nigeria during the nineteenth century, with many repatriated Sierra Leoneans who had been picked up by the British patrolling for slave ships.[18] Abeokuta, then, was a sight where the black diaspora (both near and far) was converging and in Wilson's mind, like Delany's, it may have served as an ideal alternative to the American Colonization Society sponsored Liberia. All of this is registered through language, however, more so than the image per se; for how could Wilson identifiably mark "Abeokuta" as such, distinct and differentiated from every other near likeness without the specific title that designates the location as Africa?

Wilson continues his examination of the intricacies of early national history that have produced the "Afric-American" as a particular genealogical construction in the next pair of "landscape" paintings where he contrasts Mount Vernon and the Black Forest. As he did with the first installment, Wilson presents a horrific image of violence against black bodies that is contrasted with a counter-image. If the painting of Abeokuta in the first installment serves as a counter-image to suggest emigration as a political alternative for mid-century African Americans, then physical confrontation and retribution is portrayed as a distinct possibility in the next pairing. And, if "Picture 1—The Slave Ship" is essentially a failed landscape, then "Picture 9—Mount Vernon" also seems an unfulfilled landscape painting. In "Picture 9," Wilson accentuates the scene's corrosion and decay to suggest that slavery hinders landscape painting from emerging as something closer to the picturesque proper. Ethiop recounts how the painting outlines the entire expanse of Mount Vernon, with a picture that "is of largest size, the mansion, out-house, slave huts and all" (88). The winds depicted in "Mount Vernon" bend "here and there scattering tree-tops, (land marks of the past)" and "seem to creak through the many visible crevices of the Old Mansion and sigh decay, decay! decay!!" (88). This impression of decay, Ethiop states, is "written by the Artist's pencil more legibly than in letters" (89). Here, Wilson submits that the visual supersedes the literary in its representational capacity. This moment in the story thus reverses James Heffernan's well-known understanding of ekphrastic literature as making explicit what graphic art renders through implication.[19] Importantly, Wilson's description of the treetops is also an indication of the picture's conversion away from landscape and into genre painting with its focus on everyday life, for it is the treetops, as "land marks of the past," that become correlated to the ruined social scene of Washington's estate.

As the most conspicuous aspect of "Picture 9—Mount Vernon," the slave scene demarcates the picture's ambivalent position between landscape and genre painting by exemplifying it as a crisis in the formal problems of how to represent temporality. According to Ethiop, the scene is the most compelling element of the picture:

> The first thing that here arrests the eye is the recently dug up coffin of Washington; just behind which stands the ghost of his faithful old slave and body servant; while in front, a living slave of to-day stands, with the *bones* of Washington gathered up in his arms, and labelled "For Sale" "Price $200,000; this negro included." "Money

wanted."—A number of other slaves, men, women, and children are placed in a row along the bank just beyond, bearing about the neck of each the following inscription: "*These negroes for sale. Money wanted.*" (88)

The scene is haunted by a ghost of the past who lingers in the present moment.[20] Similar to charges articulated by Douglass and Brown, "Picture 9—Mount Vernon" implies that the failures of the founding fathers to adequately address the problem of chattel slavery would return in future generations. But it is precisely the presence of the ghost that inhibits and stalls the painting's sense of nostalgia, a sensation important to the tenets of picturesque landscape painting, with its illustrations of idealized views of nature; hence, "Picture 9" cannot be about a return to a romanticized past so much as it is a representation of a miscalibrated national temporality where the past is superimposed onto the present.

The issue of how slavery confuses the teleological underpinnings of a national temporality, illustrated when the picture's landscape elements give over to the stylistic ones of genre painting, is further underscored by Ethiop's latent critique of the efforts to preserve Mount Vernon as a historical site. Ethiop notes that among the current proprietors of Mount Vernon are "a noted son of Massachusetts" and "a few pious looking old ladies" (89). The "noted son of Massachusetts" is certainly Edward Everett, whom Ethiop mentions directly in a later passage, and the women are most likely delegates of the Mount Vernon Ladies' Association of the Union. By midcentury, Mount Vernon had fallen into disrepair, and Ann Pamela Cunningham, the daughter of a South Carolina planter, and Everett, a former Harvard president and politician from Massachusetts, began efforts to resurrect the estate in the late 1850s. Everett was particularly dedicated to preserving Mount Vernon; after delivering the lecture "George Washington, Builder of the Union" in 1856, he embarked upon a more extended tour in 1858. Because Everett was one of the most highly regarded orators in the nineteenth century, his lectures became an important part of the campaign to save Mount Vernon, and the *New York Ledger* subsequently hired him to write a weekly column on U.S. history. For Everett, Washington was a perfect model of how to preserve the Union.[21]

The differences between the image of Washington described in Ethiop's "Picture 9" and his image in Everett's lectures are not simply variations of style and technique but rather illuminate a predicament of how to read national history. Whereas Everett's lectures on Washington might be thought of as oratorical portraiture, one where the figure of Washington is adumbrated again and again as a national icon, Ethiop's description of Washington disallows the body from emerging, dissolving the corpus and reducing it to a set of bones. Ethiop's suggestion that Everett himself might want to view the picture and point out any defects is more than ironic, for it is the painting, with its illustrations of black figures—both spectral and bodily—that counteracts the ways in which African Americans have been excised from the public mythology and discourse about

Washington, including Everett's own narrative. This irony is heightened further because it would be only through the sale of the slaves that the Mount Vernon site could be established, essentially consecrating a monument whereby blacks were not only removed from the grounds, so to speak, but excised from the historical channels of public memory.

However, Wilson is not only indicting the premature monumentalization of Washington through the sale of living slaves but also defacing the myth of America by accentuating that Washington's bones too are for sale. Yet, to make sure a pronouncement, even in the black public sphere, Wilson must create the convoluted apparatus of creating a persona who describes imaginary paintings to engage in such dangerous speech. It is possible that this conceit is not simply cover or protection (less than a year later Wilson would publish a nearly heretical essay entitled "What Shall We Do with the White People? [1860]); maybe this device transforms his sketches into the literary or the artistic rather than the rhetorical. Indeed, the distance Wilson puts between himself as the living, breathing author and the blasphemous violence he represents may be the result of some kind of anxiety over the potential danger that comes from expressing such ideas. But, ultimately, Wilson's use of Ethiop is one way that nineteenth-century African American sought to transpose representation in the arts as a form of representation in politics.

Whereas "Picture 4—Sunset in Abbeokuta" sheds light on the black emigration debate and "Picture 9—Mount Vernon" critiques the failures of the most venerated founding father, Wilson uses the landscape painting "Picture 11—The Black Forest" to stage a version of a black counter-public sphere. In "Afric-American Picture Gallery," "The Black Forest" is both a stylized image and a physical location, and it is significant that Ethiop travels to this location only after he has viewed the picture, for it is an implicit suggestion about how the imaginary and fantastic in art can find materialization in the real and actual of the social world. The "grand and beautiful scenery" of "The Black Forest," coupled with its "dark background," compels Ethiop to attempt a sketch of the painting to ascertain its "profound mystery" (101). Soon after sitting down to begin the sketch, Ethiop receives a letter from an unknown person from the Black Forest itself inviting him to visit and examine some of the pictures and other curiosities there. While traveling to the Black Forest, Ethiop recalls how accurately the painting portrayed the natural scene: "Here in all its grandeur and wild sublimity was the native landscape spread out before me, the same that I saw in beautiful miniature but a day before hanging on the walls of our Afric-American Gallery" (103). This moment of verisimilitude is important because later in the fourth installment Wilson will invert verisimilitude as a technique in a practice whereby art precedes actuality, fiction before fact, as a maneuver to challenge the dominant reality about chattel slavery.

In staging the Black Forest as the counterpart to the gallery, Wilson underscores it as a space of self-fashioning, one where things are depicted as they might be rather than as they exist. When Ethiop arrives at the destination, he is met by Bernice, the ninety-year-old man who presides over the Black Forest, and escorted into a deep cavern. Upon entering, he notices that it is filled with art from busts and statues to portraits and landscapes. Situated in the heart of darkness and tucked away in a cavern, this is a gallery to which only other blacks have access. After touring the art gallery, Ethiop is led to another alcove with a different scene altogether where Bernice has been keeping a man in bondage as an exhibit, which itself acts as a startling counter image to the multitudinous depictions of black slaves continually on display from slave auctions to runaway bills. Bernice explains to Ethiop that he and his family had once been owned by the captive man: "'He was brought hither, by what means I need not say.... We confronted each other. It was a sore trial to him. We conversed much and freely. He spoke of the wrong done him; I spoke of mine. He spoke of his wife and children left behind. I reminded him of the sale and separation of mine.... He pleaded earnestly for his rights. I told him he had no right that I was bound to respect'" (177). Bernice's language bears a certain cadence, a contrapuntal sonic accord that is engendered by the seeming antiphony between captor and prisoner. But Bernice is merely recounting the conversation between him and his hostage, and thus the sonic effect of this passage is more of a reverb than a strict call-and-response.

Bernice's use of the word "trial" is significant because it prefigures an African American critique of the U.S. judicial system. When Bernice replies to his captive that he has no rights that Bernice is bound to respect, he is clearly signifying on the most circulated phrase from Chief Justice Roger Taney's majority opinion in the Dred Scott decision.[22] Effectively mitigating the Missouri Compromise of 1820 even more than the Kansas-Nebraska Act of 1854, the Dred Scott decision was widely condemned by antislavery advocates at the time as an illegitimate use of judicial power, and African American activists, such as James McCune Smith, responded with tracts to contest the ruling. In the same run as Wilson's "Afric-American Picture Gallery," Smith published the treatise "Citizenship" (1859), which outlined the history of the citizen from its classical roots in antiquity and correlated this meaning to the present condition of blacks in the United States. In it, Smith exposes the logical fallacy of the majority opinion; if blacks had no rights that whites were bound to respect, why was the case before the Supreme Court at all?

While "Sunset in Abbeokuta" and "The Black Forest" are described in terms that would conventionally mark them as examples of landscape paintings, the way that Wilson has Ethiop describe "The Slave Ship" and "Mount Vernon" begs the question of whether the introduction of black bodies in a painting, even in an image as seemingly innocuous as landscape, threatens to transform that work into something perhaps closer to genre painting. Does the introduction of black bodies, regardless of the question of scale, invert the conventional properties of landscape whereby the privileging of natural scenery becomes secondary to an ostensible scene of action? To ask this question is to consider the possibilities of fulfilling a given art form or type as much as it is about reconsidering whether the introduction of black bodies into a work always transforms it into a social allegory about something else; whether the introduction of black bodies disallows that art from being anything but a representational commentary on the social meanings of race.

Wilson's use of landscape—exemplified through Ethiop's interpretation of certain paintings as well as his experiences in the countryside—exposes the fraught relationship of blacks to the territorial zones that comprise the United States. In the end, Wilson's critique of the ways African Americans have been alienated from and through the precincts of a national space, from the founding moment through the Dred Scott decision, offers little belief in the possibility that blacks could be naturalized into the territory of the United States and little relief beyond the possibilities of emigrating to Africa or forming micro enclaves of black counter-publics. In either case, Wilson's depiction of landscape painting suggests that a putative "here" might consistently elude African Americans and continually compel them to fantasize about a would-be "there" on a different horizon altogether.

■ REPRESENTING RADICAL POLITICS AND GENRE PAINTING OF EVERYDAY BLACK LIFE

While black bodies are off center and seemingly distanced from occupying the focal point of the "landscape" paintings in the gallery, they constitute the focal point—both in terms of their placement within the scenes and also the significance of their presence to the meaning of the work—in a number of genre paintings that Ethiop encounters. But, insofar as genre paintings conventionally represent scenes from everyday life, Wilson wants to suggest that there is something fantastic and exceptional in the quotidian lives of black folk as a way to foment a subversive political sensibility among his readers.

Wilson introduces a vision of such a subversive political sensibility in the initial installment of "Africa-American Picture Gallery" with "Pictures 5 and 6—The Under Ground Railroad." In two large images, the pictures illustrate different locations on the Underground Railroad, one in the South and one in the North. "Picture 5" is a composition of a portentously ominous "dark road leading through a darker forest," featuring "some twenty pairs of fine stalwart human feet and legs" scurrying northward (54). Set at night, in the distance is the North Star. "Picture 6" depicts a pastoral scene punctuated by some "twenty bold heads and fine robust faces," with a lake in the foreground and a Canadian forest in the background (54). Although the paintings are placed together side by side on the south wall of the gallery, Ethiop suggests that "Picture 6" should be relocated to the north wall as a more appropriate place for viewing.

Ethiop's suggestion about relocating "Picture 6," however, raises a number of questions about the practices of interpreting images as well as, in a larger sense, the implications of galleries as cultural and political spaces. Repositioning "Picture 6" on the north wall of the gallery would ostensibly accentuate the symbolism of the mythic North so resonant in the African American imagination. But doing so might also mitigate a latent concern of the two images with rectifying and rehabilitating the violence that has been done to the black body, violence that, as Hortense Spillers has noted, threatened to reduce the body to the mere flesh of the corpus.[23] The language of Ethiop's description itself traces the transformation from being the merely corporeal to becoming the embodied subject: "The head, the recognized seat of the mind, is useless to the slave, or, if of service to him, this thinking apparatus is not his own; it belongs to his owner; hence he makes use of his feet and legs, or the physical machinery; while in the second view, at the northern end of this undefinable [sic] Road, where liberty is, the head or mental part is presented to view. The slave,—the chattel,—the thing is a *man*" (54–55). Ethiop's interpretation of "Pictures 5 and 6" as images relies upon the rhetoric of conversion, and his language of the slave, the chattel, and the man echoes one of the most famous lines from Douglass's 1845 *Narrative*: "You have seen how a man was made a slave, you shall see how a slave was made a man."[24] Unlike Douglass's conversion, which is signaled at the moment that he physically confronts Covey, in "Picture 6," the mark of their new status as embodied subjects is signaled by their flight, a transformation of subjectivity marked not only by a change in topographical landscape but a different geopolitical location. While Wilson romanticizes Canada as, what Katherine McKittrick calls, a "finished emancipatory location," the reference is also a reminder of the wide presence of the black diaspora in the Americas.[25] The reference to the Canadian forest is both a constitutive element of the picture's formal mechanism that activates the alternation between the picture's background and foreground and also a social mark of the outer limits of a U.S. black national subjectivity, one that is figuratively hovering on the border.

If a border subjectivity is embedded in the image of "Picture 6," one that already outlines the anomalous position of blacks in the United States, then repositioning it within the gallery layout would rework the teleological underpinnings of both images as not only conjoined but sequential entities. In its current location on the south wall, "Picture 6" joins other images whose representations depict low points in the black experience of early America, including scenes of a slave ship docked at Jamestown, Virginia, and the ghosts of George Washington's Mount Vernon. "Picture 6" is immediately adjacent to "Picture 5," and the compositional arrangement of the two pieces telescopes the transition from slavery to freedom. Given their binary relationality rather than extended seriality, "Pictures 5 and 6" depict that transition as an abbreviated moment, condensed to a shortened amount of time and stylized not simply by the move from darkness to light but from the near gothic to the pastoral bucolic.

Beyond elongating the interval between slavery and an imagined freedom, disaggregating "Picture 6" from "Picture 5" would compel the would-be visitor, if walking counterclockwise through the gallery, to pass by images of the black diaspora—including Toussaint L'Ouverture, Emperor Solouque, and Phillis Wheatley—en route to the north wall with its representations of freedom and liberty. One way, therefore, to read Ethiop's suggestion about moving "Picture 6" is as a reconsideration of freedom and liberty from *within* the U.S. black imagination to one that reassesses their meanings through the representations of the hemispheric blackness of the New World. In this respect then, circum-perambulating the gallery figuratively shadows the histories of contestation regarding black freedom and liberty illustrated (or arranged) as hemispheric freedom.

Like "Pictures 5 and 6—The Under Ground Railroad," "Picture 19—Preaching" and "Picture 20—After Preaching" are offered as a companion pair and are as important for the content of their images as much as they proffer a theory of reading art. Wilson uses Ethiop's interpretation to show his readers how to read art and uncover what Barthes calls the rhetoric of the image.[26] More specifically, I want to interrogate the relational composition between different aspects of this pictorial form to reveal its latent ideological meanings. Although both sequences are preoccupied with the elapse of a time that transforms into a passageway to freedom, the incremental chronological ordering of "Preaching" and "After Preaching" belies the ways in which the paintings themselves embed a recessed futurity, one that functions as a signal of a proleptic radical black politics. Ethiop observes that "Preaching" and "After Preaching," which were featured in the July 1859 issue of the *Anglo-African Magazine*, are on the south side of the gallery, and hence share a wall with "The Under Ground Railroad" diptych. "Preaching" depicts the interior of a black church accentuated by the presence of "a double-fisted, burly, white-faced old Southern Preacher" (217). Ethiop notes that the artist has captured the preacher precisely at the moment in which he is exhorting his audience to obey their masters: "'He that knoweth his master's will and doeth it not shall be beaten with many stripes'" (217). Invoking the quotation of the well-known phrase from Luke 12:47, lines that were frequently summoned to justify the institution of chattel slavery as an imperative duty of moral necessity, Ethiop himself surmises what the preacher may have said and, in this respect, tests the limits of visual artifacts as a form of art to convey meaning by offering a narrative supplement.

Ethiop's invocation of the lines from Luke illuminates the ways in which "Preaching" operates as a social text by imagining the creation of politicized zones of communal belonging. He announces that these are the preacher's words and, in "catching the artist's conception, you *feel* them, you hear them—you put yourself in his audience, and then they are gracious words to you" (217, emphasis added). In a localized sense, this is precisely what Ethiop himself has done, but in a broader sense, it might also be thought of as theory of how one processes the aesthetic, not simply as a recognition of high art per se but as an experiential modalilty of exchange that elicits feeling. The ascription of the lines from Luke that Ethiop imagines to be emanating from the picture itself reveals the ways in which the discursive formulations used to police and regulate black bodies were rearticulated again and again. In the case of "Preaching," the invocation of Luke's lines marks their migration from the textual to the oratorical and, finally, to the visual whose compounded reverb effect makes it seem not only as if the message is being echoed but that it is endowed with the authority of coming from multiple domains when the phrase moves from the strictly scriptural to the generically idiomatic. "Preaching" circumscribes and transposes the viewer within the spatial precincts of the painting's depicted political arena, seemingly refashioning the viewer as a slave.

Indeed, "Preaching" and its counterpart, "After Preaching," manipulate space and spatialization to delimit would-be polities of black America. The most immediate and visceral way that "Preaching" experiments with compositional zones is by figuratively collapsing the space between the picture's viewer and the picture's subjects, making them an imagined, if not quicksilver and contingent, community. If "Preaching" pulls the viewer into the orbit of the picture's image, the image itself subverts the relationship between foreground and background. The bodies in the foreground of both pictures, who make up the dedicated congregation, are politicized as being from the "Uncle Tom school"; but, in "Preaching," among them are strewn "here a moody brow, and there a skeptical face, or yonder a defiant look" that, in Ethiop's estimation, "combine to form an admirable background" (217). While Wilson intimates how the black congregants (and by implication his own readers) may be too susceptible to the force of a biblical authority deployed as rhetoric to regulate socialities, he intimates that his readers can be refashioned as *disbelieving* slaves, as slaves who have not been interpellated by the preacher's Luke invocation. Here, there is no background as such; rather than a demarcated zone, the background here is imagined as a kind of constellation, one that occupies the same plane as the foreground. "After Preaching" is delineated into the more perceptible zones of background and foreground by depicting the majority of the assembly hovering outside of the church as the central scene of action while the disaffected are grouped in different quadrants of the picture altogether. It is here among those in the background that subversive black subjects coalesce as a contingency, as a kind of a constituency for a polity that is in the process of becoming:

> It is of this class comes our Nat Turners, who laid a scheme for redemption, and the *man* in Georgia who received nine hundred and ninety-nine lashes by way of gentle compulsion, and then would not so much as reveal one particle of the *plan* laid by and for the uprising of his oppressed brethren. It is of this class come the Margaret Garners, who rather than their babes even shall clank a chain, prefer to send them up to their God who gave them. It is of this class comes our Douglasses and our Browns. (217)

As important to Ethiop's litany of recognizable names, representing different forms of political dissent from reform to rebellion, is the figure of the unnamed "*man*," whose very anonymity is meant to translate his availability as a model for other African Americans, free or enslaved, to engage in the everyday practices of resistance. Ethiop's interpretation of this aspect of the painting underlines the figure of the archetype—and, significantly, the idea of reproduction. Ethiop's figuration of Turner, Garner, Douglass, Brown, and the anonymous man outlines a mode of reproduction whereby their actions might be repeated by the viewer after seeing, and properly examining, the painting "After Preaching" and thus offers a mode of reading images that obligates the viewer to imitate these still depictions by (re)animating them outside of the gallery space.

Furthermore, Ethiop's description of how space is delineated in "After Preaching" compels a reinterpretation of the practices of focalization in a wider sense. The assembly gathered immediately about the church is, in the most immediate perspective, the central scene of action and focal point of the painting. But Ethiop notes that the "faces [in the background], in contrast with the others of the congregation, give a most striking effect to the picture" and concludes that "these are good views" (217). What, then, is the function of those things of "striking effect" that might pull the viewer's eye away from the focal point itself, and, in a similar regard, what is the relationship between one background element of "striking effect" to other like elements such that, taken together, they begin to vie with the focal point as the site that most accurately and authentically renders an image's meaning? Taken together, the use of language about backgrounds in both "Preaching" and "After Preaching" needs to be analyzed for what it intimates as an articulation of an early African American theory of how to interpret art.

Wilson manipulates space in both of the paired companion pieces as a means to compress time in depicting the conversion of U.S. black subjectivity from a seemingly docile passivity to a kind of fugitive or surreptitious agency. And, like the slave ship/Abeokuta and Mount Vernon/Black Forest dyads, the subjects in the would-be diptychs of "The Under Ground Railroad" as well as "Preaching" and "After Preaching" are figured as specters of the nation—embodied as either the ever-near outer-national or as the always already embedded "constitutive outside." Wilson's curatorial efforts in depicting the paintings as having a particular arrangement in the museum is fundamental to how he seeks to induce among his readers a way of conceptualizing and operationalizing a form of black visuality. This form of black visuality allows Ethiop to trace other black figures beyond Uncle Tom whose image was rampant in popular culture.[27] In the case of "Preaching" and "After Preaching," Wilson underscores these other figures that are meant to constitute an alternative symbolic order. In a broader sense, the modes of seeing and ways of interpretation that Wilson solicits necessitate attention to the margins, the outside, and the Other.

■ ABOUT FACE

In many of the images that Ethiop encounters while walking through the gallery discussed above, Wilson is preoccupied with limning a mode of interpreting the visual that would allow Ethiop to model for the reader a way of locating and ascertaining a radical black politics. Reading between the lines for secondary and ulterior meanings in the narrative prose of the story becomes a metaphor for being able to perceive and discern the spectral presences recessed or otherwise veiled in an image's shadow. But, in a different set of images, Ethiop focuses directly on the symbolism of the head and face specifically. Of the nearly thirty paintings that Ethiop mentions, seven are referred to as portraits and Wilson's emphasis on this particular kind of painting is clearly meant to present African Americans as thinking, cognitive beings to counter commonplace assumptions that could only see them as bodies. Although whites continued to use black bodies as merely descriptive elements in their paintings well into the nineteenth century, as Gwendolyn DuBois Shaw notes, the rise of Enlightenment rhetoric about individuality and freedom in late-colonial and early-national America saw a rise in the number and types of painted portraits of African Americans by white artists and, increasingly, black artists.[28] Wilson's use of literary portraiture to fashion the heads of black subjects in high, noble, and dignified fashion counteracted the depiction of black heads in popular phrenological studies; Wilson's literary portraits also constituted an alternative to James McCune Smith's "Heads of the Colored People," a series of ten biographical sketches published in *Frederick Douglass' Paper* from 1852 to 1854.[29] In turning to portraiture, Wilson compels his reader to think about synecdochic representation whereby the head might be able to represent the whole of the body (as well as the body politic) and engage the politics of recognition by having Ethiop come head-to-head with these faces.

The first portrait that Wilson has Ethiop discuss is one of Crispus Attucks. By having Ethiop turn to "Picture 3—The First Martyr of the Revolution" first in the story, Wilson seeks to establish a black founding father as having been specifically located at the birth of the nation even though a visitor coming through the main entrance would encounter a number of other portraits, include ones of Toussaint L'Ouverture and Phillis Wheatley, before arriving at the one of Attucks. Asserting that it might not be readily known or especially desirable for the public to know that the first martyr of the revolution was an African American, Ethiop sees the painting's primary function as a factual record. In this sense, visual art might act as a corrective to the abjuration of blacks in the annals of U.S. history. But the problem with the figure of Attucks was not that he had been excised from the historical record per se but rather with how the properties of his iconicity produced a disjunction between his representation in the discourse of written texts and his representation in the visual field.

If one strategy to sanction black political dissidence in the mid-nineteenth century included overdubbing the rhetoric of the founding fathers onto rebel bodies as I discussed in Part I, then another included magnifying the visual presence of blacks in the United States at the birth of the nation, and no figure came to better exemplify that magnification than Attucks. Little is known of Attucks's life before the Boston Massacre of 1770. Born circa 1723, he was thought to be both African and Native American and employed as a sailor and, at other times, a ropemaker in Boston. And although the accounts vary—from Attucks actually leading a group of colonists to simply being a bystander—national mythology apotheosized him as the first of five to be killed on March 5 by British soldiers who had been earlier summoned to quell colonial unrest. The fact that so little was known about him allowed the single act of his death to be, and remain, the reified consummation of his devotion to the idea of liberty or, at least, his apparent opposition to the tyranny of King George III in a historic moment that precipitated the American Revolution. Almost as soon as he was carried off to Faneuil Hall, a number of competing representations of Attucks emerged. These differing representations disclose not only the particular processes in the iconicity of Attucks himself but also how African Americans, more generally, oscillated in the system of national semiotics whereby the iconicity of their blackness figured them as both an embodiment and an apparition of the country, at once at its core and its periphery.

In much of the contemporaneous written material dedicated to Attucks, his status as a racialized subject is reinscribed. In the first issue after the clash, the *Boston Gazette and Country Journal* published a story on March 12 noting that Attucks was a "mulatto" man "born in Framingham, but lately belonged to New Providence and was here in order to go for North-Carolina."[30] But, tellingly, the journal did not emphasize Attucks's political position as a runaway slave and, in a wider sense, the contemporaneous public rhetoric circumvented his personal experiences with fugitive freedom and hence hindered the figure of his person from emerging as a critique of U.S. slavery.

However, the most arrant erasure of Attucks's racialized subjectivity was Paul Revere's print *The Bloody Massacre perpetrated in King Street Boston on March 5th 1770* by a party of the 29th Regt. (1770). Revere's print (figure 7.1) was mass-produced and heavily circulated, selling in the thousands after hitting the market in late March 1770. Revere employed Christian Remick to enhance the print by colorizing it and one of the most prominent features of the coloring is the use of bright red for the garments of the British soldiers, the same shade of red that is used to mark the blood of the fallen colonialists, almost as if the state apparatus were reclaiming these bodies as subjects of the crown.[31] But the most conspicuous alteration of Revere's print was the spatial reconfiguration of Attucks within the domain of the painting's scene and the fading of his body. In an earlier version by Henry Pelham, upon which Revere based his own print, Attucks is identifiably racialized as "mulatto" or black and is at the center of the scene in heroic defiance against the British, grabbing a soldier's bayonet with his left hand and clutching a club in his right. By contrast, Revere's version depicts the immediate moment after, one where the body has been martyred. And while his name is listed among those murdered in the caption of Revere's version, if Attucks exists in the print, he has been decentered, placed in the left foreground, and, noticeably, rendered white. Here, remixing the visual field of icons,

Figure 7.1 Paul Revere, *The Bloody Massacre perpetrated in King Street Boston on March 5th 1770 by a party of the 29th Regt. 1770.* Courtesy, American Antiquarian Society.

by reproducing a reproduction, Revere's print functioned as an act of historical revisionism that elided the presence of blacks at the birth of the nation and rendered them perceptible in name only.

In the mid-nineteenth century, African Americans challenged Revere's historical revisionism in another subsequent act of revisionism by reifying Attucks's blackness to contest the institution of chattel slavery and the current asymmetrical relationship of blacks to the forms of citizenship, especially in the aftermath of the Dred Scott decision figure 7.2). A year after the Dred decision, African Americans gathered at Faneuil Hall in Boston to hold a commemorative festival honoring Attucks. As both Elizabeth Rauh Bethel and Marcus Wood have noted,

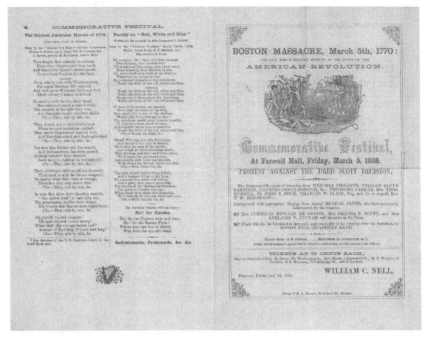

Figure 7.2 Anon., *Boston Massacre…Protest Against Dred Scott Decision*. 1858. Courtesy, American Antiquarian Society.

the festival correlated the stories of Attucks and Scott. Most likely organized by William C. Nell, author of *Colored Patriots of the American Revolution* (1855), the festival included an exhibition titled "Emblems—Relics—Engravings—Documents…of Revolutionary and other Historic association."[32] In *Blind Memory*, Wood calls the commemorative festival perhaps the first African American historical museum of slavery that exploited the "fetishisation of historical objects within museum culture to problematise the memorial agendas used to recall the War of Independence" The Attucks commemoration also revised Revere's print; the pamphlets for both the 1858 and the 1862 festivals used the same woodblock to restore Attucks's blackness.[33]

In Wilson's story, Ethiop's description of "The First Martyr of the Revolution" as a portrait shifts the visual depiction of Attucks by focusing on the head as the site of political dissent rather than the body alone. This portrait is meant to contest the prevailing images of Attucks that, from Pelham's drawings of the Boston Massacre to Revere's reproductions, all focused on the corpus. Ethiop notes that "it is a fine likeness of a bold, vigorous man,—just such, as would be likely to head a revolution to throw off oppression" (54). But how is that dissent or any other political impulse captured in the art of portraiture? What are the artistic techniques of the painting that signal to Ethiop that this is the kind of head that, in fact, "would be likely to head a revolution to throw off oppression"? If portraiture encapsulates the personal, icons might be said to invoke the historical more broadly speaking, and Wilson uses the iconicity of both Attucks and Toussaint L'Ouverture as important black figures of the Age of Revolution who were part of the historical events that instantiated and tested the limits of the rights of man in the Americas.

While Wilson stages Ethiop's encounter with the Attucks portrait as a corrective to the latter's distorted image in the visual archive, he uses Ethiop's encounter with the L'Ouverture portrait as an exemplar of a proper head of state. Wilson's description intimates that Haiti should be thought of as the incarnation of Enlightenment ideals more so than the United States. But equally important, Ethiop's assessment also reveals Wilson's own interpretation about how to read iconicity as a metacritical engagement with historiography. Wilson's engagement with the biography of L'Ouverture and the history of Haiti was part of a larger program by nineteenth-century African Americans to reframe blackness in hemispheric terms by envisioning L'Ouverture as a transnational icon.[34] Two years before Wilson creates an ekphrastic portrait of L'Ouverture in "Afric-American Picture Gallery," Frank J. Webb consecrated L'Ouverture in his 1857 novel *The Garies and Their Friends*.

Webb's novel tells the story of the Garies, a well-to-do interracial family comprised of a white husband and his "mulatta" ex-slave-turned wife, as they leave the South for Philadelphia. In the North, the Garies are situated between Philadelphia's black and white communities, represented in stark terms by the white Stevens family and the black Ellis family. Webb's novel calls attention to paintings and drawings specifically as visual artifacts simulated in narrative fiction. Webb uses literary portraiture to deploy a doubly-mediated moment of representation. These moments are accentuated by their double mediation, one where readers not only visualize the characters of the story in their own mind but are compelled to see through the eyes of these characters to perceive what they are viewing.

At an important moment in the novel where the Garies are trying to reestablish their lives by resettling in Philadelphia, they rent a home from Mr. Walters, one of the city's most affluent and wealthy African Americans. While walking through the home, Garie halts in the parlor, arrested by an image that he sees on the wall.

> "So you, too are attracted by that picture," said Mr. Walters, with a smile. "All white men look at it with interest. A black man in uniform of a general officer is something so unusual that they cannot pass it with a glance.... That is Toussaint l'Ouverture and I have every reason to believe it to be the correct likeness.... That looks like a man of intelligence. It is entirely different from any likeness I ever saw of him. The portraits generally represent him as a monkey-faced person, with a handkerchief about his head."[35]

Walters's comments to Garie about representation, that he has "every reason to believe it to be the correct likeness," circumscribes portraiture as a visual form whose artistry is tied to its claim about authenticity and accuracy less than its embellishment. It is significant that it is a portrait with its focus on the head and the face because the image functions to counter-act the discourse stemming from phrenologist about blacks as simians or a subspecies, intimated here in Walters's note that portraits of L'Ouverture "generally represent him as a monkey-faced person." But, in suggesting that the portrait "looks like a man of intelligence," Walter's comments also understand painting as a mode of representation that can translate the interior domain and render it externally visible. Here, attire designates social position—the uniform as a political emblem works against black caricature.

Equally important to the representation of L'Ouverture imagined in the portrait is its placement in the Walters's house itself. Its placement in the parlor is meant to suggest that it obeys the spatial logic of a properly decorated home. Furthermore, the interior and exterior of the home adequately portray the bourgeois class standing of the Walters; a class status that seemingly belies their progressive politics. More than simply relieving "the expanse of [wall]paper," as Edgar Allan Poe noted of most paintings in his essay "The Philosophy of Furniture" (1840), the L'Ouverture portrait in the Walters home proves to not be merely decorative but a harbinger of the fire next time.[36] As Samuel Otter notes in his reading of the scene, the "portrait links refinement to political awareness."[37] More specifically, Webb accentuates literary portraiture as a political strategy that seeks to contextualize U.S. abolitionism within a larger hemispheric framework of black resistance.

Similar to "The Slave Ship"/"Sunset at Abbeokuta" dyad featured in the first installment, the paintings of Attucks and L'Ouverture in the Afric-American Picture Gallery should be thought of as companion pieces which suggest that forms of contemporary U.S. black resistance evolve from the larger history and are part of the genealogies of the black diaspora. Whereas the "The Slave Ship" and "Sunset at Abbeokuta" paintings illustrate historical eras, respectively gothicized and romanticized, the portraits of Attuck and L'Ouverture are specifically meant to recall particular historical events. In the case of "Picture 7—Toussaint L'Ouverture," Ethiop submits that the portrait "associates in the mind of the intelligent beholder...the long and interesting trains of historical facts in relation to Hayti" (87). Even more generally, these images produce "troops of thought that paint the memory afresh," compelling the mind to "become reimpressed with the events" and "arrive at the philosophy of them" (87). Wilson's use of language here is notable for its martial tone, especially pronounced in an account of a military leader.

Beyond recalling the history of Haiti, the L'Ouverture portrait compels Ethiop to reassess the history of the American Revolution. After viewing the

L'Ouverture portrait, Ethiop offers his opinions on iconography as a specific kind of portraiture. A picture of Washington, Ethiop opines, recalls the American Revolution and the early republic; a picture of Jefferson, the Declaration of Independence and the hope that its principles "will be fully recognised by, and applied to the entire American people": "I had these conclusions forced upon me by looking not upon the picture of Washington or Jefferson in the gallery. Far from it; but by a most beautiful portrait of one of the greatest men the world ever saw—Toussaint L'Ouverture" (87). The importance of Ethiop's interpretation of the L'Ouverture portrait, then, is that it offers a new way of considering the relationship between representation and national iconography. Rather than L'Ouverture only being a representation of Haiti, Wilson's story implies that his image should also serve as a metonym for the United States. The L'Ouverture portrait in this respect is less a specific point in an alternative semiotic constellation that is patently and expressly black than it is part of a reconstructed U.S. national symbolic order.

In "Afric-American Picture Gallery," Wilson conceptualizes iconographic portraiture as the kind of painting that can seemingly speak for itself. If such an image "calls up the whole history" of the subject's time, then Wilson's concern with presenting portraits in the gallery is less about the artistry of the image's execution than as a repository of social history. Thus, rather than have him spend more time analyzing the specific features of the portraits themselves, Wilson has Ethiop recalling the black presence in the Age of Revolution in an effort to offer his mid-nineteenth century readers a reconstituted public memory.

■ A THOUSAND WORDS

Ethiop's impressions of the L'Ouverture portrait is at least as significant for situating Haiti as part of the Age of Revolution and perhaps counterintuitively as part of U.S. national history as for what they disclose about the limits of narrativity over the imagistic, prose over the pictorial. Ethiop's admission that he has "no pencil and no pen" which can properly describe "either the picture or the man" intimates that iconographic portraiture functions as an ideograph whose meaning and significance as a social text is rendered in ways that extend beyond the translative capacity of the word itself. But the hermeneutical underpinnings of Wilson's "Afric-American Picture Gallery" as an exercise in reading and seeing thematizes space as a way to continually labor through the word/image problematic.

In my reading of "Afric-American Picture Gallery," I have implicitly suggested that Wilson's story is less important for how it presents a public institution that displays images of the black diaspora than for how it is uses the display of these images as a means of institutionalizing a subversive politics. If nineteenth-century

African Americans embraced daguerrotypy and photography as authentic mediums that could depict the truth about slavery and inequality, my return to fiction
and its embedded forms of visuality decenters the documentary charge of photography's ability to capture a present politics to theorize the ways that Wilson
stylizes his readers as "picture-making animals," in the words of Douglass, and
imagine a proleptic politics of a democracy to come.[38]

Conclusion: Shadow and Act Redux

More than a hundred years after African Americans began reconceptualizing the image of Crispus Attucks through a number of cultural performances, including speeches and dance, Stevie Wonder invoked him in "Black Man" in his now-classic double album *Songs in the Key of Life* (1976). With the bicentennial as its backdrop, "Black Man" continued a theme of social commentary evident in Wonder's earlier songs such as "Big Brother" (1972) and "Living for the City" (1973).[1] "Black Man" opens with a reference to Attucks as a way to subvert the conventional pantheon of U.S. national icons and offer a new vision of a wider America:

> First man to die
> For the flag we now hold high
> Was a black man
> The ground were we stand
> With the flag held in our hand
> Was first the red man's
> Guide of a ship
> On the first Columbus trip
> Was a brown man
> The railroads for trains
> Came on tracking that was laid
> By the yellow man[2]

Wonder's "Black Man" might seem to be a variation of Brown's *Black Man*, as well as its twentieth-century counterparts, including Carter G. Woodson's book *The Negro in Our History* (1922), Lerone Bennett's *Before the Mayflower* (1963), and, later, Kareem Abdul-Jabbar's *Black Profiles in Courage* (1997). But, with an emphasis on multiple ethnicities, Wonder's song deconstructs the black-white dyad that has been so fundamental to the binary logic of U.S. national identity formation. The song also moves away from the prevailing consensus histories of the United States offered by writers such as Daniel J. Boorstin and Arthur M. Schlesinger and toward those of Howard Zinn and Ronald Takaki.[3] While the different figures in Wonder's song are neither strict portraits nor vignettes, their symbolic equality is translated by his flash-frame stills that are rendered equivalent through their forms as tercets that approximate the aural calibration of a haiku. A seeming misnomer, Wonder's title demarcates a number of racialized subjectivities in the United States. By registering these subjectivities, Wonder delineates a panorama of America that is less parochial than the more conventional images of the United States, almost as the apotheosis to Langston Hughes's poem "Let America Be America Again" (1936).[4]

By alternating representations of the iconic with the anonymous, the famous with the unnamed, Wonder diminishes the symbolism of status as a social differential to envision a sequence where egalitarianism is made quotidian. The song catalogs a number of people who have influenced the making and remaking of America: Pedro Alonzo Nino, Hiawatha, Lincoln, and César Chávez, among others. But equally important to the thematic meaning of the song and its visual correlative of frame switching are the anonymous subjects who represent the many thousand gone, unnamed subjects unacknowledged in the traditional narratives of U.S. history, who must be recognized as citizens, even if only momentarily in the sonic space of a song.

Manipulating narrativization to create images, both Wilson and Wonder engage in practices of visualization. Both "Afric-American Picture Gallery" and "Black Man" call attention to the function of the mind's eye as the site of the artistic processes that create and re-create alternative visions of the nation. As significant as these processes are in terms of how they figuratively make every reader or listener an artist, they are equally important for what they suggest about politics. Almost as the inverse of Sojourner Truth's distribution of her *cartes-de-visite*, which disseminated her representation throughout different states and thereby constellated an imagined community, Wilson and Wonder conceptualized a black or multiethnic public sphere and interiorized it in the corridors of the mind—a veritable political aesthetic emblematized perhaps no better than by Wonder's own notion of the democratic potentialities of the "innervision."[5]

While Wonder's "Black Man" offers a reconstituted, if not alternative, symbolic order of different (primarily male) icons that have lingered in the shadows of the national imaginary, the hip-hop artist Common conceptualizes music, and art more broadly, as a means that can repair the fractured subjectivities of African Americans in his 2005 album *Be*. Using Lonnie "Pops" Lynn as a figure that is equal parts community elder and griot historian, the album's reprise references the violence done to black bodies by their having been made fractional subjects through the Constitution's Three-fifth clause. Appearing as he does at the end of each album, his reflections are extemporaneous and contemplative, often riffing on the theme announced by the title of the album. He considers temporality in the 2008 album *Finding Forever*; in *Be*, he ruminates on ontology. At the conclusion of "It's Your World," Pops enters after a train of children's voices. These young voices are all wishful, projecting hopes to be any number of things from astronauts to obstetricians, rendered in the future conditional of "I wanna be" while Pops delivers his words in the declarative and indicative tense of "be":

Be amended
Five fifths.
Be amended
Five fifths human![6]

Pops's meditation is noteworthy because it reveals that African Americans are too frequently still not considered full citizens, let alone fully human, even after the Thirteenth, Fourteenth, and Fifteenth Amendments and, later, the Civil Rights Act of 1964 and Voting Rights Act of 1965. In a metacritical sense, his words intimate how black cultural production might work to counteract the mandates of the conventional political sphere or even at times influence the direction of political institutions themselves.

Hip-hop music from its inception—from Grandmaster Flash and the Furious Five's "Message" to Public Enemy's "Fight the Power" to Mos Def's "Dollar Day"—has been a vehicle of social protest, but no better recent example of how African American popular music has influenced American politics exists than will.i.am's song "Yes We Can."[7] Inspired by Barack Obama's speech after the New Hampshire primary in January 2008, "Yes We Can" featured cameos from celebrities whose voices formed the refrain around the song's lyrics as well as samples from the New Hampshire speech itself. Commenting on the speech, will.i.am stated: "It made me reflect on the freedoms I have, going to school where I went to school, and the people that came before Obama like Martin Luther King, presidents like Abraham Lincoln that paved the way for me to be sitting here on ABC News and making a song from Obama's speech."[8] Accompanied by a video shot by Jesse Dylan, "Yes We Can" became the signature song of the campaign before Obama secured the Democratic nomination. Whereas the slogan "Change You Can Believe" was idiomatic, "Yes We Can" was a proleptic anthem for a nation on the precipice of becoming, a theme song for a sociality that was concretizing as a distinct polity.

Perhaps the most striking aspect of "Yes We Can" is its use of the overdub and collage as artistic devices that engage a political semiotic and, more critically, constitute a veritable mode of, if not model for, democratic participation. In a number of sequences, the video uses one of the most fundamental aspects of collage filming techniques, the split screen, to place Obama next to one of the celebrities, sometimes featuring celebrities on both sides of him. Although African American celebrities are featured most prominently, with appearances by Kareem Abdul-Jabbar, John Legend, and Herbie Hancock, the video also includes other artists and performers. Among these are the Hawaiian and Chinese Kelly Hu, Israeli-born Maya Rubin, and Adam Rodríguez, of Cuban and Puerto Rican descent. Beyond the immediacy of their fame, the majority of these celebrities were under forty-five and represented a clear appeal by the Obama campaign to compel younger voters to the electorate. In a strategic use of overdubbing, the song parallel-tracks the voices of two or more people with Obama's own and synchronizes them to the words of his speech such that it produces a discernible echo, one that is extended by the visual optics of the video montage that make it seem as if that echo is an embodied chorus. This echo is as much an approximation of a chorus as it is polyvocal in its articulation as a discourse formation, with Shoshannah Stern using sign language, Rubin uttering "Kein, Annu

Yecholim" in Hebrew, and Rodríguez adding "Sí se puede" in Spanish. Beyond the possible extension of the phrase into the transnational sphere of geopolitics and culture, Rodríguez's "Sí se puede" was less a translation of the English per se than an allusion to the fact that Obama's slogan itself was a riff on the United Farm Workers' motto conceptualized by César Chávez and Dolores Huerta from the early 1970s and hence has a transhistorical dynamic as well. Obama's "Yes We Can" also riffed on the Pointer Sisters's "Yes We Can Can," a 1973 pop anthem of interracial unity.[9]

As with the sublimated presence of the labor movement embedded in the catchphrase "Yes We Can," the discursive mechanism of Obama's political artistry simultaneously invoked and ensconced, summoned and veiled, the most identifiable figure of the modern civil rights movement: Martin Luther King Jr. King was everywhere in Obama's speeches but also nowhere; even at the Denver convention to accept the Democratic nomination on the forty-fifth anniversary of the March on Washington, King is alluded to but not mentioned explicitly by name. There is a sense, as critics such as political scientist Cathy Cohen have noted, that Obama strategically distanced himself from a manifestly patent African American genealogy of political engagement to cultivate a more explicit multiracial constituency.[10] And as commentators such as David Remnick of the New Yorker have noted, Obama, like King and many others, invoked the words of Abraham Lincoln to herald a new day.[11]

If King remained the most haunting ghost in the machine of Obama's campaign, other significant African American figures and historical moments were intimated but not rendered wholly visible. The commercial success of Shepard Fairey's Obama posters has received much comment, if not for their artistry per se than for what they illustrate about the institutional practices of the art world, but there has been little discussion about the texts themselves that undergird these images. As keywords from his speeches, "Progress," "Change," and "Hope" constitute a particular lexicon for Obama. But, to those especially versed in African American rhetorical arrangements, Obama was also signifying or referencing key moments of black activist engagement with the U.S. political system. Distilled to a single word, to the atom if you will, "Change" harkens back to Sam Cooke's song "A Change Is Gonna Come" (1964), a veritable anthem for the civil rights movement. In a similar vein, "Hope" recalled the most memorable turn of phrase from Jesse Jackson's address at the 1988 Democratic National Convention in Atlanta, Georgia: "Keep hope alive. Keep hope alive! Keep hope alive! On tomorrow night and beyond, keep hope alive!"[12] Like Frederick Douglass in the nineteenth century, Obama conjured up a cadre of his own founding fathers that included George Washington, Lincoln, and Franklin D. Roosevelt, as well as a group of more spectral figures like King and Chávez.

But even more noteworthy than Obama's rhetorical strategies of invoking the spirit of past ghosts to bring into being a political materiality of the present are the practices that everyday African Americans employed to shape their own discourse about Obama and the contemporary moment of black civic engagement. In particular, as soon as it was announced that Obama won the election, underground or so-called informal economies immediately linked the image of Obama with other notable African Americans. In Chicago, for example, on the night of the election, street vendors lined lower Michigan Avenue selling T-shirts that collated the visual imagery of Douglass and Obama. An even more suggestive indication of the use and manipulation of political aesthetics are the T-shirts that revised the already iconic image of the meeting between King and Malcolm X. Although the encounter lasted less than a minute, their brief meeting on March 26, 1964, has been romanticized as a vision of what might have occurred had they not been assassinated. Consecrated as an emblem of two seemingly competing modes of black political activism, however, the image has been fetishized in the visual circuits of African American cultural production, notably in Spike Lee's film *Do the Right Thing* (1989).[13] In T-shirts that appeared during the inauguration ceremonies, the iconic image of Martin and Malcolm had been revised to depict Martin and Obama. On the one hand, the image could be said to offer a radicalized representation of Obama, with undertones of his being characterized as a Muslim, as a substitute of either Malcolm X or El-Hajj Malik El-Shabazz. On the other hand, the image could signal the excision of the ostensibly more radical politics often used to distinguish Malcolm from King. What seems important to note here are the ways that African Americans encounter and manipulate art—even in the most basic and seemingly disposable forms of ephemera, paraphernalia, curios, and quotidian objects of everyday life—to revise and imagine cultural production as an avenue into the political.

The anonymous producers of the T-shirts on the streets of Chicago, Washington, D.C., and elsewhere also need to be understood in relation to their earlier fictional counterparts in Stowe's novel *Uncle Tom's Cabin* and Wilson's story "Afric-American Picture Gallery." In Stowe's novel, when guided into the home of Uncle Tom and Aunt Chloe, the reader is ushered to a wall that depicts an episode of how African Americans have recodified the meanings of art objects: "The wall over the fireplace was adorned with some very brilliant scriptural prints, and a portrait of General Washington, drawn and colored in a manner which would certainly have astonished that hero, if ever he happened to meet with its like" (68). Stowe is clearly implying that the portrait has been shaded darker such that the president probably appears black. Rather than read the scene as simply an example of a didactic episode that instructs slaves how they might become Americans proper—via the authenticating documents of biblical scripture and the iconic image of Washington—the drawing room moment illustrates how U.S. blacks have rescripted the signs of a national semiotics.

Whether in public festivals, performances of song and dance, through fictional characters created by black (and sometimes white) authors or the informal economy sector, African Americans have continually made tropes of national icons, illustrated in works such as Robert Colescott's *George Washington Carver Crossing the Delaware* (1975). Colescott's painting, like Wonder's "Black Man," used the backdrop of the impending bicentennial to reassess the birth of the nation. As much as the occasion of the bicentennial was a backdrop of Colescott's *George Washington Carver Crossing the Delaware*, so too was perhaps the most famous iconic national painting: Emanuel Gottlieb Leutze's *Washington Crossing the Delaware* (1851). In *George Washington Carver Crossing the Delaware*, Colescott parodies an assortment of stereotypical figures, including Aunt Jemima, Uncle Ben, and other "darkies." Washington is not rendered in black, as implied in Stowe's novel or on a recent cover of the *New Yorker* that depicts Obama donning Washington's signature white wig, but rather is replaced by George Washington Carver.[14] In this regard, Colescott depicts all African Americans as apparitions of the state, facsimiles of the citizen proper, even a respected figure like Carver the renowned agriculturalist.

Recasting *Washington Crossing the Delaware*, Colescott dramatically altered the setting, changed all the figures, and detached the painting's stylistics from the Romantic school of art.[15] Part of the iconography of Leutze's painting is determined by the heroic figuration of Washington, as well as the idealized ship of state that includes depictions of a man in a Scottish bonnet, western riflemen, farmers, and a man of African descent.[16] While Colescott's painting implies that African Americans have been part of the country since its very founding, the use of caricature also discloses how blacks and the image of them have been distorted in the public imaginary as disfigured national subjects. *George Washington Carver Crossing the Delaware* does not rectify these so much as it exposes the multiple genealogies of visual iconography that have worked in conjunction with one another to render blacks as the abnegated sign of the nation. As much as Colescott's painting recast Leutze, so too has Colescott been recast. Works like Titus Kaphar's *George, George, George* (2008) and the RZA's canvas prints *Victory of Death* (2010) return to both Leutze and Colescott to reconsider the meanings of blackness and national sensibility. As an abrogated facsimile and approximation of the genuine article, the work of Colescott, Kaphar, and the RZA revisits the seeming anomaly of an African American as a head of state that is both already present and not yet existent.

While Washington, D.C., has long been referred to as "Chocolate City" by African Americans, Obama's election gives new resonance to George Clinton's charge to paint the White House black, a charge that was not mollified with Toni Morrison's pronouncement that Bill Clinton was America's first black president. Itself a rhetorical expression, the song "Chocolate City" from Parliament's 1975 eponymous album signifies on a number of idioms that encapsulated the histories of contested moments in African American history. For example, the lines "Hey, uh, we didn't get our forty acres and a mule / But we did get you CC" are a reference to General William T. Sherman's Special Field Orders, Number 15, one of the most compelling and controversial features of Radical Reconstruction. The order to award land to freed African American slaves who lived near the coasts of South Carolina, Georgia, and Florida was subsequently revoked by Andrew Johnson after Lincoln's assassination and has remained ever since in the popular, if not political, discourse as an emblem of how the state abrogates the rights of African Americans. A number of hip-hop artists from Public Enemy and Tupac Shakur to Jay-Z and Kanye West have all made various references to the order, with Nas's lines "Owe me back like you owe your tax / Owe me back like 40 acres to blacks" being some of the most trenchant.[17]

More than simply a moan of an offer rescinded, Parliament's allusion to the Sherman order implies a causal link between its withdrawal and the later establishment of urban black cities. In the southeast region where Sherman's order was meant to be applied, many of the beneficiaries would have used their homesteads as farms. Beyond dispossessing them, the annulment, in one fell swoop, disallowed thousands of African Americans from embodying the classic Jeffersonian yeoman farmer archetype. Instead of expansive farms in the nineteenth century, condensed urban areas awaited African Americans in the twentieth century:

> There's a lot of chocolate cities around
> We've got Newark, we've got Gary
> Somebody told me we got L.A.
> And we're working on Atlanta
> But you're the capitol, CC.

The Chocolate Cities in Parliament's litany were all areas that suffered from the cataclysms of urban unrest and race riots in the late 1960s.

While Parliament alludes to Sherman's orders, the group also signifies on one of the most important rhetorical expressions from within black America: Malcolm X's famous phrasing about the ballot or the bullet. "You don't need the bullet," George Clinton offers, "when you got the ballot." In the midst of the debates on the legislation of what would become the Civil Rights Act of 1964, Malcolm delivered his speech "The Ballot or the Bullet" in Cleveland, Ohio, on April 3. The speech, in which he implored African Americans to use the suffrage not just judiciously but strategically, was criticized for its ostensible strident militancy, but what seems important to note here is one of the rhetorical strategies that Malcolm used to legitimate his claim. The architecture of Malcolm's oratorical formulations made frequent use of contrapuntal rhythmic alternation as well as irony to create his rhetorical style, but at a key moment in the speech, he simultaneously invokes the Patrick Henry maxim only to immediately evacuate it: "It'll be ballots, or it'll be bullets. It'll be liberty, or it will be death. The only difference about this kind of death—it'll be reciprocal."[18] Rather than simply reiterate that blacks might continue to die for the state as the supreme sign of their allegiance to the country, what Russ Castronovo has called "necro citizenship," Malcolm tropes Henry to suggest that white bodies themselves might be sacrificed in the perennial ritual to maintain the state through racial violence. Malcolm's ballot or bullet speech, then, transformed the Hegelian dialectic into a Manichaean confrontation for African Americans.[19]

While the abatement of Sherman's orders is bemoaned in "Chocolate City," the song suggests that the vote might be one way to redress past grievances and, more important, bring forth an alternative, if not utopian, society. Malcolm begins to suggest as much in his speech when he encourages African Americans to vote as a political bloc.[20] As a moniker, "Chocolate City" is not simply a name for metropolises with large African American populations, but it comes to represent a romanticized state governed by cultural practitioners.

> And when they come to march on ya
> Tell 'em to make sure they got their James Brown pass
> And don't be surprised if Ali is in the White House
> Reverend Ike, Secretary of the Treasury
> Richard Pryor, Minister of Education
> Stevie Wonder, Secretary of Fine Arts
> And Miss Aretha Franklin, the First Lady.[21]

Because the song intimates a causal relationship between electoral politics and the concentration of African Americans in certain municipalities, the would-be federal cabinet depicted here suggests that blacks might become the majority demographic at the national level.

If "Chocolate City" imagines a possibility whereby a predominantly African American constituency could gain control over a precinct, if not its governmental institutions, then Parliament's *Mothership Connection* (1975) imagines a possibility whereby citizenship is no longer bound and determined by the nation. Released in the same year, *Mothership Connection* needs to be thought of as the counterpart to *Chocolate City*. Where *Chocolate City* is national, *Mothership Connection* is intergalactic; where *Chocolate City* is utopian, *Mothership Connection* is fantastic. As George Clinton has said of the album: "We had put black people in situations nobody ever thought they would be in, like the White House. I figured another place you wouldn't think black people would be was outer space. I was a big fan of *Star Trek*, so we did a thing with a pimp sitting in a spaceship shaped like a Cadillac, and we did all these James Brown–type grooves, but with street talk and ghetto slang."[22]

Where the cover art to *Chocolate City* is geographically situated by the national monuments of the Capitol, Lincoln Memorial, and Washington obelisk, *Mothership Connection* is set in space. It is significant that Clinton mentions the television series *Star Trek*, since it and its later science fiction counterparts of the 1970s, including *Battlestar Galactica* and *Buck Rogers*, were allegories of the United States and illustrations of a future temporality where blacks, perhaps not coincidentally, had little presence in the last and final frontier of human existence. The album *Mothership Connection* not only imagines a cosmos where blacks will exist, in ways that will be more fully animated in the novels of Octavia

Butler and Samuel R. Delaney, but evinces that an adoption of the funk aesthetic as a political program will produce the quintessential egalitarian subject—the "citizen of the universe."

Although a number of artists have sampled Parliament/Funkadelic's music, the group that has perhaps most fully adopted the idea that funk can fashion a counterreality to the U.S. is the hip-hop duo Outkast. Coming out of Atlanta, Georgia, Outkast has continually contested the representations of the South as the alterity or underside of the United States while reformulating it as a kind of utopia.[23] The title of its album *ATLiens* (1996) simultaneously gestures to how blacks are sometimes seen as aliens and to how Atlanta might be thought of as an other-worldly or outer-national zone that makes use of music to coalesce social-ities of belonging. The idea of an outer-national zone is reiterated in the group's later album *Stankonia* (2000), where "Stankonia" is described as "the center of the earth" and "7 light-years below sea level."

As much as Big Boi and Andre 3000 imagine Stankonia as an outer-national zone within the lyrical content of their songs, the cover art to the album visually correlates this place specifically to the United States. Importantly, while all three of their previous album covers were drawn illustrations, this one is a photograph. Perhaps the most conspicuous feature of the image is the backdrop of the U.S. flag where the primary colors of red and blue have been excised, almost as if to symbolically distill the United States to the binary codes that have underlined so much of the nation's history. In this respect, the flag depicted here is reminiscent of Gordon Parks's photograph "American Gothic" (1942). Distilling the flag to black and white, accentuated by the contrast of Big Boi's white T-shirt and Andre 3000's bare black skin, is also a reminder of the histories of racism that are partic-ular to the South. In this respect, the album cover recalls the South of novels such as Jean Toomer's *Cane* (1923) and Nella Larsen's *Passing* (1929).

What Atlanta is to Outkast's concept of Stankonia, Harlem is to Langston Hughes's idea of Jazzonia. Initially included in *The Weary Blues*, "Jazzonia" is a poem, but it also might be thought of as an imaginary place, one where the sen-sual and sensational might overcome the parochialism of rigid social positions. Both the blues and jazz informed Hughes's vision of how music could shape the line, if not the word, of a poem and, in a larger sense, present a different rhythm of America altogether.[24] Hughes's writings include numerous examples where the improvisational impulse of a jazz poetic is less pronounced in favor of the tech-nique of riffing or quoting.

By quoting Jefferson, Lincoln, and Douglass in "Freedom's Plow," Hughes not only presents a reconfigured cadre of founding fathers but extends the founding moment itself to suggest that the U.S. experiment with democracy is still contin-uing. Like "I, Too," which alludes to Whitman with its imagery of landscape, labor, and expedition, "Freedom's Plow" is reminiscent of Whitman's "Song of the Broad-Axe." Using both metonymy and synecdoche, Hughes takes some of the most famous phrases from the three men to underline the poem as both an artistic and political project. Their interpolated words form a kind of discourse conjoined with the lyricism of the poem, engendered by its use of anaphora. Importantly, the words of Jefferson, Lincoln, and Douglass, formerly spread throughout the poem, are collated together near the end to form a reconstituted statement on democracy and race in the United States. But the most salient feature of the poem's formal workings is how it moves from the quote to the riff by creating a sonic overlay that uses one of the most important songs in the African American folk tradition—"Keep Your Hands on the Plow"—as a sound system that makes the poem's statement on democracy and race discernibly resonant.

The way that Hughes deploys an African American folk song as a sound track to the cultures of America, if not the political discourse of the United States, is symbolic of the larger claims that Ralph Ellison explores in "What America Would Be Like without Blacks." Ellison published this essay originally in *Time* magazine on April 6, 1970, at a moment when many African Americans were growing disillusioned with the continued promises of equality. In castigating the "fantastic vision of a lily-white America," Ellison turns his attention to culture and especially literature to contend that, without blacks in America, there would be no Walt Whitman, no Mark Twain, no Stephen Crane, no Ernest Hemingway, no William Faulkner as we know them now, a sentiment similarly reiterated more than three decades later in Morrison's *Playing in the Dark*.[25] Without blacks, Ellison continues, the entire political history of the United States would be markedly different: "Absent, too, would be the need for that tragic knowledge which we try ceaselessly to evade: that the true subject of democracy is not simply well-being, but the extension of the democratic process in the direction of perfecting itself. The most obvious test and clue to that perfection is the inclusion, *not* assimilation, of the black man."[26]

The black presence in the United States is important not simply to its material history but to its own (self-created) ideologem as a democracy. In an essay later collected in *Going to the Territory*, Ellison spoke of the relation of the novel to American democracy—the novel, as Ellison saw it, could "produce imaginative models of the *total* society" (764, emphasis added). Extrapolating Ellison's reading to include other literary and cultural forms, *Specters of Democracy* has approached a number of texts to explore the national antinomy that has simultaneously rendered blacks the antithesis and the apotheosis of American democracy. Cognizant that Ellison opens his classic *Invisible Man* (1952) with Melville's lines about the shadow from "Benito Cereno," this project has tried to resurrect the voices on the other side of the veil, conscious of the concluding epilogue of Ellison's novel where his protagonist asks plaintively, "Who knows but that, on the lower frequencies, I speak for you?"[27]

■ NOTES

▦ Introduction

1. Butler, "Restaging the Universal," 11 (emphasis added).

2. Truth, *Narrative*, 147.

3. Painter, *Sojourner Truth*, 196.

4. Butler, "Restaging the Universal," 11; Rancière, "Ten Theses on Politics," 38. Derrida's understanding that "the expression 'democracy to come' does indeed translate or call for a militant and interminable political critique" provides an apt frame for my reading of how antebellum free blacks participated in democratic discourse from their own "rogue" or alien status (*Rogues*, 86).

5. For a sustained engagement with the idea of a "democracy to come" where Derrida takes up Kant to militate against the allure and force of the regulatory idea and any vision that democracy is palpably immanent, see *Rogues*, 78-94.

6. Ellison, *Invisible Man*, 3.

7. Moten, *In the Break*, 68.

8. Melville, "Benito Cereno," 353.

9. See Anderson, "Black Shadow Politics in Midwestville." Important recent extensions of Anderson include Glenn Altschuler and Stuart Blumin's *Rude Republic*.

10. Newman, "Black Shadow Politics in the Antebellum North."

11. In a similar vein, Moten puts the predicament of alienation in these terms: "This is to say that if alienation and distance represent the critical possibility of freedom, they do so where the question of the human is most clearly rendered as the question of a kind of competence that is performed as an infinite set of variations of blackness" (*In the Break*, 256).

12. One of the earliest and still classic works on African Americans and the North is Leon Litwack's *North of Slavery*. It has since been refined with many studies of individual states and cities. An important legal history of various forms of African American citizenship is Paul Finkelman's "Prelude to the Fourteenth Amendment."

13. Smith, *Civic Ideals*, 257.

14. Lenox Remond, "Resolved, That to Secure Funds."

15. Delany, "Political Destiny of the Colored Race on the American Continent," 227.

16. Douglass, *My Bondage and My Freedom*, 346.

17. Quoted in Foster, *Brighter Coming Day*, 99.

18. Quoted in Foner, *Life and Writings*, II, 235.

19. On the correlation between the written word and the nation, see Warner, *Letters of the Republic*; Ziff, *Writing in the New Nation*; Gustafson, *Representative Words*; and Kramer, *Imagining Language in America*. On the correlation between vocal expression and performance, see Fliegelman, *Declaring Independence*; Portelli, *The Text and the Voice*; Looby, *Voicing America*; Ruttenberg, *Democratic Personalities*; and Gustafson, *Eloquence Is Power*.

20. My invocation of Spivak and postcolonial criticism here to interrogate the conditions of antebellum U.S. blacks is not meant as a facile collapse of different imperial

systems of colonization with racialized hegemony in the United States but rather as a way to illuminate the social machinations that constructed U.S. blacks, in the words of Martin R. Delany, as a "nation within a nation"; see Delany, "A Project for an Expedition of Adventure, to the Eastern Coast of Africa," 320. Earlier in *The Condition... of the Colored People of the United States,* Delany writes: "That there have in all ages, in almost every nation, existed a nation within a nation, a people who although forming a part and parcel of the population, yet were form forces of circumstances, known by the peculiar position they occupied, forming in fact, by the deprivation of political equality with others, no part, and if any, but a restricted part of the body politic of such nations, is also true" (190).

21. Spivak, "Can the Subaltern Speak?" 275–76.

22. African Americans, most notably those in the North, did have uneven experiences with the forms of citizenship that marked their asymmetrical relationship to U.S. polities; see Finkelman's "Prelude to the Fourteenth Amendment" and Litwack's *North of Slavery.*

23. Iton, *In Search of the Black Fantastic,* 17.

24. See Rancière, *The Politics of Aesthetics.* Similarly, in the context of American Studies specifically, Heinz Ickstadt has advocated for "the reinstatement of the aesthetic as a distinct discourse not *separate* from or *against* American (Culture) Studies but emphatically *within* it, since the aesthetic does not deny the political, ethical, or historical dimensions of literary texts but engages them and mediates between them" ("Toward a Pluralist Aesthetics," 265).

25. Among this work on aesthetics and nineteenth-century U.S. literature, I would note in particular the essays of the special volume on "Aesthetics and the End(s) of Cultural Studies" of *American Literature* edited by Christopher Castiglia and Russ Castronovo; Dorrie Beam's *Style, Gender, and Fantasy in Nineteenth-Century American Women's Writing;* Castronovo's *Beautiful Democracy;* Theo Davis's *Formalism, Experience, and the Making of American Literature in the Nineteenth Century;* Paul Gilmore's *Aesthetic Materialism: Electricity and American Romanticism;* Samuel Otter and Geoffrey Sanborn's forthcoming collection on Herman Melville and aesthetics; Eric Slaughter's *The State as a Work of Art;* and Cindy Weinstein and Christopher Looby's forthcoming *American Literature's Aesthetic Dimensions.*

26. See Castiglia, *Interior States;* Castronovo, *Beautiful Democracy;* and Nelson, "Representative/Democracy" that respectively take up the marvelous, the beautiful, and the ugly respectively as they intersect with democratic discourse.

27. See especially Derrida's *Limited Inc.*

28. Bhabha, *Location of Culture,* 86.

29. Ibid.

30. See Gates, *Figures in Black,* 236, and, more generally, *Signifying Monkey.*

31. The potential for repetition or the remix that I limn throughout *Specters of Democracy* is just as susceptible to neo-conservative impulses as it is to radicalizing democratic futurities. As an example, one might note, in passing, Malcolm X's famous, militant epigrammatic phrase "By any means necessary" being inverted and indeed converted, in the Marxist sense of transubstantiation, into a veritable advertisement for liberal capitliasm itself with Kanye West's edict to "buy any jeans necessary." For a recent different perspective on West's political sensibilities, see Cathy Cohen, *Democracy Remixed,* 110–14.

32. Hartman, *Scenes of Subjection,* 115–25, 130–40, 171–75; Johnson, "On Agency," 113–24; and Kazanjian, "The Speculative Freedom of Colonial Liberia."

33. Among others, Eric J. Sundquist's essay "Benito Cereno and New World Slavery" is perhaps the most important and representative of this historicist impulse.

34. Although he examines the post–civil rights era, my impulse here is influenced by Richard Iton's focus on the relationship between popular culture and in/formal politics; see *In Search of the Black Fantastic*.

■ Chapter One

1. Douglass, *Narrative*, 65.

2. Ibid., 83.

3. Allen, "Orators and Oratory," 243.

4. McCune Smith, "Introduction," xxv. Part of McCune Smith's evaluation regarding the pragmatism (and utility) of *My Bondage and My Freedom* depended upon an understanding that it was not embellished but rather factual: "The reader's attention is not invited to a work of ART, but to a work of FACTS" (v).

5. While historians such as Benjamin Quarles, John Blassingame, and David Blight have tended to emphasize Douglass's position as an orator, literary critics have tended to de-emphasize his position as an orator. Important work focusing on Douglass as orator includes O'Meally's "Frederick Douglass' 1845 *Narrative*" and Andrews's "Frederick Douglass, Preacher."

6. Both Peterson and Mullen are specifically concerned with the ways that nineteenth-century African American women used their voice to gain agency. For Peterson, black women were "doers of the world," compelled to civic action by a near spiritual, if not religious, motivation whose "speaking and writing constituted a form of doing, of social action continuous with their social, political, and cultural work" (3). Mullen locates in black women "a tradition of resistant orality, or verbal self-defense, which included speech acts variously labeled sassy or saucy, impudent, impertinent, or insolent" ("Runaway Tongue," 245).

7. Gustafson, *Eloquence Is Power*, xvi–xvii.

8. Gregory, *Frederick Douglass*, 93.

9. As Fishkin and Peterson write: "The oppressed group most often asserts itself, not by creating a new discourse, but by 'using the same categories [of the dominant discourse] by which it was…disqualified' and simply reversing these or the values that had been assigned to them" ("'We Hold These Truths to Be Self-Evident,'" 191–92).

10. Bhabha, *Nation and Narration*, 292.

11. Brown, "I Have No Constitution, And No Country," 215.

12. Remond, "An Anti-Slavery Discourse," *Liberator*, July 10, 1857.

13. In his study of Douglass's use of irony that focuses on this particular passage of the speech, John Louis Lucaites notes that Douglass spoke "*to* his audience as a dialogical other, rather than to speaking for them as a duly constituted member of their community" ("The Irony of 'Equality' in Black Abolitionist Discourse," 57).

14. On Bakhtin's notion of heteroglossia, see "Discourse in the Novel" in *The Dialogic Imagination*.

15. In the January 24, 1786, letter to Jean Nicholas Démeunier, Jefferson writes: "What a stupendous, what an incomprehensible machine is man! Who can endure toil, famine, stripes, imprisonment, and death itself, in vindication of his own liberty, and, the next moment, be deaf to all those motives whose power supported him through his trial, and inflict on his fellow men a bondage, one hour of which is fraught with more misery, than ages of that which he rose in rebellion to oppose" (Jefferson, *Answers to Démeunier's First Queries*, 582).

16. Douglass, "To Horace Greeley," 28.

17. Douglass would use this Jefferson line again more than twelve years later in the midst of the Civil War. In an address in Baltimore on November 17, 1864, Douglass declared: "The fathers of this republic waged a seven years war for political liberty. Thomas Jefferson taught me that my bondage was, in its essence, worse than ages of that which your fathers rose in rebellion to oppose" ("A Friendly Word to Maryland," 42).

18. Andrews, "Frederick Douglass, Preacher," 593.

19. See Douglass, "The Present Condition and Future Prospects of the Negro People," 251.

20. Stanley, "What, to the Toiling Millions There, Is This Boasted Liberty?" 286.

21. Douglass, *Narrative*, 38.

22. In addition to the sorrow songs, Douglass also conceded that some minstrel songs had the capability to mobilize antislavery political consciousness through affect. In his 1855 address "The Anti-Slavery Movement," Douglass wrote: "It would seem almost absurd to say it, considering the use that has been made of them, that we have allies in the Ethiopian songs; those that constitute our national music, and without which we have no national music. They are heart songs, and the finest feelings of human nature are expressed in them. 'Lucy Neal,' 'Old Kentucky Home,' 'Uncle Ned,' can make the heart sad as well as merry, and call forth a tear as well as a smile. They awaken the sympathies for the slave, in which Anti-Slavery principles take root, grow up and flourish" ("The Anti-Slavery Movement," 48).

23. For more on Douglass's use of humor see Ganter, "'He Made Us Laugh Some.'"

24. Douglass, "Let All Soil Be Free Soil," 390.

25. Ibid., 391.

26. Ibid., 392.

27. In describing this notion of the runaway tongue, Mullen writes: "The oral tradition often permitted a directness of expression (particularly within family networks in less Europeanized slave communities) about matters of sex, violence, and sexual violence that literary convention—particularly the indirection and euphemistic language of sentimental fiction in its concern with modesty and decorum—rendered 'unspeakable'" ("Runaway Tongue," 245).

28. See Blight, *Beyond the Battlefield*, 77; O'Meally, "Frederick Douglass's 1845 *Narrative*."

29. Douglass addresses the issue in *My Bondage and My Freedom*: "'Let us have the facts,' said the people. So also said Friend George Foster, who always wished to pin me down to my simple narrative. 'Give us the facts,' said Collins, 'we will take care of the philosophy.' . . . 'Tell your story, Frederick,' would whisper my then revered friend, William Lloyd Garrison, as I stepped upon the platform. I could not always obey, for I was now reading and thinking. . . . It was said to me, 'Better have a little of the plantation manner of speech than not; 'tis not best that you seem too learned.' These excellent friends were actuated by the best of motives, and were not altogether wrong in their advice; and still I must speak just the word that seemed to me the word to be spoken by me" (361–62). Douglass would in fact develop the ability to alter the intonation of his voice—perfected by his mimicry of speeches by Henry Clay and John C. Calhoun as well as sermons—but the request to put on a little "plantation manner of speech" for his own self-(re)presentation probably seemed somewhat disingenuous and possibly politically dangerous even at this relatively early moment in his public life. Putting on a little "plantation manner" might serve the immediate cause of illustrating the debasing effects of slavery, but parading such caricatures could

also have negative consequences on the larger question of black citizenship in the United States.

30. See Ward, *Autobiography of a Fugitive Negro*.

31. Douglass himself recalled Ward in this manner: "As an orator and thinker he was vastly superior, I thought, to any of us [Henry Highland Garnet, Charles Lenox Remond, and Henry Bibb], and being perfectly black and of unmixed African descent, the splendors of his intellect went directly to the glory of race. In depth of thought, fluency of speech, readiness of wit, logical exactness, and general intelligence, Samuel R. Ward has left no successor among the colored men amongst us, and it was a sad day for our cause when he was laid low in the soil of a foreign country" (*Life and Times*, 345).

32. For more on the convention movements, see Ernest, *Liberation Historiography*, 219–77, and Philip S. Foner and George E. Walker, *Proceedings of the Black State Conventions, 1840–1865*.

33. "Resolved, That the Constitution of the United States, in Letter, Spirit, and Design, Is Essentially Anti-Slavery: A Debate between Samuel Ringgold Ward and Frederick Douglass in New York, New York, on 11 May 1849," 194.

34. Ibid., 197.

35. Throughout the study, I refer to Frances Ellen Watkins Harper as Watkins Harper to signal her literary production and political career both before and after her marriage to Fenton Harper in 1860. Brown, "I Have No Constitution, and No Country," 216.

36. Watkins Harper, "Miss Watkins and the Constitution," 48.

37. Quoted in Fabre, "African American Commemorative Celebrations in the Nineteenth Century," 83.

38. Remond, "For the Dissolution of the Union."

39. Douglass, "Is the Plan of the American Union under the Constitution," 155, 152–53.

40. When Douglass revises his speech for print in his pamphlet, he writes the passage this way: " 'We, the people'—not we, the privileged class, and excluding all other classes but we, the people; not we, the horses and cattle, but we the people—the men and women, the human inhabitants of the United States, do ordain and establish this Constitution, &c." ("Dred Scott Decision," 176). For more on pamphleteering see Richard Newman, Patrick Rael, and Philip Lapsansky, eds., *Pamphlets of Protest*.

41. Douglass, "Is the Plan of the American Union under the Constitution," 152.

42. Wilson, "Leaf from My Scrap Book," 167.

43. Ibid., 168.

44. Ibid., 169.

45. Ibid.

46. Douglass, "Men and Brothers," 238–39.

47. Ibid., 237.

48. Quoted in Blassingame, "Introduction," xxxii.

49. Andrews, "Novelization of Voice in Early African American Narrative," 24.

50. Ellison, *Invisible Man*, 581.

51. I am referring here to Saidiya Hartman's deft maneuver to refuse to re-print the passage from Douglass's *Narrative* describing Aunt Hester's beating as a way to give pause to the ways in which accounts of violence against black bodies have been so utterly naturalized in our ecology that they almost cease to be phenomenal at all, being reduced, as it were, to being mere quotidian; see *Scenes of Subjection*, 3.

52. Stauffer, "Frederick Douglass and the Aesthetics of Freedom," 115.

53. As Franchot writes: "Situating himself in the American Revolutionary tradition of self-reliant opposition to tyranny, Douglass strove to negate the vestiges of any 'effeminate' dependence or vulnerability" (149).

54. Andrews, "Novelization of Voice in Early African American Narrative," 28.

55. The language that Brown uses in describing Susan's body—which gains its effect from a kind of phantasmagoric gaze on her as a specter of the sexual and racial economies of nationalism—was almost the same that he used in developing Clotel. Child's depiction, which likely made use of Brown's, portrayed her similarly.

56. Douglass, *The Heroic Slave*, 138. All later references to this edition will be cited in the text with page number in parentheses.

57. Franchot, "Douglass and the Construction of the Feminine," 161.

58. Castronovo and Nelson, "Fahrenheit 1861," 335.

59. As Sundquist points out, Washington's role as a founding father is exemplified in both the personal and national sense; see Sundquist, *To Wake the Nations*, 120.

60. Sale, "Critiques from Within," 711–12.

61. For more on the ontology of national belonging as a category of existence that necessitates the availability of death itself as a formative act of constitutive inclusion, see Castronovo, *Necro Citizenship*.

62. In chapter 18, "Months of Peril," Jacobs writes: "When I started upon this hazardous undertaking, I had resolved that, come what would, there should be no turning back. 'Give me liberty, or give me death,' was my motto" (80). Earlier, in chapter 12, "Fear of Insurrection," Jacobs writes: "Not far from this time Nat Turner's insurrection broke out; and the news threw our town into great commotion. Strange that they should be alarmed, when their slaves were so 'contented and happy'! But so it was" (53).

63. For example, Douglass later echoes his description of Madison Washington as a veritable Patrick Henry in his description of his own escape. In *My Bondage and My Freedom*, Douglass writes: "Patrick Henry...thrilled by his magic eloquence, and ready to stand by him in his boldest flights, could say, 'GIVE ME LIBERTY OR GIVE ME DEATH,' and this saying was a sublime one, even for a freeman; but incomparably more sublime, is the same sentiment, when practically asserted by men accustomed to the last and chain—men whose sensibilities must have become more or less deadened by their bondage. With us it was a doubtful liberty, at best, that we sought; and a certain, lingering death in the rice swamps and sugar fields, if we failed" (284).

64. See Castronovo and Nelson, "Fahrenheit 1861," esp. 332–33.

65. Examining the textual connections between *Uncle Tom's Cabin* and *The Heroic Slave* as they relate to antislavery politics, Robert S. Levine has written that "sympathy allows for the possibility of dialogue and influence; and I do not think it too farfetched to read "The Heroic Slave," in part, as an allegory of Douglass's relationship to Stowe, particularly if we take Listwell's overhearing of Washington's soliloquy and subsequent conversion to antislavery as analogous to Stowe's reading of Douglass's *Narrative* and eventual authoring of *Uncle Tom's Cabin*" (*Politics of Representative Identity*, 85). Although Levine is primarily concerned with hypothesizing a "model of influence" where "power is shared and mutually constitutive" (85), it is worth noting that, within the story of *The Heroic Slave*, Grant's conversion comes with no corollary sense that blacks are the equals of whites. However, as I am trying to insist here, in order for the latent impulse of Douglass's political message to gain currency, he needs both the example of Listwell and Grant as versions of transformed white political subjectivity—one that is going to accept blacks as

equals and the other that is willing, or is forced to concede, that African Americans are indeed part of the nation.

66. Foreman, "Sentimental Abolition in Douglass's Decade," 200.

67. See Yarborough, "Race, Violence, and Manhood: The Masculine Ideal in Frederick Douglass's 'The Heroic Slave.'"

■ Chapter Two

1. Bhabha, *Location of Culture*, 123.

2. In *Narrative*, Douglass is keen to note the influence of *The Columbian Orator* (1797) in helping him situate his opposition to chattel slavery in the United States within a longer history of antislavery and emancipation movements over the course of centuries. *The Columbian Orator* did more than inform Douglass's philosophy about the injustices of slavery as a human rights issue. By focusing on the master-slave dialogue and the speeches on Catholic emancipation in the *Orator*, Douglass also shaped his sense of rhetoric and oratory.

3. Brown, "Sketch of the Author's Life," 38.

4. Stepto, *From behind the Veil*, xv.

5. "Outsider art" is one of the most ill-defined and contentious designations in modern aesthetics. As a term, it is broad enough to encapsulate or reference a number of different kinds of works, including assemblages, drawings, paintings, sculptures, and the architectural design of gardens and other outdoor constructions. But one of the central ideas of outsider art, related to other modes such as folk art, primitive art, and vernacular art, is that its practitioners are self-taught. Importantly, its practitioners are often "outside of" or antagonistic to the conventions of both traditional art training and art's institutionalization via commercial art houses and dealers. Although the field has expanded significantly since it appeared in 1972, Roger Cardinal's *Outsider Art* remains the seminal book on the topic.

6. My contention here is similar to Robert Reid-Pharr's claim that *Clotel* "is not best understood as the seminal text of the Black American novelistic tradition, but instead a self-consciously racialist (though anti–white supremacist) meditation on the tragedy and promise of American republicanism that…are immediately apparent in the distinctly American, distinctly hybrid body of the mulatto" (*Conjugal Union*, 38).

7. Among the many critics, including Vernon Loggins, Arthur Davis, and Blyden Jackson, who have noted the disjointed nature of the text as a novel, Addison Gayle's notion of *Clotel*'s "structural chaos" is representative. See Gayle, *The Way of the New World*, 5.

8. Fabi correlates the "sketchiness" of the novel to its sensational effect: "the oft-noted sketchiness that results from this narrative mode not exclusively as an instance of artistic ineptitude but as a deliberate strategy that succeeds…in making the reader experience the powerlessness, the uncertainty, the absurdities that characterize slave life" ("The 'Unguarded Expressions of the Feelings of the Negroes,'" 642). In *Resistance and Reformation*, Ernest argues that the novel is an index to the social confusion of a national political system attempting to reconcile the existence of slavery in a democratic state: "Brown brings together the various fragmented fabrications that constitute the social masquerade created by an uneasy reliance on and obfuscated devotion to the national system of slavery and racial domination" (54).

9. Reid-Pharr, *Conjugal Union*, 57, 64.

10. In the introduction to his edition, Robert S. Levine identifies *Clotel* as pastiche and bricolage. See Levine, "Introduction," 7.

11. Nabers, "Problem of Revolution in the Age of Slavery," 93.

12. Laclau, *Reflections on the Revolution of Our Time*, 9. My own consideration of the remix aesthetic in African American culture and politics has benefitted from Butler's summary and analysis of Laclau and Chantal's notion of radical democracy in her *Bodies That Matter* where she writes: "Against a causal theory of historical events or social relations, the theory of radical democracy insists that political signifies are contingently related, and that hegemony consists in the perpetual rearticulation of these contingently related political signifiers, the weaving together of a social fabric that has no necessary ground, but that consistently produces the 'effect' of its own necessity through the process of rearticulation" (192).

13. Young, "Communication and Other," 120. This expanded field of communication is central to my consideration of how African American cultural production is simultaneously an alternative and constitutive component of U.S. political discourse.

14. For more on the circulation of the idea that Jefferson fathered children with Sally Hemmings, see Schweninger, "*Clotel* and the Historicity of the Anecdote."

15. Fabi writes: "Cognizant of the appeal that 'white slaves' elicited on a white abolitionist audience and concerned with his heroines' gentility and higher moral standards, Brown casts their story in the sentimental patterns of female virtue, distress, death, and/ or marriage" ("The 'Unguarded Expressions of the Feelings of the Negroes,'" 642).

16. Ellison has written one of the most trenchant essays on the American novel's democratizing potential in "The Novel as a Function of American Democracy." (1967).

17. The literature on Jefferson and race is extensive. On Jefferson's understanding of blacks, see Shuffleton's "Thomas Jefferson," Holland's "Notes on the State of America," and, more recently, Hardt's "Jefferson and Democracy." For a reading that recovers his radical (egalitarian) thought, see Erkkilä, "Radical Jefferson."

18. Jefferson, *Notes on the State of Virginia*, 288.

19. Brown, *Clotel*, 160. All later references to this edition will be cited in the text with page numbers in parentheses.

20. Samuels's discussion of *Uncle Tom's Cabin* might be similarly extrapolated to Brown's *Clotel*: "If to see race in *Uncle Tom's Cabin* means to see miscegenation, what image of miscegenation is presented? What we see when we see race in these representations is sexual—that is to say, both sexual availability and the promise or threat of miscegenation"; see Samuels, "Miscegenated America," 493–94.

21. Farrison, *Clotel*, 250n.

22. See duCille, *Coupling Convention*, 17–29, and Reid-Pharr, *Conjugal Union*, 37–64. In particular, Reid-Pharr reads Brown's depiction of the mulatto woman as the author's attempt to illustrate a specific "American nativity": "Clotel's mixed-race body is understood by Brown as the very site at which the splits (racial, sexual, psychological, and ideological) that plague America can be healed—domesticated, if you will—thus producing in one not so dark body that which is properly and inevitably American" (45).

23. In outlining the ways in which Brown makes a distinction between genteel and confrontational forms of resistance that split along gender lines, Fabi notes that Brown reproduced many of the tenets of midcentury white womanhood in the characterization of his mulatta characters: "On the one hand, the mulatto qualifies as a device of meditation both for her mixed genealogy and her gender: As a 'white Negro,' she appropriates the qualities of ideal white womanhood and complements them with loyalty, understanding,

and support for individual black men" ("The 'Unguarded Expressions of the Feelings of the Negroes,'" 641).

24. Nancy Bentley has astutely outlined the rules of corporeal representation for white and black bodies in prewar fiction with particular attention to the question of the male body and violence; see Bentley, "White Slaves." Importantly, Althesa's struggle for freedom concerns not her own freedom but Salome's and is engendered not through physical violence but through discourse.

25. I borrow this term from Stepto, who, in cataloging the prevalence of white-authored introductions and prefaces to texts written by African Americans, identified their use as "authenticating documents," substantiating, verifying, and in some respects instantiating the black self as an authorial self. See *From behind the Veil*, 4–6.

26. Nelson, "Representative/Democracy," 242, n19.

27. Fliegelman, *Declaring Independence*, 4.

28. Ibid., 197.

29. Stowe's George Harris utters, "You say your fathers did it; if it was right for them, it is right for me!" and Douglass's Madison Washington proclaims, "God is my witness that LIBERTY, not *malice*, is the motive for this night's work. I have done no more to those dead men yonder than they would have done to me in like circumstances. We have struck for our freedom, and if a true man's heart be in you, you will honor us for the deed. We have done that which you applaud your fathers for doing, and if we are murderers, *so were they*." See, respectively, Stowe, *Uncle Tom's Cabin*, 187; Douglass, *Heroic Slave*, 161.

30. In Tompkins's words, it is not the words of sentimental fiction "but the emotions of the heart [which] bespeak a state of grace, and these are known by the sound of a voice, the touch of a hand, but chiefly in moments of greatest importance, by tears" (*Sensational Designs*, 131-32).

31. Bentley, "White Slaves," 501–22.

32. Fisher, *Hard Facts*, 115.

33. Questioning Carlton, Georgiana asks him: "'Is this not their native land? What right have we, more than the Negro, to the soil here, or to style ourselves native Americans? Indeed it is as much their home as ours, and I have sometimes thought it was more theirs.... Who fought more bravely for American independence than the blacks? A Negro, by the name of Attucks, was the first that fell in Boston at the commencement of the revolutionary war; and, throughout the whole struggles for liberty in this country, the Negroes have contributed their share'" (Brown, *Clotel*, 163).

34. Reid-Pharr, *Conjugal Union*, 45.

35. The sensational sentimentalism of this scene is underlined by the fact that Clotel has been at pains trying to make her way into the city to reunite with her daughter. Brown's narrative asserts, and the illustration reiterates, that slavery performs extreme violence on the black family and to the very idea of the bonds of motherhood.

36. Castronovo, *Necro Citizenship*, 41.

37. Of the four images reproduced in *Clotel*, only two identify the artist. The first, which features a young mulatto boy being sold upon a gambling table aboard the ship the *Patriot* (from the chapter "Going to the South"), carries the name "J. Johnston." The second, which caricatures Sam as a dentist (from the chapter "A Night in the Parson's Kitchen"), lists "H. Amelay" and "J. Johnston." The last two, from the chapters "A Slave Hunting Parson" and "Death Is Freedom," apparently have no identifiable name ascribed to them. Given his work for Alfred Elwes's *Paul Blake; or, The Story of a Boy's Peril in the*

Islands of Corsica and Monte Cristo (1859), it is conceivable that Amelay was an English illustrator. Johnston perhaps may have produced the engravings upon which the illustrations for *Clotel* were based.

38. As Gilmore writes, "Brown redeploys the standard conceits of the minstrel show—slaves singing and dancing on the plantation—in order to uncover its antislavery possibilities. Brown's rewriting of Foster's 'Massa's in De Cold Ground' makes its possibly subversive meaning explicit" ("De Genewine Artekil," 758).

39. Jefferson, "A Summary View of the Rights of British America," 263.

40. On the notion of the "hidden transcript," see Scott, *Domination and the Arts of Resistance*.

■ Chapter Three

1. Wheatley, "America," 6–7.

2. In Berlant's words, the "National Symbolic" is "the order of discursive practices whose reign within a national space produces, and also refers to, the 'law' in which the accident of birth within a geographic/political boundary transforms individuals into subjects of a collectively held history. Its traditional icons, its metaphors, its heroes, its rituals, and its narratives provide an alphabet for a collective consciousness or national subjectivity" (*Anatomy*, 20). Both Berlant and Slavoj Žižek are extending Jacques Lacan's notion of "Symbolic Order" in various way. For Berlant she extends the primacy that language plays in Lacan's understanding of the Symbolic Order to all discursive forms but especially iconographic ones that help to regulate socialities. Žižek extends Lacan by taking the latter's analysis of the Self and subjectivization from the psychoanalytic and local to the political and social.

3. Whereas Brown's publication simply identifies the air intended to accompany the lyrics, Clark's version includes the sheet music itself to the composition. Even more compelling as a mode of political articulation is the route of circulation of "A Song for Freedom." Brown's text includes no sheet music, perhaps a sign of the popularity of these particular songs or an indication of how well versed his own particular intended audience was with the songs. In *The Harp of Freedom*, Clark states that he takes the words as they appeared in Douglass's periodical. Douglass reprinted "A Song for Freedom" on July 14, 1848, a month after Brown had included it in *The Anti-Slavery Harp*. "A Song for Freedom" migrates from Brown's *Anti-Slavery Harp* and Douglass's *North Star* in 1848 to reemerge in Clark's collection with details of full accompaniment. As a veritable example of an organic political discourse, the transmission of the lyrics from Brown's transcription to their publication in Douglass's periodical to their inclusion in Clark's collection produced a reverb effect, one where the words of the slave-singer and his compatriots find voice again and again as a kind of echo.

As William John Maher points out, "Dandy Jim" or "Dandy Jim of Caroline" was one of the most popular minstrel songs. As its title indicates, it focuses on the dandy figure who, as depicted in the song, imagines himself to be the finest export from South Carolina. In the song's various iterations, Dandy Jim boasts about his superlative qualities. But in at least one version, "Dandy Jim from Carolina" No. 3 (New York: Firth, Hall, and Pond, 1844), Dandy Jim offers an explicit reference to politics: "Oh white folks jis as sure as fate, / Dat Carolina is de nullify state, / It hab de finest nigger and e best yellow pine, / An a tall sample is dandy Jim ob Caroline." The "nullify state" phrase alludes to South Carolina's attempt during Andrew Jackson's presidency to nullify a federal law that South Carolinians, led by John C. Calhoun, felt disproportionately affected their state negatively. Importantly, its opponents argued, the tariff would unfairly tax slaveholders and make them less able to oversee their plantations, which might lead to misrule—logic that was exploited when word of Nat Turner's Rebellion reached South Carolina. On the slavery subtext of the nullification ordinance, see Niven, *John C. Calhoun and the Price of the Union*, 181–84; for more on "Dandy Jim of Caroline" and a study of the musical notations of minstrel songs, see Maher, *Behind the Burnt Cork Mask*, 210–28; and for studies that turns more toward the cultural politics of black face minstrelsy, see Lott,, *Love and Theft* and Lhamon, *Raising Cain*.

4. Short entries on Watkins Harper (ranging from two to four pages) are included in Redding, *To Make a Poet Black*; Wagner, *Black Poets of the United States*; Loggins, *Negro Author*; Sherman, *Invisible Poets*; and Redmond, *Drumvoices*. More sustained analyses of her poetry appear in Robinson, *Early Black American Poets*; Foster, *Written by Herself*; Boyd, *Discarded Legacy*; Peterson, *"Doers of the Word"*; Loeffelholz, *From Schools to Salons*; and Bennett, *Democratic Discourses*.

One of the underlining reasons Watkins Harper's poetry has been relatively neglected is because of the still-lingering question concerning the literary merits of her verse. Despite the notable work of Foster and Peterson, there has been only slight interest in the aesthetic aspects of Watkins Harper's poetry. Even the most sustained commentary on her poetry, Melba Joyce Boyd's *Discarded Legacy*, more or less consists of selected quotes from Watkins Harper's writings. An earlier essay by Patricia Liggins Hill exemplifies another kind of approach to Watkins Harper which suggests that the modes of evaluating aesthetics have been circumscribed by certain presuppositions that regulate criteria, judgment, and value: "Moreover, she [Watkins Harper], like the new black poets, embraces an 'art for people's sake' aesthetic, rather than a Western Caucasian assumption, 'an art for art's sake' principle" ("'Let Me Make Songs for the People,'" 60).

While Watkins Harper's novel *Iola Leroy* has long been recovered as an object of literary study, the same cannot yet be said to be true of her poetry. What is needed most is the kind of close attention to Watkins Harper's poetry that one finds in Foster's reading of *Moses: A Story of the Nile* and *Sketches of Southern Life*; in Carolyn Sorisio's commentary on Watkins Harper's antebellum poetry; and in Mary Loeffelholz analysis of Watkins Harper's post–Civil War verse. My focus in this chapter is on the forms of Watkins Harper's poetry that make it both topical and tropic.

5. One of the most conspicuous facets of the criticism on Watkins Harper's poetry is that it is so nominal in comparison to her novels. For someone who was the most prolific nineteenth-century African American poet and as someone who is regularly cited as laying the foundation for much of the protest poetry of the modern civil rights movement, much of the criticism on Watkins Harper has focused on her novel *Iola Leroy* rather than her verse. In this regard, the relative neglect of Watkins Harper's poetry is characteristic of a larger trajectory in much of U.S. literary studies on nineteenth-century poetry, which, as Mary Loeffelholz has noted, have not moved much beyond "Whitman and Dickinson, in the course of explicating U.S. cultural histories of race, ethnicity, class, gender, and other national thematics" (*From Schools to Salons*, 2). Too often when her poetry is acknowledged, it is usually only mentioned as part of an undifferentiated corpus of her writings, as if there were little need to make distinctions between the forms and mediums of her writings themselves. Her numerous volumes of poetry—*Poems on Miscellaneous Subjects* (1854), *Moses: A Story of the Nile* (1869), *Poems* (1871), *Sketches of a Southern Life* (1872), *The Martyr of Alabama and Other Poems* (1894), *The Sparrow's Fall*

and Other Poems (n.d.), *Atlanta Offering: Poems* (1895), and *Light beyond the Darkness* (n.d.)—have received relatively less attention than even *Minnie's Sacrifice* (1869), one of her three recently rediscovered novels.

The framework of certain strands of U.S. literary studies—including those undergirded by the impulses of the Black Arts Movement, black feminist historiographies, and, more recently, the critical theories of affect, especially as they pertain to sentimentalism— has not generated a substantial body of interpretative criticism to accompany the recent moves in nineteenth-century literary scholarship of reshaping the archives by recovering many a forgotten poet. Why has there been such reluctance to engage with Watkins Harper's poetry qua poetry and, equally important, what does such a dearth indicate about how African American literary history is being constructed?

6. On Watkins Harper see Foster, *Written by Herself*, 131–53; Peterson, "*Doers of the Word*," 119–35; and Carby, *Reconstructing Womanhood*, 62–94. On the role of African American women in the church and the role of the church in black politics, see Higginbotham, *Righteous Discontent*; on the formation of independent women's clubs, see White, *Too Heavy a Load*; on the interplay between religious and secular domains of women's activism, see Gilmore, *Gender and Jim Crow*; and on how black women exercised autonomy and authority within their community's public culture, see Jones, *All Bound Up Together*.

7. For more on Watkins Harper as orator and rhetorician, see Boyd, *Discarded Legacy*, 43–49; Logan, "Black Speakers, White Representations"; Stancliff, *Frances Ellen Watkins Harper*; and on her antebellum speeches especially, Peterson, "*Doers of the Word*," 121–24. For more biographical details on Watkins Harper's life more generally, see Foster, *Brighter Day*, 3–40.

8. G., "From Indianapolis, Ind."

9. Boyd, *Discarded Legacy*, 67.

10. Redding, *To Make a Poet Black*, 44.

11. Foster, *Brighter Coming Day*, 25–26; Peterson, "*Doers of the Word*," 125.

12. Sorisio, *Fleshing Out America*, 62, 47.

13. Morrison, "Unspeakable Things Unspoken."

14. Although it contains a number of subsets including compassion, empathy, and feeling, the broader set of the (cultural or formal) politics of emotion is the subject of an overwhelming amount of scholarship. On formal politics and emotion see, for example, Henderson, *Legality and Empathy*; Morrell, *Empathy and Democracy*; and Nussbaum, *Upheavals of Thought*, esp. 297–456. On sentimentality, feminism, and slavery, see Berlant, "Poor Eliza"; Douglas, *Feminization of American Culture*; Hartman, *Scenes of Subjection*; Romero, *Home Fronts*, 52–88; Samuels, *The Culture of Sentiment*; Sánchez-Eppler, *Touching Liberty*, 14–49 and 83–104; and Tompkins, *Sensational Designs*.

15. I am thinking especially of chapters 6 through 9 of Aristotle's *Poetics*.

16. Redding, *To Make a Poet Black*, 39.

17. Hollander, *Vision and Resonance*, 8, 116. One way to de-center Hollander's emphasis on the primacy of the eye and ear is to think about another site of the senses—the heart—as an important and necessary location in the creation of the aesthetic. In a different context, Dillon makes a similar observation when she notes that sentimental fiction can become aesthetic if we think about the aesthetic in terms of sensation, emotion, and affect (see Dillon, "Sentimental Aesthetics, 496).

18. Davis, *Women, Race, and Class*, 12.

19. By examining Watkins Harper's poetry, Peterson describes what might be called the ontological publicity of black female corporeality in this way: "Yet in Watkins Harper's poems the public-private dichotomy finds itself repeatedly deconstructed. Thus, if the public history of African Americans is seen most often to unfold within the 'private' familial sphere, the poems' depiction of the slave mother's or the fugitive's wife fate, for example, historicizes African-American family life and demonstrates the degree to which it is never 'private'" (127).

20. See Morrison, "Home," 3–12. A number of recent studies have explored the idea of "interiority" in American literature; among these are Stacy Margolis's *Public Life of Privacy* (2005), where she invokes the notion of "public affects" through which a private self can be made to emanate.

21. Neal, "Sold Out on Soul," 119.

22. See C. B. McPherson's *The Political Theory of Possessive Individualism* (1962).

23. Compare, for example, Watkins Harper's "Free Labor" to Marx's famous passage in *Capital* where the sweater speaks. Does not Watkins Harper's "Free Labor" literalize the social hieroglyphic of commodity fetishism by revealing the labor processes entailed therein? In a letter to Still she wrote, "I have reason to be thankful that I am able to give a little more for a Free Labor dress, if it is coarser. I can thank God that upon its warp and woof I see no stain of blood and tears; that to produce a little finer muslin for my limbs no crushed and broken heart went out in sighs, and that from the field where it was raised went up no wild and startling cry unto the throne of God to witness there in language deep and strong, that in demanding that cotton I was nerving oppression's hand for deeds of guilt and crime" (Still, *Underground Railroad*, 788).

24. Ibid., 759.

25. Brown, *Clotel*, 119.

26. Levine, "*Uncle Tom's Cabin* in *Frederick Douglass' Paper*," 71–94.

27. Derrida, *Of Grammatology*, 144–45.

28. Stepto, "Sharing the Thunder," 137.

29. On violence, see Fisher, *Hard Facts*, 115; on suffering, see Berlant, "Poor Eliza," 646.

30. Bentley, "White Slaves," 503.

31. Berlant, "The Queen Goes to Washington," 564.

32. Stowe, *Uncle Tom's Cabin*, 119.

33. See Ryan, "Charity Begins at Home," 751–82.

34. Whittier's poem "Democracy" (1841) begins with an epigraph from the lines from Matthew.

35. See the heading for chapter 2 of *Clotel* and Whitfield's poem "America."

36. Watkins Harper offered a rather sobering critique of the Constitution in a letter she published in the *National Anti-Slavery Standard* on April 9, 1859: "I never saw so clearly the nature and intent of the Constitution before. Oh, was it not strangely inconsistent that men fresh, so fresh, from the baptism of the Revolution should make such concessions to the foul spirit of Despotism! That, when fresh from gaining their own liberty, they could permit the African slave trade—could let their national flay hang a sign of death on Guinea's coast and Congo's shore!"

37. Peterson writes about the contemporaneous assessment of Watkins Harper's speeches in this way: "What is at stake when a black woman's physical comportment and verbal expression are described in such terms in the nineteenth century? I suggest that these comments, in contrast to those about [Sojourner] Truth, constitute attempts to

decorporealize Watkins Harper by emphasizing the quietness of her body, the chastity of her language, and the purity of her voice" (122).

38. Moten urges that we turn to the category of sound in his reinterpretation of the visual and Douglass's Aunt Hester scene, writing: "In this sense utterance and response, seen together as encounter, form a kind of call wherein Hester's shrieks improvise both speech and writing. What they echo and initiate in their response to the oaths—that must be heard as the passionate utterance or call—of the master helps to constitute a question, musical encounter" (*In the Break*, 21).

39. Sale, "Critiques from Within," 702.

40. See, for example, Benjamin Quarles, "Antebellum Free Blacks and the 'Spirit of '76."

41. For more on the permutations of "America" from the early national period through the twentieth century, see, Branham, "Of Thee I Sing," 623–52. Whitfield's most famous poem turns the anthem into a kind of sound bite, extracting it from its honorific domain to excoriate the nation in a feigned elegy for democracy. For more on Whitfield's only volume of poetry see Whitley, *American Bards,* 21–65 and Levine and Wilson, *The Works of James M. Whitfield*, 31–34.

42. Smith's "America" itself was an adaption of one of the most popular British tunes "God Save the King For more on Smith's "America" and African American adaptions and appropriations of the song, see Branham's "'Of Thee I Sing,'" esp. 630–34.

43. Dimock, "A Theory of Resonance," 1061–62. As she notes early in the essay, her theory of resonance is influenced by, or at least takes one of its cues from, Ellison's notion of the frequency (1061).

44. Simpson, *Original Anti-Slavery Songs*, 3.

45. Barrett, *Blackness and Value*, 83.

46. Herrington, "Poems by Charlotte Forten and Frances Watkins Harper," 5.

47. Harper would have been thoroughly conscious of the reference from Garrison's *Liberator,* if not from the anthology published by New England abolitionists Maria Weston and Lydia Maria Child entitled *The Liberty Bell*, which ran for years in the 1840s. For more on the symbolism as antislavery icon, see David Hackett Fischer, *Liberty and Freedom*, 282.

48. Foster, *Brighter Coming Day*, 27–28.

49. For more on "Home, Sweet Home," see Sylvester, *Journeys Through Bookland*, 221.

▪ Chapter Four

1. Ellison, "What America Would Be Like Without Blacks," 581.

2. Whitman, *Leaves of Grass: A Textual Variorum, Three Volumes,* I: 114–15. All later references to this edition will be cited in the text with abbreviated title, original publication date, and page number in parentheses.

3. Aspiz, *Walt Whitman and the Body Beautiful*.

4. Sánchez-Eppler, "To Stand Between," 924.

5. Moon, *Disseminating Whitman*.

6. Moon, *Disseminating Whitman*, 18.

7. In his 1881 essay "The Poetry of the Future," Whitman lamented that "the prevailing flow of poetry...is (like music) an expression of the mere surface of melody," which, while pleasant nonetheless "shrinks with aversion from the study, the universal, the democratic" (*Prose Works*, II: 490, 481). For more on Whitman and musical composition, especially in comparison to Sidney Lanier, see Kerkering, *The Poetics of National and Racial Identity*, 113–51.

8. Whitman, *Prose Works 1892*, II: 724.

9. In *Love and Theft*, Lott writes that "Whitman was a great lover of the minstrel show, seeing in it an American example of what he had found in opera, but he could never quite decide whether it represented the best or worst America had to offer in the way of a national art. He avidly attended blackface performances, as he did many Bowery productions, and he praised them in print" (78). Kaplan contends that "Alboni [the opera singer] and her music liberated him from the metrical, rhymed, 'ballad-style' of poetry" (*Walt Whitman*, 178).

10. Whitman, *An American Primer*, 24.

11. See Appadurai, "Disjuncture and Difference in the Global Cultural Economy," 2–3.

12. Whitman's complicated and fraught negotiations with racialized bodies, and especially black bodies, has been the subject of much criticism. My critique of Whitman and blackness has benefitted from analyses in Beach, *The Politics of Distinction*; Coviello, "Intimate Nationality"; Erkkilä, *Whitman the Political Poet*; Grossman, *Reconstituting the American Renaissance*; Folsom, "Lucifer and Ethiopia"; Hutchinson, "Race and the Family Romance"; Klammer, *Whitman, Slavery, and the Emergence of "Leaves of Grass"*; Mancuso, *The Strange Sad War Revolving*; Price, "The Lost Negress and the Jolly Young Wenches"; Sánchez-Eppler, "To Stand Between"; and Sill, "Whitman and 'The Black Question."

13. Trachtenberg, "Democracy and the Poet," 277.

14. Importantly, Whitman underscored the performative dynamic of "Song of Myself" by amending these lines to read in the final two editions of *Leaves of Grass*: "I celebrate myself, and sing myself, / And what I assume you shall assume, / For every atom belonging to me as good belongs to you" (*LG* 1881–82, 29).

15. For a different reading of the performativity of Whitman's poetry, see Stephen Railton, "As If I Were With You," 7–26.

16. As Wai Chee Dimock has argued, Whitman develops "a series of complexly articulated and carefully differentiated uses of 'me,' 'mine,' and 'myself,'" through a process of "accumulation" and "divestment," adding that "the 'myself' who is both author and subject of his song" can only remain "democratically defensible" insofar as it "can remain structurally inviolate" (*Residues of Justice*, 113).

17. Horace Kallen likened America to an orchestra, imagining a form of "cultural pluralism" where different peoples might come together as different instruments to produce a common symphony of civilization. See Kallen, "Democracy versus the Melting-Pot" and *Cultural Pluralism and the American Idea*.

18. For an extended discussion of Whitman's relationship to the temperance, suffrage, and other social issues of the day, see Reynolds, "Politics and Poetry."

19. See Von Frank, *Trials of Anthony Burns*.

20. Grossman, *Reconstituting the American Renaissance*, 51.

21. Whitman, *Prose Works 1892*, II: 363.

22. Here, I am drawing upon Kerry C. Larson's important study *Whitman's Drama of Consensus* as a way to reconsider the forms of conflict and resolution embodied in Whitman's poetry.

23. Whitman, "The Eighteenth Presidency!," 2120. All later references to this edition will be cited in the text with the abbreviated title "Eighteenth" and page number in parentheses.

24. The subject of Whitman and the white working-class is a vast topic. Important considerations of the theme include Garman, *A Race of Singers*, 43–80; Thomas, "Whitman

and the Dreams of Labor"; and Trachtenberg, "The Politics of Labor ad the Poet's Work" among others.

25. Whitman, *The Gathering of Forces*, I: 208–09.

26. Emerson, *Essays and Lectures*, 867.

27. Dimock, *Residues of Justice*, 117.

28. In one of the most acute studies of Whitman, Coviello interrogates the meanings of race and sexuality to Whitman's concept of attachment and identification; see his essay "Intimate Nationality."

29. Buell, "Transcendentalist Catalogue Rhetoric," 329.

30. Buell, *Literary Transcendentalism*, 167. More recently Robert Belknap has examined how Whitman maneuvers and contorts positions within the catalogues themselves. Belknap notes, for example, that "a purposeful paratactic structure, in which the poet arranges items side by side, may challenge other spatial and temporal relations if the context provides for some sort of parity between members" (*The List*, 86).

31. Betsy Erkkilä notes that Whitman's desire to express the special nature of American political culture compelled him experiment with language in an attempt to evolve the national idiom; see "The Politics of Language," 25. For an extended treatment of Whitman and language specifically see Bauerlein, *Whitman and the American Idiom*.

32. Quoting Whitman's statement that "my form has strictly grown from my purports and facts, and is the analogy of them," Jack Kerkering has written that "free verse is the 'analogy' of a 'revolutionary age'" for Whitman. See Whitman, *Prose Works* 1892, II: 430; and Kerkering, *The Poetics of National and Racial Identity*, 148.

33. For my purposes, I will focus on the version of "Ethiopia Saluting the Colors" published initially in the 1871–72 edition of *Leaves of Grass*. For more on the permutations of the poem and its placement relative to other poems in the various editions of *Leaves of Grass*, see Herrington, "Fit Compositions," 35.

34. Folsom, "Lucifer and Ethiopia," 67.

35. Erkkilä, *Whitman the Political Poet*, 122.

36. As Martin Klammer notes the black presence continually diminishes in the second and third editions of *Leaves of Grass* such that none of the poems contain passages longer than two lines on slavery; see "Slavery and Abolitionism," 642. The comprehensive treatment of post-war Whitman and African American is Luke Mancuso's *The Strange Sad War Revolving*.

37. Johnson, *Black Manhattan*, 116–18.

38. Offering that the "mental attitude" of the nation regarding African Americans can be changed once it recognizes their contribution to literature and art, Johnson writes in the preface to *Book of American Negro Poetry*: "I make here what may appear to be a more startling statement by saying that the Negro has already proved the possession of these powers by being the creator of the only things artistic that have yet sprung from American soil and have been universally acknowledged as distinctive American products.... The first two are the Uncle Remus stories, which were collected by Joel Chandler Harris, and the 'spirituals' or slave songs, to which the Fisk Jubilee Singers made the public and the musicians of both the United States and Europe listen. The Uncle Remus stories constitute the greatest body of folk lore that America has produced, and the 'spirituals' the greatest body of folk song. I shall speak of the 'spirituals' later because they are more than folk songs, for in them the Negro sounded the depths, if he did not scale the heights, of music." For more on Burleigh and Negro spirituals, see Southern, *Music of Black Americans*, 284; and Southall, "Black Composers and Religious Music," 48.

39. Whitman, *An American Primer*, 24.

40. Nettles, *African American Concert Singers before 1950*, 40.

41. As Nettles writes: "The music moves upon the discordant tread of the marching army. A barbaric melody calls to mind the dark continent where it and "Ethiopia" were both fetched over sea, and now and then the opening phrase of 'Marching through Georgia' enters to give life to the picture" (ibid., 40). Importantly, while the black woman in Whitman's poem is overtaken by a sense of confusion that can yield only a nominal sound, the black subjects of Work's "Marching through Georgia" are vociferous, if not caricaturized as such: "How the darkies shouted when they heard the joyful sound / How the turkeys gobbled which our commissary found / How the sweet potatoes even started from the ground / While we were marching through Georgia."

42. I am grateful for my exchanges with Shana Redmond where her deep understanding of popular and religious African American music greatly shaped my own analysis here.

43. For more on Burleigh, black music, and "race anthems," see Floyd, *The Power of Black Music*, 101.

44. On March 10, 1917, a writer for the *Boston Evening Transcript* noted that Burleigh's song possessed "a marked facility in the invention of melody, an unusual cleverness in the construction of rich yet clear accompaniment, and a marked power of musical articulation." The writer continued, saying "*The Young Warrior* has gained great popularity in Italy as a sort of patriotic anthem of the present war." For more on the reception of McKay's "If We Must Die," especially Winston Churchill's invocation of the poem to urge U.S. support, see Ramesh and Rani, *Claude McKay*, 69–70.

45. Kaplan quotes Whitman as saying, "I wonder if the lady Marietta Alboni will ever know that her singing, her method, gave the foundation, the start, thirty years ago, to all my poetic literary efforts since" (*Walt Whitman*, 178).

■ Chapter Five

1. Whitman, *Uncollected Poetry and Prose*, 1: 238.

2. Ibid.

3. Lott, *Love and Theft*, 78.

4. Here I am extending Berlant's reading of the mulatta/o archetype where she differentiates the normative white person as an icon and the light-skinned person who is of African descent as a hieroglyph; see "National Brands/National Body," 110.

5. Bachelard, *The Poetics of Space*.

6. When William Schaus, the Manhattan agent for the French lithography outfit Goupil, Vibert and Co. pursued Mount to reproduce ten of his paintings as lithographs to be widely disseminated in Europe and America, he insisted that six of them picture African Americans. This had the effect of increasing Mount's profile at home and making him one of the most widely viewed American artists in Europe; see Reilly, "Translation and Transformation," 141.

7. See, for example, Berger's *Sight Unseen*; Harris's *Colored Pictures*; McElroy's *Facing History*, and Shaw's *Portraits of a People*. Earlier work on this topic includes Boime's *The Art of Exclusion* and chapters in Lubin's *Picturing a Nation* as well as Johns's *American Genre Painting*.

8. Frankenstein, *Painter of Rural America*, 14.

9. Harris, *Colored Pictures*, 42.

10. Foucault, "Of Other Spaces," 23.

11. Johns, *American Genre Painting*, 119–20.

12. Novak, *American Painting of the Nineteenth Century*, 139.

13. Laclau, *Emancipation(s)*, 53, 61.

14. Mount offers a trio of genre paintings of black musicians. *Right and Left* (1850), *The Banjo Player* (1856), and *The Bones Player* (1856) all present a close study of a sole black musician.

15. Jones, "Sketch of the Life and Character of William S. Mount," 122–27.

16. Powell, *Cutting a Figure*, 39.

17. Hills, "Painting Race: Eastman Johnson's Pictures of Slaves, Ex-Slaves, and Freedmen," 125, 121, 128.

18. Quoted in Hills, "Painting Race: Eastman Johnson's Pictures of Slaves, Ex-Slaves, and Freedman,"125.

19. Davis, "Eastman Johnson's 'Negro Life at the South' and Urban Slavery in Washington, D.C.," 70.

20. Johns, *American Genre Painting*, 135.

21. Davis, "Eastman Johnson's 'Negro Life at the South' and Urban Slavery in Washington, D.C," 69, 76.

22. Groseclose, *Nineteenth-Century American Art*, 79.

23. For more on the formation of Liberia, see Foster, "Colonization of Free Negroes, in Liberia."

24. One of the starkest aspects of the scene in White's painting is not simply the sparse quality of the room but the subject's sense of desolation, underscored by his acute attention to the paper before him. In *Forgotten Readers*, Elizabeth McHenry traces the genealogies of literary societies among African Americans through which they could discuss their civic ambitions, intellectual pursuits, and social activities as a mode of collectivity; there is no trace of such a collectivity in White's painting.

25. Warner, *Letters of the Republic*.

26. Wolf, "All the World's a Code," 332.

27. Habermas, *The Structural Transformation of the Public Sphere*.

28. For more on the numerous rectangular forms that frame Woodville's painting, see Wolf, "All the World's a Code," 332.

29. Adams, "Black Image in the Paintings of William Sidney Mount," 49.

30. Young, "Communication and Other," 120.

■ Chapter Six

1. Gilroy, *The Black Atlantic*, 16.

2. Melville, *Moby-Dick*, 62.

3. Casarino, *Modernity at Sea*, 12.

4. Extending some of the claims of his foundational *Slave Culture*, Stuckey has offered the most trenchant analyses of Melville and an emergent, coalescing African (American) culture in a pair of essays; see "The Tambourine in Glory" and "Cheer and Gloom." These essays from the basis for his recent book *African Culture and Melville's Art* (2009). For more on the formation of an interstitial "black" culture borne out of the travel across the Atlantic and elsewhere, see Stuckey, *Slave Culture*, 3–97 and Gilory, *The Black Atlantic*, 1–40.

5. See, for example, Pease, "*Moby-Dick* and the Cold War"; on "Benito Cereno" specifically, see Emery, "'Benito Cereno' and Manifest Destiny" and Franklin, "'Apparent Symbol of Despotic Command."

6. Melville, *Moby-Dick*, 557.

7. Melville, "Hawthorne and His Mosses," 246.

8. See, for example, Eaton, "'Lost in their Mazes,'" 218–24; Levine, *Conspiracy and Romance*, 200–02; Nelson, *The Word in Black and White*, 109; and Sundquist, *To Wake the Nations*, 151.

9. See Lott, *Love and Theft*, 234–35 and Baker, "Staging Revolution in Melville's *Benito Cereno*." Other works which address the actions of the Africans, especially Babo's "show" and Atufal's masquerade, as performance include Franklin, "Past, Present, and Future Seemed One," 243; Levine, *Conspiracy and Romance*, 208; and Sundquist, *To Wake the Nations*, 135–82.

10. Mitchell, "Narrative, Memory, and Slavery," 220.

11. I draw the term "damaged space" from Philip Fisher. In one of the most insightful essays on "Benito Cereno" and indeed the post-New Critical American literary studies, Fisher urges that we attend to issues of space. Outlining four principal characteristics of what he calls a "democratic social space," an infinitely reproducible cellular zone, he finds in Whitman's poetry the promise of such a domain, while in "Benito Cereno" its very abnegation. See Fisher, "Democratic Social Space," 62, 77.

12. Fisher, "Democratic Social Space," 96; Bentley, *Frantic Panoramas*, 22–68.

13. Chaney, *Fugitive Vision*, 211.

14. Melville, "Benito Cereno," 354. All later references to this edition will be cited in the text with page number in parentheses.

15. In *The Political Unconscious*, Jameson writes: "For the sea is the empty space between the concrete places of work and life; but it is also, just as surely, itself a place of work and the very element by which an imperial capitalism draws its scattered beach-heads and outposts together, through which it slowly realizes its sometimes violent, sometimes silent and corrosive, penetration of the outlying precapitalist zones of the globe" (205).

16. Spillers, "Mama's Baby, Papa's Maybe," 72. It is no surprise that Toni Morrison's *Beloved* and other writings, such as Paule Marshall's *Praisesong for the Widow* and Audre Lorde's *Zami*, call for either a literal or a metaphoric journey across the Atlantic as an essential component in healing the wounds produced by enslavement and slavery.

17. For more on the political implications of this form of decadence and the "dandiacal body," see Nicola Nixon's essay "Men and Coats," 360.

18. Writing specifically on photography, Barthes has noted that images can have at least three messages: a linguistic message, a coded iconic message, and a non-coded iconic message; see *Image, Music, Text*, 36.

19. Foucault borrows Bentham's concept for his study on surveillance and the birth of the prison in his book *Discipline and Punish*. For a commentary on Foucault's reading of Bentham, see Jay, *Downcast Eyes*, 384.

20. Fisher, "Democratic Social Space," 82.

21. On the topic of Delano's benevolence and, by extension, U.S. charity, see Andrews, "No Charity on Earth, Not Even at Sea"; Coviello, "The American in Charity"; and Downes, "Melville's *Benito Cereno* and the Politics of Humanitarian Intervention."

22. Herman Melville to Nathaniel Hawthorne, June 1 [?], 1851, in *Correspondence*, 191.

23. Deception, imitation, and performativity function as subversive mechanisms for black liberation in a process that Sundquist calls a "tautology." According to Sundquist, this tautology "defines not just the perceptual apparatus that occludes Delano's recognition but also the relationship of Benito Cereno and Babo, whose enacted revolt has been contained as something that *is* and *is not*" (*To Wake the Nations*, 156).

24. Yet what initially seems a performance is in fact no performance to Babo. That is, the "play of the barber" scene can only be maintained as such a posteriori and from the viewpoint of Delano, not in real time and from the perspective of Babo or any of the other black subjects for whom these actions are anything but play. From the perspective of the black subjects aboard the ship, there is no delineation between the cultural performance of their ostensible subservience, scripted as nonaction, versus the physical action of the revolt itself in part because the end game remains the same: either they will be returned into bondage, or they will gain their freedom.

25. Wharton, *The Decoration of Houses*, xix.

26. Debord, *The Society of the Spectacle*, 7.

27. By contrast, Charles Berryman contends that the "repetition of words like 'prostrate' and 'writhing' follows the movement of Babo from slave to master and back to slave again, and the symbolic stern-piece of the *San Dominick* finally suggests the interchangeability of master and slave" ("'Benito Cereno' and the Black Friars," 164).

28. This concept of the "Revolutionary Atlantic" is from Peter Linebaugh and Marcus Rediker's *Many-Headed Hydra* where they reconstruct and analyze the complicated cultural interchanges between merchant seamen, sailors, and slaves in the maritime world.

29. For discussions of the significance of the appended documents to the text and story of "Benito Cereno," see Robertson-Lorant, *Melville: A Biography*, 350 and Sundquist, *To Wake the Nations*, 179. For more on these documents specifically as legal text in "Benito Cereno," see Lee *Slavery, Philosophy, and American Literature*, 144–45; DeLombard, "Salvaging Legal Personhood"; and Weiner, "'Benito Cereno' and the Failure of Law." For more on Melville and the law more generally, see Thomas, "The Legal Fictions of Herman Mevlille and Lemuel Shaw."

30. Time has emerged as one of the most salient units of critical inquiry in recent criticism on "Benito Cereno"; see, for example, Luciano, "Melville's Untimely History." On time, chronology, and memory in Melville's later work, see Trodd, "A Hid Event, Twice Lived," esp. 56–59.

31. The meanings of Melville's decision to have Babo remain silent is heavily contested, with opinions ranging from Melville's sympathy with Babo to an illustration of his own ostensible racism; see, for example, Colatella, "The Significant Silence of Race"; Goldberg, "*Benito Cereno*'s Mute Testimony"; Haegert, "Voicing Slavery through Silence"; Jones, "Dusky Comments of Silence" and Lee, "Melville's Subversive Political Philosophy."

32. Bartley, "'The Creature of His Own Tasteful Hands,'" 451.

33. I am signifying here on Gilroy's well-known concept of "roots and routes" where he suggests that black identity in particular but all identity in general might relinquish the illusion of a fixed rootedness and let the self accept its continual mediation through various routes or itineraries of being; see *The Black Atlantic*, 19, 133.

34. Agamben, *Coming Community*, 18–19.

35. Stuckey, *Slave Culture*, 3.

36. Heavily critiqued, the notion of a "closed system" is most closely associated with John Rawls's *Theory of Justice*.

37. Ankersmit, *Political Representation*, 158.

38. Spillers, "Mama's Baby, Papa's Maybe," 67.

39. Melville, *Moby-Dick*, 847.

40. Quoting Michael P. Clark's introduction to *Revenge of the Aesthetic* (2000), Castiglia and Castronovo make this point in their own introduction for the special issue of *American Literature*; see "A 'Hive of Subtlety,'" 426.

41. See Rancière, *The Politics of Aesthetics*, 12–19 and "Ten Theses on Politics," especially numbers 8 and 10. Rancière's understanding of dissensus runs counter to various political theorists and philosophers from Habermas's "communicative action," Rawl's "closed system," and Young's "communicative democracy" and, especially with respect to what might be called the liberal democratic practices of the black writers I discussed in Part I.

42. Derrida, "The Spatial Arts," 18.

43. Stuckey and Leslie, "Death of Benito Cereno," 297. According to Harold Scudder, in Delano's *Narrative of Voyages and Travels*, it was the whites who shaved the Africans: "On going aboard the next morning with hand-cuffs, leg irons, and shackled bolts, to secure the hands and feet of the negroes, the sight which presented itself to our view was truly horrid. They had got all of the men who were living made fast, hand and feet, to the ring bolts in the deck; some of them had parts of their bowels hanging out, and some with half their backs and thighs shaved off" (Scudder, "Melville's 'Benito Cereno' and Captain Delano's 'Voyages,'" 510).

44. Spillers, "Mama's Baby, Papa's Maybe," 67.

45. DuBois, *Souls of Black Folk*, 2.

46. Ezekiel cried them dry bones.
Now hear the word of the Lord
Ezekiel connected them dry bones.
Now hear the word of the Lord.
Your toe bone connected to your foot bone.
Your foot bone connected to your ankle bone.
Your ankle bone connected to your leg bone.
Your leg bone connected to your thigh bone.
Your thigh bone connected to your hip bone.
Your hip bone connected to your back bone.
Your back bone connected to your shoulder bone.
Your shoulder bone connected to your neck bone.
Your neck bone connected to your head bone.
Now hear the word of the Lord.
Them bones gonna walk around.
Now hear the word of the Lord.

47. Sundquist, *To Wake the Nations*, 156.

48. Gates, *Signifying Monkey*, 236.

■ Chapter Seven

1. Douglass, "Pictures and Progress," 452.

2. Smith, "Our Correspondence." *Frederick Douglass' Paper*, October 5, 1855.

3. As Jean Fagan Yellin notes, Wilson was part of the abolitionist movement who were calling for separate black institutions that were "complexionally distinct"; see *Harriet Jacobs: A Life*, 124.

4. Brown, *The Black Man*, 230.

5. Relatively little is known about Wilson, with basic biographical details about his still uncovered. The best contemporary account of him is in Craig Steven Wilder's book on Brooklyn; see *A Covenant with Color*, 72–74, 110. My reading of Wilson has benefitted from conversations with John Ernest, Radi Clytus, Erica Ball and especially Anthony Foy.

6. I invoke Jean Baudrillard's notion of "simulation" to underscore not only the modes of representation within art and politics but also between them. By underscoring simulation over simulacra, I mean to accentuate the idea of motion and specifically animation within the mind's eye of the reader of the *Anglo-African*. See Baudrillard, *Simulacra and Simulation* (1985).

7. Bentley, *Frantic Panoramas*, 24.

8. Wilson, "From Our Brooklyn Correspondent," *Frederick Douglass's Paper*, March 11, 1853.

9. Wilson, "From Our Brooklyn Correspondent," *Frederick Douglass' Paper*, March 25, 1853.

10. Wilson, "From Our Brooklyn Correspondent," *Frederick Douglass' Paper*, March 11, 1853.

11. While speaking specifically of land-ownership, one of the places where Wilson first expresses the idea of the "peculiar position" of free blacks is in an 1853 report published in *Frederick Douglass' Paper* that noted that they were a "floating people" ("Report of the Committee on Social Relations and Polity"). Two years later, in the call for the National Convention of Colored Americans to be held in Philadelphia, Wilson, Stephen Lewis, and John W. Lewis used the term to refer to all free blacks in the United States: "The present aspect of the times, and the condition of our brethren in bonds, and our own peculiar position as Free-man, require of us some well-directed effort to counteract the debasing influence that holds us in our present anomalous condition in their sour native country" ("A Call for a National Convention of Colored Americans").

12. Mitchell, "Word and Image," 54.

13. By focusing on Wilson's use of ekphrasis I am not simply detailing his preoccupation with a certain form of writing but how it attempts to bring forward images which, like antebellum free blacks, "cannot literally come into view." As Mitchell writes: "This figurative requirement puts a special sort of pressure on the genre of ekphrasis, for it means that the textual other must remain completely alien; it can never be present, but must be conjured up as a potent absence or a fictive, figural present" (*Picture Theory*, 158).

14. For extended discussions of the convention movement see Ernest, *Liberation Historiography*, 219–76; Glaude, *Exodus!*, 107–25; and Jones, *All Bound Up Together*, 87–118.

15. For discussions of Peter Williams and Theodore S. Wright, see Glaude, *Exodus*, 20, 107–08.

16. I am thinking here of Fred Wilson's exhibit *Mining the Museum* at the Maryland Historical Society in Baltimore beginning in 1992 and Kara Walker's exhibit *My Complement, My Enemy, My Oppressor, My Love* at the Whitney Museum of Art in 2007.

17. Melville, "Benito Cereno," 353.

18. Waterman, "'Our Tradition Is a Very Modern Tradition,'" 370.

19. See Heffernan, "Ekphrasis and Representation," especially where he writes that ekphrastic literature delivers "from the pregnant moment of graphic art its embryonically narrative impulse, and thus make[s] explicit the story that graphic art tells only by implication" (301).

20. The convoluted relationship between slavery, time, and the countermonumental impulse is explored with deft acuity by Dana Luciano; see *Arranging Grief*, 169–214.

21. In this regard, Everett might be said to have modeled his own actions as a politician too closely after those of Washington. As U.S. senator in 1853, he failed to vote when Stephen A. Douglas's Kansas-Nebraska Act came to the floor, angering Massachusetts's

antislavery supporters and precipitating his early resignation from office. Although, like Washington, Jefferson, and Lincoln, Everett disliked slavery, he believed in the necessity of preserving the Union.

22. In Taney's opinion, he noted that it "is difficult at this day to realize the state of public opinion in regard to that unfortunate race which prevailed in the civilized and enlightened portions of the world at the time of the Declaration of Independence, and when the Constitution of the United States was framed and adopted; but the public history of every European nation displays it in a manner too plain to be mistaken. They had for more than a century before been regarded as beings of an inferior order, and altogether unfit to associate with the white race, either in social or political relations, and so far unfit that they have no rights which the white man was bound to respect."

23. The distinction that I draw here recalls Spillers's language of "body" and "flesh" from "Mama's Baby, Papa's Maybe."

24. Douglass, *Narrative*, 65.

25. McKittrick, "Freedom Is a Secret," 99. In a metacritical sense, McKittrick is also concerned with the ways that certain conceptions of Canada emanating from U.S. scholarship on abolitionism, especially emblematized through the Underground Railroad, has occluded Canada's own history of racist and colonial practices: "Thus, *within and beyond* nineteenth-century black diaspora histories, one region of North America (the United States) is 'out of time' while another region (Canada) is simultaneously advanced, socially evolved, and, perhaps most importantly, only engaging blackness as it escapes to Canada in search of liberation" (98).

26. Barthes, *Image, Music, Text*, 49.

27. For an extended discussion on the circulation of Uncle Tom images, see Morgan, Uncle Tom's Cabin *as Visual Culture*, 20–63.

28. Shaw, *Portraits of a People*, 23.

29. Smith's "word paintings," as John Stauffer has called them, were impressionistic sketches done in an experimental style that portrayed New York City's black working class (Stauffer, *Works*, 187).

30. *Boston Gazette and Country Journal*, March 12, 1770.

31. Fischer, *Paul Revere's Ride*, 24.

32. Quoted in Bethel, *Roots of African-American Identity*, 7.

33. For example, five years after the initial Attucks commemorative festival, Brown included a sketch of him in *The Black Man*. Because the sketch was published in the midst of the Civil War, Brown, like Nell, was at pains to denote that African Americans had willingly participated in major conflicts such as the War of Independence and the War of 1812. Noting the black presence in battles at Bunker Hill, Red Bank, and Groton, Brown insisted that African Americans went into "battle feeling proud of the opportunity of imitating the first martyr of the American revolution" (*Black Man*, 109). Brown's estimation, however romantic, is noteworthy because it intimates that African Americans held an image of Attucks racialized distinctly as black that traveled among a discrete subcircuit that mitigated the fading of his racial identity in the public registers of visual artifacts.

34. Nineteenth-century African American male intellectuals were keen to signal the importance of L'Ouverture to freedom struggles in the United States including such examples of James McCune Smith's 1841 speech at the Stuyvesant Institute; William Wells Brown's entry in *The Black Man*; and Richard Charles O'Hara Benjamin's *Life of Toussaint L'Ouverture, Warrior and Statesman* (1888).

35. Webb, *The Garies and Their Friends*, 122–23.

36. Poe, "The Philosophy of Furniture," 107–08.

37. Otter, *Philadelphia Stories*, 247.

38. On the appeal of African Americans to subject themselves to the lens of camera as a capture the "true" reality of their condition, see Stauffer, "Creating a Black Image," 258.

■ Conclusion

1. On the politics of Stevie Wonder's *Innervisions* (1973) album, see *"Who Set You Flowin'*," 94–99.

2. Stevie Wonder, "Black Man," *Songs in the Key of Life* (1776).

3. I am thinking here of Boorstin's trilogy *The Americans: The Colonial Experience* (1958), *The Americans: The National Experience* (1965), *The Americans: The Democratic Experience* (1973); of Arthur S. Schlesinger's *The Disuniting of America* (1991); and Howard Zinn's *A People's History of the United States* (1980).

4. Take, for example, this stanza from Hughes's "Let America Be America Again":
Who said the free? Not me?
Surely not me? The millions on relief today?
The millions shot down when we strike?
The millions who having nothing for our pay?
For all the dreams we've dreamed
And all the songs we've sung
And all the hopes we've held
And all the flags we've hung,
The millions who have nothing for our pay—
Except the dream that's almost dead today. (53–62)

5. Stevie Wonder, *Innvervisions* (1973).

6. Common, *Be* (2005).

7. Grandmaster Flash and the Furious Five, "The Message"; Public Enemy, "Fight the Power"; Mos Def, "Dollar Day."

8. "Celeb-Filled Music Video for Obama: Black Eyed Peas' will.i.am Inspired by Obama Speech."

9. Written by Allen Toussaint, the Pointer Sister's version was a remake of the original recorded by Lee Dorsey in 1970. I am grateful to Imani Perry pointing this out to me and for our conversations about black popular music and culture more generally.

10. Cohen, "Politics in the Age of Obama."

11. Remnick, "Joshua Generation."

12. Jackson, "Keynote Address."

13. Lee, *Do the Right Thing*.

14. The issue of a black head of state and iconography was illustrated, in living color, in Barry Blitt's cover for the July 21, 2008, issue of the *New Yorker*, which depicted the Obamas as subversives—Michelle Obama as an Angela Davis–type black militant and Barack Obama, presumably, as an Islamacist. *Vanity Fair* riffed the *New Yorker* in August 2008 with a cover of Cindy and John McCain in a similar setting and poses with conspicuously less stereotypical, although equally caricaturized, appearances. The cover for the January 26, 2009, issue of the *New Yorker*, where Obama is transfigured as George Washington, is yet another remix of black iconography. Rather than the antithesis of an American democracy, Obama is illustrated as its progenitor.

15. For more on Leutze's painting, see Groseclose, "'Washington Crossing the Delaware,'" 70–78; for more on Colescott's painting, see Gubar, *Racechanges*, 46–48.

16. The black man is believed to be Prince Whipple, an enslaved African who was emancipated during the war. As an early biographer said of him: "Prince Whipple was born in Amabou, Africa, of comparatively wealthy parents. When about ten years of age, he was sent by them, in company with a cousin, to America to be educated.... The captain who brought the two boys over proved to be a treacherous villain, and carried them to Baltimore, where he exposed them for sale, and they were both purchased by Portsmouth men, Prince falling to Gen. Whipple" (Nell, *Colored Patriots*, 198).

17. Nas, "You Owe Me."

18. Malcolm X, "The Ballot or the Bullet," 32.

19. I invoke the term here as Fanon discusses it in *Wretched of the Earth*, where he argues for the possibility, if not necessity, of an "absolute violence" to divest and purge the categories of blackness and whiteness (37).

20. While Malcolm remains skeptical that the United States could develop into a racist-free society, he nonetheless believed that African Americans should use the vote to work for their political well-being: "Well, what does this mean? It means that when white people are evenly divided, and black people have a bloc of votes of their own, it is left up to them to determine who's going to sit in the White House and who's going to be in the dog house" (26).

21. Parliament, "Chocolate City."

22. "Turn This Mutha Out," *New Times Media*, September 13, 2006.

23. For more on the construction of the South as the underside of the United States, see Greeson, "Figure of the South and the Nationalizing Imperatives of Early United States Literature."

24. For more on Hughes and jazz, see Patterson, "Jazz, Realism, and the Modernist Lyric"; for more on jazz and American society more generally, see O'Meally, *Jazz Cadence of American Culture.*

25. Ellison, "What America Would Be Like without Blacks," 584.

26. Ibid., 582.

27. Ellison, *Invisible Man*, 581.

■ WORKS CITED

Adams, Karen. "The Black Image in the Paintings of William Sidney Mount." *American Art Journal* 7, no. 2 (November 1975): 42–59.

Adler, Joyce. "Melville's 'Benito Cereno': Slavery and Violence in the Americas." *Science and Society* 38 (1974): 19–48.

Agamben, Giorgio. *The Coming Community*. Minneapolis: University of Minnesota Press, 1990.

Allen, William G. "Orators and Oratory." *Frederick Douglass' Paper*, October 22, 1852.

Altieri, Charles. "Spectacular Antispectacle: Ecstasy and Nationality in Whitman and His Heirs." *American Literary History* 11, no. 1 (Spring 1999): 34–62.

Altschuler, Glenn and Stuart Blumin. *Rude Republic: Americans and Their Politics in the Nineteenth Century*. Princeton, N.J.: Princeton University Press, 2000.

Anderson, Benedict. *Imagined Communities: Reflections on the Origin and Spread of Nationalism*. New York: Verso, 1983.

Anderson, Elijah. "Black Shadow Politics in Midwestville: The Insiders, the Outsiders, and the Militant Young," *Sociological Inquiry* 42, no. 1 (January 1972): 19–27.

Andrews, David. "'Benito Cereno': No Charity on Earth, Not Even at Sea." *Leviathan: A Journal of Melville Studies* 2.1 (2000): 83–103.

Andrews, William L. "Frederick Douglass, Preacher," *American Literature* 54, no. 4 (December 1982): 592–97.

———. "The Novelization of Voice in Early African American Narrative." *PMLA* 105, no. 1 (January 1990): 23–34.

———., ed. *The Oxford Frederick Douglass Reader*. New York: Oxford University Press, 1996.

Ankersmit, Frank. *Aesthetic Politics: Political Philosophy Beyond Fact and Value*. Palo Alto, Calif.: Stanford University Press, 1996.

———. *Political Representation*. Palo Alto, Calif.: Stanford University Press, 2002.

Anonymous. "A Song for Freedom" (n.d.). In Brown, *The Anti-Slavery Harp: A Collection of Songs for Anti-Slavery Meetings, Compiled by William Wells Brown, A Fugitive Slave*. 1848. 57–60. Whitefish, MT: Kessinger Publishing, 2004.

Appadurai, Arjun. "Disjuncture and Difference in the Global Cultural Economy." *Public Culture* 2, no. 2 (1990): 1–24.

Aspiz, Harold. *Walt Whitman and the Body Beautiful*. Urbana: University of Illinois Press, 1980.

Bachelard, Gaston. *The Poetics of Space*. 1958. Reprint, New York: Beacon Press, 1994.

Baker, Jennifer Jordan. "Staging Revolution in Melville's *Benito Cereno*: Babo, Figaro, and the 'Play of the Barber.'" *Prospects: An Annual Journal of American Cultural Studies* 26 (2001): 91–107.

Bakhtin, Mikhail. *The Dialogic Imagination: Four Essays*. Ed. Michael Holquist. Austin: University of Texas Press, 1981.

Barrett, Lindon. *Blackness and Value: Seeing Double*. New York: Cambridge University Press, 1999.

Barthes, Roland. *Image/Music/Text*. Trans. Stephen Heath. New York: Hill & Wang, 1977.

Bartley, William. "'The Creature of His Own Tasteful Hands': Herman Melville's *Benito Cereno* and the 'Empire of Might.'" *Modern Philology* 93, no. 4 (May 1996): 445–67.

Baudrillard, Jean. *Simulacra and Simulation*. Ann Arbor: University of Michigan Press, 1994.

Bauerlein, Mark. *Whitman and the American Idiom*. Baton Rouge: Louisiana State University Press, 1991.

Beach, Christopher. *The Politics of Distinction: Whitman and the Discourses of Nineteenth-Century America*. Athens, Ga.: University of Georgia Press, 1996.

Beam, Dorri. *Style, Gender, and Fantasy in Nineteenth-Century American Women's Writing*. New York: Cambridge University Press, 2010.

Belknap, Robert. *The List: The Uses and Pleasures of Cataloguing*. New Haven: Yale University Press, 2004.

Bennett, Michael. *Democratic Discourses: The Radical Abolition Movement and Antebellum American Literature*. New Brunswick, N.J.: Rutgers University Press, 2005.

Bentley, Nancy. *Frantic Panoramas: American Literature and Mass Culture, 1870–1920*. Philadelphia: University of Pennsylvania Press, 2009.

———. "White Slaves: The Mulatto Hero in Antebellum Fiction." In "Subjects and Citizens: Nation, Race, and Gender from *Oroonoko* to Anita Hill." Special issue, *American Literature* 65, no. 3 (September 1993): 501–22.

Bercovitch, Sacvan, ed. *Reconstructing American Literary History*. Cambridge, MA: Harvard University Press, 1986.

Berger, Martin A. *Sight Unseen: Whiteness and American Visual Culture*. Berkeley: University of California Press, 2005.

Berlant, Lauren. *Anatomy of National Fantasy: Hawthorne, Utopia, and Everyday Life*. Chicago: University of Chicago Press, 1991.

———. "National Brands/National Body: *Imitation of Life*." In *Comparative American Identities*, ed. Hortense Spillers, 110–40. New York: Routledge, 1991.

———. "The Queen Goes to Washington: Harriet Jacobs, Frances Harper, Anita Hill." In "Subjects and Citizens: Nation, Race, and Gender from *Oroonoko* to Anita Hill." Special issue, *American Literature* 65, no. 3 (September 1993): 549–74.

———. "Poor Eliza." In "No More Separate Spheres!" ed. Cathy N. Davidson. Special issue, *American Literature* 70, no. 3 (September 1998): 635–68.

Berryman, Charles. "'Benito Cereno' and the Black Friars." *Studies in American Fiction* 18, no. 2 (Autumn 1990): 159–70.

Bethel, Elizabeth Rauh. *The Roots of African-American Identity: Memory and History in Free Antebellum Communities*. London: Macmillan, 1997.

Bhabha, Homi K. *The Location of Culture*. New York: Routledge, 1994.

———., ed. *Nation and Narration*. New York: Routledge, 1990.

Biome, Albert J. *The Art of Exclusion: Representing Blacks in the Nineteenth Century*. Washington, D.C.: Smithsonian Institution Press, 1990.

Blassingame, John W. "Introduction to Series One." In *The Frederick Douglass Papers, Series One, Volume One, 1841–1846*, ed. John W. Blassingame et al., xxi–lxix. New Haven: Yale University Press, 1979.

Blight, David W. *Beyond the Battlefield: Race, Memory, and the American Civil War*. Amherst: University of Massachusetts Press, 2002.

Boston Evening Transcript, March 10, 1917.

Boston Gazette and Country Journal, no. 779 (March 12, 1770): 1–3.

Boyd, Melba Joyce. *Discarded Legacy: Politics and Poetics in the Life of Frances E. W. Harper, 1825–1911*. Detroit, Mich.: Wayne State University Press, 1994.

Branham, Robert James. "'Of Thee I Sing': Contesting America," *American Quarterly* 48.4 (1996): 623–52.

Brown, William Wells. *The Anti-Slavery Harp: A Collection of Songs for Anti-Slavery Meetings, Compiled by William Wells Brown, A Fugitive Slave*. 1848. Whitefish, MT: Kessinger Publishing, 2004.

———. *The Black Man: His Antecedents, His Genius, and His Achievements*. Boston: R. F. Wallcut, 1863.

———. *Clotel; or, The President's Daughter*. 1853. Ed. William Edward Farrison. New York: University Books, 1969.

———. *Clotel; or, The President's Daughter*. 1853. A Bedford Cultural Edition. Ed. Robert S. Levine. Boston: Bedford, 2011.

———. "I Have No Constitution, And No Country." 1849. In *Lift Every Voice: African American Oratory 1787–1900*, ed. Philip S. Foner and Robert James Branham, 214–17. Tuscaloosa, AL: University of Alabama Press, 1998.

———. *Narrative of the Life and Escape of William Wells Brown* (1853). In *Clotel; or, The President's Daughter: A Narrative of Slave Life in the United States. By William Wells Brown, Author of "Three Years in Europe." With A Sketch of the Author's Life.* 1–52. London: Partridge and Oakley, 1853.

Buckley, Peter G. "'The Place to Make an Artist Work': Micah Hawkins and William Sidney Mount." In *Catching the Tune: Music and William Sidney Mount*, ed. Janice Gray Armstrong, 22–39. Stony Brook, N.Y.: The Museums at Stony Brook, 1984.

Buell, Lawrence. *Literary Transcendentalism: Style and Vision in the American Renaissance*. Ithaca, N.Y.: Cornell University Press, 1973.

———. "Transcendentalist Catalogue Rhetoric: Vision Versus Form." *American Literature* 40, no. 3 (November 1968): 325–39.

Butler, Judith. *Bodies That Matter: On the Discursive Limits of "Sex."* New York: Routledge, 1993.

———. "Restaging the Universal: Hegemony and the Limits of Formalism." In *Contingency, Hegemony, Universality: Contemporary Dialogues on the Left*, ed. Judith Butler, Ernesto Laclau, and Slavoj Zizek, 11–43. New York: Verso, 2000.

Carby, Hazel V. *Reconstructing Womanhood: The Emergence of the Afro-American Woman Novelist*. New York: Oxford University Press, 1987.

Cardinal, Roger. *Outsider Art*. London: Studio Vista, 1972.

Casarino, Cesare. *Modernity at Sea: Melville, Marx, Conrad in Crisis*. Minneapolis: University of Minnesota Press, 2002.

Castiglia, Christopher and Russ Castronovo. "A 'Hive of Subtlety': Aesthetics and the End(s) of Cultural Studies." Special issue, *American Literature* 76, no. 3 (September 2004): 423–35.

Castiglia, Christopher. *Interior States: Institutional Consciousness and the Inner Life of Democracy in the Antebellum United States*. Durham, N.C.: Duke University Press, 2008.

Castronovo, Russ and Dana D. Nelson. "Fahrenheit 1861: Cross Patriotism in Melville and Douglass." In *Frederick Douglass and Herman Melville: Essays in Relation.*

Ed. Robert S. Levine and Samuel Otter, 329–48. Chapel Hill: University of North Carolina Press, 2008.

Castronovo, Russ. *Beautful Democracy: Aesthetics and Anarchy in a Global Age.* Chicago: University of Chicago Press, 2007.

———. *Necro Citizenship: Death, Eroticism, and the Public Sphere in the Nineteenth-Century United States.* Durham, N.C.: Duke University Press, 2001.

"Celeb-Filled Music Video for Obama: Black Eyed Peas' will.i.am Inspired by Obama Speech." *ABC News,* February 2, 2008.

Chaney, Michael A. *Fugitive Vision: Slave Image and Black Identity in Antebellum Narrative.* Bloomington: Indiana University Press, 2008.

Child, L. Maria. "Madison Washington." In *The Freedman's Book,* ed. Lydia Maria Child, 147–53. Boston: Ticknor, 1865.

Clark, George Washington. *Liberty Minstrel.* New York: Published by the Author, 1844.

Cohen, Cathy. *Democracy Remixed: Black Youth and the Future of American Politics.* New York: Oxford University Press, 2010.

———. "Politics in the Age of Obama." Allison Davis Lecture. Northwestern University, Evanston, Illinois, November 6, 2008.

Colatrella, Carol. "The Significant Silence of Race: *La Cousine Bette* and 'Benito Cereno.'" *Comparative Literature* 46, no. 3 (1994): 240–66.

Common. "It's Your World/Pop's Reprise," *Be.* Arista Records, 2005.

Coviello, Peter. "The American in Charity: 'Benito Cereno' and Gothic Anti-Sentimentality." *Studies in American Fiction* 30, no. 2 (2002): 155–80.

———. "Intimate Nationality: Anonymity and Attachment in Whitman." *American Literature* 73, no. 1 (March 2001): 85–119.

Davis, Angela. *Women, Race, and Class.* New York: Vintage, 1983.

Davis, John. "Eastman Johnson's 'Negro Life at the South' and Urban Slavery in Washington D.C." *Art Bulletin* 80, no. 1 (March 1998): 67–92.

Davis, Theo. *Formalism, Experience, and the Making of American Literature in the Nineteenth Century.* New York: Cambridge University Press, 2007.

Debord, Guy. *The Society of the Spectacle.* 1967. Reprint, London: Rebel Press, 2002.

Delano, Amasa. *A Narrative of Voyages and Travels, in the northern and southern hemispheres: comprising three voyages around the world, together with a voyage and survey in the Pacific Ocean and Oriental Islands.* Boston: E. G. House, 1817.

Delany, Martin R. *The Condition, Elevation, Emigration, and Destiny of the Colored People of the United States.* 1852. In *Martin R. Delany: A Documentary Reader,* ed. Robert S. Levine, 189–216. Chapel Hill: University of North Carolina Press, 2007.

———. "Political Destiny of the Colored Race on the American Continent." 1854. In *Pamphlets of Protest: An Anthology of Early African-American Protest Literature, 1790–1860,* ed. Richard Newman, Patrick Rael, and Philip Lapsansky, 226–39. New York: Routledge, 2001.

———. "A Project for an Expedition of Adventure, to the Eastern Coast of Africa." In *Martin R. Delany: A Documentary Reader,* ed. Robert S. Levine, 320–24. Chapel Hill: University of North Carolina Press, 2007.

DeLombard, Jeannine Marie. "Salvaging Legal Personhood: Melville's *Benito Cereno.*" *American Literature* 81, no. 1 (March 2009): 35–64.

Derrida, Jacques. *Of Grammatology.* Baltimore: Johns Hopkins University Press, 1976.

———. *Limited Inc.* Trans. Samuel Weber and Jeffrey Mehlman. Evanston, IL: Northwestern University Press, 1988.

———. "The Spatial Arts: An Interview with Jacques Derrida." In *Deconstruction and the Visual Arts: Art, Media, Architecture*, ed. Peter Brunette and David Willis, 9–32. New York: Cambridge University Press, 1994.

———. *Rogues: Two Essays on Reason*. Trans. Pascale-Anne Brault and Michael Nass. Stanford, Calif.: Stanford University Press, 2005.

———. *Specters of Marx: The State of the Debt, the Work of Mourning, and the New International*. Trans. Peggy Kamuf. New York: Routledge, 1994.

Dillon, Elizabeth. "Sentimental Aesthetics." In "Aesthetics and the End(s) of Cultural Studies" ed. Christopher Castiglia and Russ Castronovo. Special issue, *American Literature* 76, no. 3 (September 2004): 495–523.

Dimock, Wai Chee. "A Theory of Resonance." *PMLA* 112, no. (October 1997): 1060–71.

———. *Residues of Justice: Law, Literature, Philosophy*. Berkeley: University of California Press, 1996.

Downes, Paul. "Melville's *Benito Cereno* and the Politics of Humanitarian Intervention," *South Atlantic Quarterly* 103, no. 2–3 (2004): 465–88.

Douglass, Frederick. "The American Constitution and the Slave." 1860. In *The Frederick Douglass Papers: Series One, Volume Three, 1855–63*, ed. John W. Blassingame et al., 340–66. New Haven, Conn.: Yale University Press, 1985.

———. "The Anti-Slavery Movement." 1855. In *The Frederick Douglass Papers: Series One, Volume Three, 1855–63*, ed. John W. Blassingame et al., 14–50. New Haven, Conn.: Yale University Press, 1985.

———. "Citizenship and the Spirit of Caste." 1858. In *The Frederick Douglass Papers: Series One, Volume Three, 1855–63*, ed. John W. Blassingame et al., 208–12. New Haven, Conn.: Yale University Press, 1985.

———. "Colored Men's Rights in This Republic." 1857. In *The Frederick Douglass Papers: Series One, Volume Three, 1855–63*, ed. John W. Blassingame et al., 143–50. New Haven, Conn.: Yale University Press, 1985.

———. "The Dred Scott Decision: An Address Delivered, in Part, in New York, New York, in May 1857." 1857. In *The Frederick Douglass Papers: Series One, Volume Three, 1855–63*, ed. John W. Blassingame et al., 163–83. New Haven, Conn.: Yale University Press, 1985.

———. "A Friendly Word to Maryland." 1864. In *The Frederick Douglass Papers: Series One, Volume Four, 1864–1880*, ed. John W. Blassingame et al., 38–50. New Haven, Conn.: Yale University Press, 1991.

———. "The Heroic Slave." 1853. In *The Oxford Frederick Douglass Reader*, ed. William L. Andrews, 132–63. New York: Oxford University Press, 1996.

———. "To Horace Greeley." 1846. In *Frederick Douglass: Selected Speeches and Writings*, ed. Phillip S. Foner. 27–30. New York: Lawrence Hill Books, 1999.

———. "Is the Plan of the American Union under the Constitution, Anti-Slavery or Not?" 1857. In *The Frederick Douglass Papers: Series One, Volume Three, 1855–63*, ed. John W. Blassingame et al., 151–62. New Haven, Conn.: Yale University Press, 1985.

———. "Let All Soil Be Free Soil." 1852. In *The Frederick Douglass Papers: Series One, Volume Two, 1847–1854*, ed. John Blassingame et al., 388–92. New Haven, Conn.: Yale University Press, 1982.

———. *Life and Times of Frederick Douglass*. Boston: De Wolfe and Fiske Co., 1892.

———. "Men and Brothers: An Address Delivered in New York, New York, on May 7, 1850." 1850. In *Frederick Douglass Papers, Series One, Volume Two, 1847–1854*, ed. John W. Blassingame et al., 235–42. New Haven: Yale University Press, 1982.

Douglass, Frederick. *My Bondage and My Freedom*. New York: Miller, Orton and Mulligan, 1855.

———. *Narrative of the Life of Frederick Douglass, an American Slave, Written by Himself.* 1845. In *The Oxford Frederick Douglass Reader*, ed. William L. Andrews, 23–97. New York: Oxford University Press, 1996.

———. "Pictures." Holographs. N.d. [ca. late 1864]. Frederick Douglass Papers, Library of Congress.

———. "Pictures and Progress." 1861. In *The Frederick Douglass Papers: Series One, Volume Three, 1855–63*, ed. John W. Blassingame et al., 452–73. New Haven, Conn.: Yale University Press, 1985.

———. "The Present Condition and Future Prospects of the Negro People." 1853. In *Frederick Douglass: Selected Speeches and Writings*, ed. Philip S. Foner. 250–59. New York: Lawrence Hill Books, 1999.

———. "Resolved, That the Constitution of the United States, in Letter, Spirit, and Design, Is Essentially Anti-Slavery: A Debate between Samuel Ringgold Ward and Frederick Douglass in New York, New York, on 11 May 1849." 1849. In *The Frederick Douglass Papers: Series One, Volume One, 1847–1854*, ed. John Blassingame et al., 193–97. New Haven, Conn.: Yale University Press, 1982.

———. "The Revolution of 1848." In *Frederick Douglass: Selected Speeches and Writings*, ed. Philip S. Foner, 103–11. New York: Lawrence Hall Books, 1999.

———. "We Ask Only for Our Rights." 1855. In *The Frederick Douglass Papers: Series One, Volume Three, 1855–63*, ed. John W. Blassingame et al., 91–96. New Haven, Conn.: Yale University Press, 1985.

———. "What to the Slave Is the Fourth of July? An Address Delivered in Rochester, New York, on 5 July 1852." In *The Oxford Frederick Douglass Reader*, ed. William L. Andrews, 109–30. New York: Oxford University Press, 1996.

Douglas, Ann. *Feminization of American Culture*. New York: Knopf, 1977.

DuBois, W. E. B. "Criteria For Negro Art," *The Crisis* 32 (October 1926): 290–97.

———. *The Souls of Black Folk*. 1903. Reprint, New York: Penguin, 1989.

duCille, Ann. *The Coupling Convention: Sex, Text, and Tradition in Black Women's Fiction*. New York: Oxford University Press, 1993.

Eaton, Mark A. " 'Lost in their Mazes': Framing Facts and Fictions in *Benito Cereno*." *Journal of Narrative Technique* 24, no. 3 (1994): 212–36.

Elliott, Emory, Lou Freitas Caton, and Jeffrey Rhyne, ed. *Aesthetics in a Multicultural Age*. New York: Oxford University Press, 2002.

Ellison, Ralph. *Invisible Man*. New York: Vintage, 1952.

———. "The Novel as a Function of Democracy." 1967. In *The Collected Essays*, ed. John Callahan, 755–65. New York: Modern Library, 1995.

———. "The Shadow and the Act." 1964. In *The Collected Essays*, ed. John Callahan, 302–9. New York: Modern Library, 1995.

———. "What America Would Be Like without Blacks." 1970. In *The Collected Essays*, ed. John Callahan, 577–84. New York: Modern Library, 1995.

Emerson, Ralph Waldo. *Essays and Lectures*. Ed. Joel Porte. New York: Library of America, 1983.

Emery, Allan Moore. " 'Benito Cereno' and Manifest Destiny." *Nineteenth-Century Fiction* 39, no. 1 (1984): 48–68.

Erkkilä. Betsy. "Radical Jefferson." *American Quarterly* 59, no. 2 (June 2007): 277–89.

——. *Walt Whitman the Political Poet*. New York: Oxford University Press, 1989.

——. "Walt Whitman: The Politics of Language," *American Studies* 24 (Fall 1983): 21–34

Ernest, John. *Liberation Historiography: African American Writers and the Challenge of History, 1794–1861*. Chapel Hill: University of North Carolina Press, 2004.

——. *Resistance and Reformation in Nineteenth-Century African-American Literature: Brown, Wilson, Jacobs, Delany, Douglass, and Harper*. Jackson: University Press of Mississippi, 1995.

Fabi, M. Giulia. "The 'Unguarded Expressions of the Feelings of the Negroes': Gender, Slave Resistance, and William Wells Brown's Revisions of Clotel." *African American Review* 27, no. 4 (Winter 1993): 639–54.

Fabre, Geneviève. "African American Commemorative Celebrations in the Nineteenth Century." In *History and Memory in African-American Culture*, ed. Geneviève Fabre and Robert O'Meally, 72–91. New York: Oxford University Press, 1994.

Fairfax, Colita Nichols. *Hampton, Virginia*. Charlotte, Va: Arcadia, 2005.

Fanon, Frantz. *The Wretched of the Earth*. New York: Grove Press, 1963.

Farrison, William Edward, ed. *Clotel; or, The President's Daughter*. 1853. New York: University Books, 1969.

Finkelman, Paul. "Prelude to the Fourteenth Amendment: Black Legal Rights in the Antebellum North," *Rutgers Law Journal* 17 (1986): 415–82.

Fischer, David Hackett. *Liberty and Freedom: A Visual History of America's Founding Ideas*. New York: Oxford University Press, 2005.

——. *Paul Revere's Ride*. New York: Oxford University Press, 1994.

Fisher, Dexter and Robert B. Stepto, eds. *Afro-American Literature: The Reconstruction of Instruction*. New York: Modern Language Association of America, 1979.

Fisher, Philip. "Democratic Social Space: Whitman, Melville, and the Promise of American Transparency." In "America Reconstructed, 1840–1940." Special issue, *Representations* 24 (Summer 1988): 60–101.

——. *Hard Facts: Setting and Form in the American Novel*. New York: Oxford University Press, 1987.

Fishkin, Shelley Fisher, and Carla L. Peterson. "'We Hold These Truths to Be Self-Evident': The Rhetoric of Frederick Douglass's Journalism." In *Frederick Douglass: New Literary and Historical Essays*, ed. Eric J. Sundquist, 189–204. Cambridge: Cambridge University Press, 1990.

Fliegelman, *Declaring Independence: Jefferson, National Language, and the Culture of Performance*. Stanford, Calif.: Stanford University Press, 1993.

Floyd, Samuel A., Jr. *The Power of Black Music: Interpreting Its History from Africa to the United States*. New York: Oxford University Press, 1995.

Folsom, Ed. "Lucifer and Ethiopia: Whitman, Race, and Poetics before the Civil War and After." In *A Historical Guide to Walt Whitman*, ed. David S. Reynolds, 45–95. New York: Oxford University Press, 2000.

Foner, Philip S. and Robert James Branham, eds. *Lift Every Voice: African American Oratory 1787–1900*. Tuscaloosa, AL: University of Alabama Press, 1998.

Foner, Philip S. and George E. Walker, eds. *Proceedings of the Blacks State Conventions, 1840–1865, Volume One*. Philadelphia: Temple University Press, 1979.

——. *Proceedings of the Black State Conventions, 1840–1865, Volume Two*. Philadelphia: Temple University Press, 1980.

Foner, Philip S., ed. *Frederick Douglass: Selected Speeches and Writings*. New York: Lawrence Hill Books, 1999.

———. *Life and Writings of Frederick Douglass*. Vol. 1. New York: International Publishers, 1950.

Forbes, Esther Hoskins. *Paul Revere and the World He Lived In*. New York: Mariner Books, 1999.

Foreman, P. Gabrielle. "Sentimental Abolition in Douglass's Decade: Revision, Erotic Conversion, and the Politics of Witnessing in 'The Heroic Slave' and *My Bondage and My Freedom*." In *Criticism and the Color Line: Desegregating American Literary Studies*, ed. Henry B. Wonham, 191–204. New Brunswick, N.J.: Rutgers University Press, 1996.

Foster, Charles I. "The Colonization of Free Negroes, in Liberia, 1816–1835." *Journal of Negro History* 38, no. 1 (January 1953): 41–66.

Foster, Frances Smith. *A Brighter Coming Day: A Frances Ellen Watkins Harper Reader*. New York: Feminist Press, 1990.

———. *Written by Herself: Literary Production by African American Women, 1746–1892*. Bloomington: Indiana University Press, 1993.

Foucault, Michel. "Of Other Spaces." *Diacritics* 16 (Spring 1986): 22–27.

Franchot, Jenny. "Douglass and the Construction of the Feminine." In *Frederick Douglass: New Literary and Historical Essays*, ed. Eric J. Sundquist, 141–65. New York: Cambridge University Press, 1990.

Frankenstein, Alfred. *Painter of Rural America: William Sidney Mount*. Stony Brook, N.Y.: Suffolk Museum of Stony Brook, 1968.

Franklin, H. Bruce. "'Apparent Symbol of Despotic Command': Melville's *Benito Cereno*." *New England Quarterly* 34, no. 4 (1961): 462–77.

———. "Past, Present, and Future Seemed One." In *Critical Essay on* "Benito Cereno," ed. Robert E. Burkholder, 230–46. Boston: G. K. Hall, 1992.

Frank, Jason. "Aesthetic Democracy: Walt Whitman and the Poetry of the People." *Review of Politics* 69.2 (2007): 402–30.

Ganter, Granville. "'He Made Us Laugh Some': Frederick Douglass's Use of Humor." *African American Review* 37.4 (Winter 2003): 535–52.

Garman, Bryan K. *A Race of Singers: Whitman's Working-Class Hero from Guthrie to Springsteen*. Chapel Hill, N.C.: University of North Carolina Press, 2000.

Gates, Henry Louis, Jr. *Figures in Black: Words, Signs, and the "Racial" Self*. New York: Oxford University Press, 1987.

———. *The Signifying Monkey: A Theory of African-American Literary Criticism*. New York: Oxford University Press, 1988.

Gayle, Addison, Jr. *The Way of the New World: The Black Novel in America*. New York: Anchor, 1976.

Gayle, Addison, Jr., ed. *The Black Aesthetic*. Garden City, N.Y.: Doubleday, Anchor, 1971.

Gilmore, Glenda E. *Gender and Jim Crow: Women and the Politics of White Supremacy in North Carolina, 1896–1920*. Chapel Hill, N.C.: University of North Carolina Press, 1996.

Gilmore, Paul. *Aesthetic Materialism: Electricity and American Romanticism*. Palo Alto, Calif.: Stanford University Press, 2009.

———. "De Genewine Artekil: William Wells Brown, Blackface Minstrelsy, and Abolitionism." *American Literature* 69, no. 4 (December 1997): 743–80.

Gilroy, Paul. *The Black Atlantic: Modernity and Double Consciousness.* Cambridge, Mass.: Harvard University Press, 1993.

Goldberg, Shari. "*Benito Cereno*'s Mute Testimony: On the Politics of Reading Melville's Silences." *Arizona Quarterly* 65, no. 2 (2009): 1-26.

Goss, Thomas J. *The War within the Union High Command: Politics and Generalship during the Civil War.* Lawrence: University Press of Kansas, 2003.

Glaude, Eddie S., Jr. *Exodus! Religion, Race, and Nation in Early Nineteenth-Century Black America.* Chicago: University of Chicago Press, 2000.

Graham, Maryemma. "Introduction." In *Complete Poems of Frances E. W. Harper,* ed. Maryemma Graham, xxxiii-lvii. New York: Oxford University Press, 1988.

Grandmaster Flash and the Furious Five. "The Message." *The Message.* Sugar Hill Records, 1982.

Greeson, Jennifer R. "The Figure of the South and the Nationalizing Imperatives of Early United States Literature." *Yale Journal of Criticism* 12, no. 2 (1999): 209-48.

Gregory, James M. *Frederick Douglass: The Orator.* Springfield, Mass.: Willey, 1893.

Griffin, Farah Jasmine. "*Who Set You Flowin'?*": *The African-American Migration Narrative.* New York: Oxford University Press, 1995.

Groseclose, Barbara. *Nineteenth-Century American Art.* New York: Oxford University Press, 2000.

———. "'Washington Crossing the Delaware': The Political Context." *American Art Journal* 7, no. 2 (November 1975): 70-78.

Grossman, Allen R. "The Poetics of Union in Whitman and Lincoln: An Inquiry toward the Relationship of Art and Policy." In *The American Renaissance Reconsidered,* ed. Walter Benn Michaels and Donald E. Pease, 183-208. Baltimore: Johns Hopkins University Press, 1985.

Grossman, Jay. *Reconstituting the American Renaissance: Emerson, Whitman, and the Politics of Representation.* Durham, N.C.: Duke University Press, 2003.

Gubar, Susan. *Racechanges: White Skin, Black Face in American Culture.* New York: Oxford University Press, 1997.

Gustafson, Sandra M. *Eloquence Is Power: Oratory and Performance in Early America.* Chapel Hill: University of Chapel Hill Press, 2000.

Gustafson, Thomas. *Representative Words: Politics, Literature, and the American Language, 1776-1864.* Cambridge: Cambridge University Press, 1992.

Habermas, Jürgen. *The Structural Transformation of the Public Sphere: An Inquiry into a Category of Bourgeois Society.* Cambridge, Mass.: MIT Press, 1991.

Haegert, John. "Voicing Slavery through Silence: Narrative Mutiny in Melville's *Benito Cereno*." *Mosaic* 26, no. 2 (Spring 1993): 21-38.

Hardt, Michael. "Jefferson and Democracy." *American Quarterly* 59, no. 1 (March 2007): 41-78.

Harper, Frances Ellen Watkins. "Eliza Harris." 1853. In *Complete Poems of Frances E. W. Harper,* ed. Maryemma Graham, 6-7. New York: Oxford University Press, 1988.

———. "The Fifteenth Amendment." 1871. In *Complete Poems of Frances E. W. Harper,* ed. Maryemma Graham, 108. New York: Oxford University Press, 1988.

———. "The Freedom Bell." 1871. In *Complete Poems of Frances E. W. Harper,* ed. Maryemma Graham, 94-95. New York: Oxford University Press, 1988.

Harper, Frances Ellen Watkins. "Miss Watkins and the Constitution." 1859. In *Brighter Day Coming*, ed. Frances Smith Foster, 47–48. New York: Feminist Press, 1990.

——. *Poems on Miscellaneous Subjects*. Boston: J. B. Yerrington and Son, 1854.

——. "To Mrs. Harriet Beecher Stowe," *Frederick Douglass' Paper*, January 27, 1854.

——. "The Slave Auction." 1854. In *Complete Poems of Frances E. W. Harper*, ed. Maryemma Graham, 10. New York: Oxford University Press, 1988.

——. "The Slave Mother." 1854. In *Complete Poems of Frances E. W. Harper*, ed. Maryemma Graham, 4–5. New York: Oxford University Press, 1988.

Harris, Michael D. *Colored Pictures: Race and Visual Representation*. Chapel Hill, N.C.: University of North Carolina Press, 2003.

Hartman, Saidiya. *Scenes of Subjection: Terror, Slavery, and Self-Making in Nineteenth-Century America*. New York: Oxford University Press, 1997.

Heffernan, Jeffrey. "Ekphrasis and Representation." *New Literary History* 22, no. 2 (Spring 1991): 297–316.

Henderson, Lynne N. "Legality and Empathy." *Michigan Law Review* 85 (1987): 1574–1653.

Henderson, Mae Gwendolyn. "Speaking in Tongues: Dialogics, Dialectics, and the Black Woman Writer's Literary Tradition." In *Feminists Theorize the Political*, ed. Judith Butler and Joan W. Scott, 144–66. New York: Routledge, 1992.

Herrington, Eldrid. "Fit Compositions: Whitman's Revisions to *Drum-Taps*." In *Rebound: The American Poetry Book*, eds. Michael Hinds and Stephen Matterson, 29–43. Amsterdam: Rodopi, 2004.

——. "Poems by Charlotte Forten and Frances Ellen Watkins Harper Found in AAS Collection," *The Book* 64 (November 2004): 5–6.

Higginbotham, Evelyn Brooks. *Righteous Discontent: The Women's Movement in the Black Baptist Church, 1880–1920*. Cambridge, Mass.: Harvard University Press, 1993.

Hill, Patricia Liggins. "'Let Me Make Songs for the People': A Study of Frances Watkins Harper's Poetry." *Black American Literature Forum* 15, no. 2 (Summer 1981): 60–65.

Hills, Patricia, Teresa A. Carbone, and Patricia Hills. "Painting Race: Eastman Johnson's Pictures of Slaves, Ex-Slaves, and Freedmen." In *Eastman Johnson: Painting America*, ed. eresa A. Carbone and Patricia Hills, 121–65. New York: Brooklyn Museum of Art in association with Rizzoli International Publications, 1999.

Holland, Catherine. "Notes on the State of America: Jeffersonian Democracy and the Production of a National Past." *Political Theory* 29, no. 2 (2001): 190–216.

Hollander, John. *Vision and Resonance: Two Senses of Poetic Form*. New York: Oxford University Press, 1975.

Hughes, Langston. "Let America Be America Again." 1938. In *The Collected Poems of Langston Hughes*, ed. Arnold Rampersad, 189–91. New York: Vintage, 1994.

——. "The Negro Artist and the Racial Mountain," *The Nation* 23 (June 1926): 692–94.

Hurston, Zora Neale. "Characteristics of Negro Expression." In *Negro: An Anthology*, ed. Nancy Cunard. London: Wishart, 1934. 39–46.

Hutchinson, George. "Race and the Family Romance: Whitman's Civil War." *Walt Whitman Quarterly Review* 20 (Winter 2003): 134–50.

Ickstadt, Heinz. "Toward a Pluralist Aesthetics." In *Aesthetics in a Multicultural Age*, ed. Emory Elliott, Lou Freitas Caton, and Jeffrey Rhyne, 263–78. New York: Oxford University Press, 2002.

Iton, Richard. *In Search of the Black Fantastic: Politics and Popular Culture in the Post-Civil Rights Era*. New York: Oxford University Press, 2008.

Jacobs, Harriet A. *Incidents in the Life of a Slave Girl, Written by Herself*. 1861. Ed. Jean Fagan Yellin. Cambridge: Harvard University Press, 1987.

Jackson, Jesse. "Keynote Address: Keep Hope Alive." Democratic National Convention, Atlanta, Georgia, July 19, 1988.

Jameson, Fredric. *The Political Unconscious: Narrative as a Socially Symbolic Act*. Ithaca, N.Y.: Cornell University Press, 1981.

Jay, Martin. *Downcast Eyes: The Denigration of Vision in 20th Century French Thought*. Berkeley: University of California Press, 1994.

"Jefferson and Slavery." *Frederick Douglass' Paper*, April 1, 1852.

Jefferson, Thomas. *Answers to Démeunier's First Queries, January 24, 1786*. In *Jefferson: Writings*, ed. Merrill D. Peterson, 575–92. New York: Library of America, 1984.

———. *Notes on the State of Virginia*. 1787. In *Jefferson: Writings*, ed. Merrill D. Peterson, 123–325. New York: Library of America, 1984.

———. "A Summary View of the Rights of British America." In *Tracts of the American Revolution, 1763–1776*, ed. Merrill Jensen, 256–76. Indianapolis: Hackett Publishing, 2003.

Johnson, Oliver. "Our Correspondence." *Frederick Douglass' Paper*, October 5, 1855.

Johns, Elizabeth. *American Genre Painting: The Politics of Everyday Life*. New Haven, Conn.: Yale University Press, 1991.

Johnson, James Weldon. *Black Manhattan*. New York: Da Capo Press, 1930.

———. *The Book of American Negro Poetry, Chosen and Edited with an Essay on the Negro's Creative Genius*. New York: Harcourt, Brace, 1922.

Johnson, Walter. "On Agency." *Journal of Social History* 37, no. 1 (2003): 113-24.

Jones, Gavin. "Dusky Comments of Silence: Language, Race, and Herman Melville's 'Benito Cereno.'" *Studies in Short Fiction* 32, no. 1 (1995): 39–50.

Jones, Martha S. *All Bound Up Together: The Woman Question in African American Public Culture, 1830–1900*. Chapel Hill, N.C.: University of North Carolina Press, 2007.

Jones, W. Alfred. "A Sketch of the Life and Character of William S. Mount." *American Whig Review* 14, no. 80 (August 1851): 122–27.

Kaplan, Justin. *Walt Whitman: A Life*. New York: Simon and Schuster, 1980.

Kallen, Horace. *Cultural Pluralism and the American Idea: An Essay in Social Philosophy*. Philadelphia: University of Pennsylvania Press, 1956.

———. "Democracy versus the Melting-Pot." *The Nation* 100 (February 18, 25, 1915): 190–94, 217–20.

Kateb, George. "Walt Whitman the Culture of Democracy." *Political Theory* 18 (November 1990): 545–71.

Kavanagh, James H. "That Hive of Subtlety: 'Benito Cereno' and the Liberal Hero." In *Ideology and Classic American Literature*, ed. Sacvan Bercovitch and Myra Jehlen, 352–83. New York: Cambridge University Press, 1986.

Kazanjian, David. "The Speculative Freedom of Colonial Liberia" (unpublished manuscript).

Kerkering, Jack. "'Of Me and Mine': The Music of Racial Identity in Whitman and Lanier, Dvorak and DuBois." *American Literature* 73, no. 1 (March 2001): 147–84.

Klammer, Martin. *Whitman, Slavery, and the Emergence of* Leaves of Grass. University Park, Pa.: Pennsylvania State University Press, 1995.

———. "Slavery and Abolitionism." In *Walt Whitman: An Encyclopedia*, ed. J.R. LeMaster and Donald D. Kummings, 640–42. New York: Routledge, 1998.

Kramer, Michael P. *Imagining Language in America: From the Revolution to the Civil War.* Princeton, N.J.: Princeton University Press, 1992.

Laclau, Ernesto. *Emancipation(s).* New York: Verso, 1996.

———. *New Reflections on the Revolution on Our Time.* London: Verso, 1990.

Larson, Kerry C. *Whitman's Drama of Consensus.* Chicago: University of Chicago Press, 1988.

Lee, Maurice S. "Melville's Subversive Political Philosophy: 'Benito Cereno' and the Fate of Speech." *American Literature* 72, no. 3 (2000): 495–519.

———. *Slavery, Philosophy, and American Literature, 1830–1860.* New York: Cambridge University Press, 2005.

Lee, Spike. *Do the Right Thing.* 40 Acres and a Mule, 1989.

Levine, Robert S. *Conspiracy and Romance: Studies in Brockden Brown, Cooper, Hawthorne, and Melville.* New York: Cambridge University Press, 1989.

———. "Introduction." In *Clotel: A Bedford Cultural Edition*, ed. Robert S. Levine, 3–27. Boston: Bedford, 2011.

———. *Martin R. Delany: A Documentary Reader.* Chapel Hill: University of North Carolina Press, 2007

———. *Martin Delany, Frederick Douglass, and the Politics of Representative Identity.* Chapel Hill: University of North Carolina Press, 1997.

———. "*Uncle Tom's Cabin* in *Frederick Douglass' Paper*: An Analysis of Reception." *American Literature* 64, no. 1 (March 1992): 71–93.

Levine, Robert S. and Samuel Otter, eds. *Frederick Douglass and Herman Melville: Essays in Relation.* Chapel Hill: University of North Carolina Press, 2008.

Levine, Robert S. and Ivy G. Wilson, eds. *The Works of James M. Whitfield: America and Other Works by a Nineteenth-Century African American Poet.* Chapel Hill, N.C.: University of North Carolina Press, 2011.

Lhamon, W.T., Jr. *Raising Cain: Blackface Performance from Jim Crow to Hip Hop.* Cambridge, Mass.: Harvard University Press, 1998.

Lincoln, Jairus. *Anti-Slavery Melodies: For the Friends of Freedom. Prepared for the Hingham Anti-Slavery Society.* Hingham, MA: Elijah B. Gill, 1843.

Linebaugh, Peter and Marcus Rediker. *The Many-Headed Hydra: Sailors, Slaves, Commoners, and the Hidden History of the Revolutionary Atlantic.* Boston: Beacon Press, 2000.

Litwack, Leon F. *North of Slavery: The Negro in the Free States, 1790–1860.* Chicago: University of Chicago Press, 1961.

Loeffelholz, Mary. *From Schools to Salons: Reading Nineteenth-Century American Women's Poetry.* Princeton, N.J.: Princeton University Press, 2004.

Logan, Shirley Wilson. "Black Speakers, White Representations: Frances Ellen Watkins Harper and the Construction of a Public Persona." In *African American Rhetoric(s): Interdisciplinary Perspectives*, ed. Elaine B. Richardson and Ronald L. Jackson II, 21–36. Carbondale, IL: Southern Illinois University Press, 2004.

Loggins, Vernon. *The Negro Author: His Development in America to 1900.* Port Washington, N.Y.: Kennikat Press, 1964.

Looby, Christopher. *Voicing America: Language, Literary Form, and the Origins of the United States.* Chicago: University of Chicago Press, 1996.

Lott, Eric. *Love and Theft: Blackface Minstrelsy and the American Working Class*. New York: Oxford University Press, 1993.

Lubin, David M. "Reconstructing Duncanson." In *Picturing a Nation: Art and Social Change in Nineteenth-Century America*, ed. David M. Lubin, 108–57. New Haven, Conn.: Yale University Press, 1994.

Lucaites, John Louis. "The Irony of 'Equality' in Black Abolitionist Discourse: The Case of Frederick Douglass's 'What to the Slave Is the Fourth of July?'" In *Rhetoric and Political Culture in Nineteenth-Century America*, ed. Thomas W. Benson, 47–69. East Lansing: Michigan State University Press, 1997.

Luciano, Dana. *Arranging Grief: Sacred Time and the Body in Nineteenth-Century America*. New York: New York University Press, 2007.

———. "Melville's Untimely History: 'Benito Cereno' as Counter-Monumental Narrative." *Arizona Quarterly* 60, no. 3 (2004): 33–60.

Maher, William John. *Behind the Burnt Cork Mask: Early Blackface Minstrelsy and Antebellum American Popular Culture*. Urbana: University of Illinois, 1999.

Mancuso, Luke. *The Strange Sad War Revolving: Walt Whitman, Reconstruction, and the Emergence of Black Citizenship, 1865–1876*. Columbia, S.C.: Camden House, 1997.

Margolis, Stacy. *Public Life of Privacy in Nineteenth-Century American Literature*. Durham, N.C.: Duke University Press, 2005.

Marx, Karl. *Capital*. Vol. 1. 1867. Reprint, New York: Penguin, 1990.

McCarthy, Timothy Patrick and John Stauffer, eds. *Prophets of Protest: Reconsidering the History of American Abolitionism*. New York: New Press, 2006.

McElroy, Guy. *Facing History: The Black Image in American Art, 1710–1940*. San Francisco: Bedford Arts; Washington, D.C.: Corcoran Gallery of Art, 1990.

McHenry, Elizabeth. *Forgotten Readers: Recovering the Lost History of African American Literary Societies*. Durham, N.C.: Duke University Press, 2002.

McKittrick, Katherine. "'Freedom Is a Secret': The Future Usability of the Underground." In *Black Geographies and the Politics of Place*, ed. Katherine McKittrick and Clyde Woods, 97–114. Cambridge, Mass.: South End Press, 2007.

McPherson, C. B. *The Political Theory of Possessive Individualism: Hobbes to Locke*. Oxford: Oxford University Press, 1962.

Melville, Herman. "Benito Cereno." Pts. 1, 2, and 3. *Putnam's Monthly* 6, no. 34 (October 1855): 353–67; no. 35 (November 1855): 459–74; no. 36 (December 1855): 633–44.

———. *Billy Budd and Other Stories*. Ed. Frederick Busch. New York: Penguin, 1986.

———. "Hawthorne and His Mosses." In *The Piazza Tales, and Other Prose Pieces, 1839–1860*, ed. Harrison Hayford, Alma A. MacDougall, G. Thomas Tanselle, et al., 239–53. Evanston and Chicago, Ill.: Northwestern University Press and Newberry Library, 1987.

———. Letter to Nathaniel Hawthorne, June 1 [?], 1851. In *Correspondence*, ed. Lynn Horth, 190–94. Evanston and Chicago, Ill.: Northwestern University Press and Newberry Library, 1993.

———. *Moby-Dick; or, The Whale*. 1851. Ed. Harrison Hayford, Hershel Parker, and G. Thomas Tanselle. Evanston and Chicago, Ill.: Northwestern University Press and Newberry Library, 1988.

Michaels, Walter Benn and Don E. Pease, eds. *The American Renaissance Reconsidered*. Baltimore: Johns Hopkins University Press, 1985.

Mitchell, W. J. T. *Iconology: Image, Text, Ideology.* Chicago: University of Chicago, 1987.

———. "Narrative, Memory, Slavery." In *Cultural Artifacts and the Production of Meaning: The Page, the Image, and the Body,* ed. Margaret J. M. Ezell and Katherine O'Brien O'Keefe, 199–222. Ann Arbor: University of Michigan Press, 1995.

———. *Picture Theory: Essays on Verbal and Visual Representation.* Chicago: University of Chicago Press, 1994.

———. "Word and Image." In *Critical Terms for Art History,* ed. Robert Nelson and Richard Shiff, 47–57. Chicago: University of Chicago Press, 1996.

Moon, Michael. *Disseminating Whitman: Revision and Corporeality in* Leaves of Grass. Durham, N.C.: Duke University Press, 1991.

Morgan, Jo-Ann. Uncle Tom's Cabin *as Visual Culture.* Columbia: University of Missouri Press, 2007.

Morrell, Michael E. *Empathy and Democracy: Feeling, Thinking, and Deliberation.* University Park: Pennsylvania State University Press, 2010.

Morrison, Toni. *Beloved.* New York: Knopf, 1987.

———. "Home." In *The House That Race Built: Black Americans, U.S. Terrain,* ed. Wahneema Lubiano, 3–12. New York: Pantheon, 1997.

———. *Playing in the Dark: Whiteness and the Literary Imagination.* Cambridge, Mass.: Harvard University Press, 1992.

———. "Unspeakable Things Unspoken: The Afro-American Presence in American Literature." *Michigan Quarterly Review* 28, no. 1 (Winter 1989): 1–34.

Mos Def. "Dollar Day." *True Magic.* Geffen Records, 2006.

Moten, Fred. *In the Break: The Aesthetics of the Black Radical Tradition.* Minneapolis: University of Minnesota Press, 2003.

Mullen, Harriet. "Runaway Tongue: Resistant Orality in *Uncle Tom's Cabin, Our Nig, Incidents in the Life of a Slave Girl,* and *Beloved.*" In *The Cultures of Sentiment: Race, Gender, and Sentimentality in Nineteenth-Century America,* ed. Shirley Samuels, 244–64. New York: Oxford University Press, 1992.

Murray, Albert. *Blues Devil of Nada: A Contemporary American Approach to Aesthetic Statement.* New York: Pantheon, 1996.

Nabers, Deak. "The Problem of Revolution in the Age of Slavery: *Clotel,* Fiction, and the Government of Man." *Representations* 91 (Summer 2005): 84–108.

Nas. "You Owe Me." *Nastradamus.* Columbia Records, 1999.

Neal, Mark Anthony. "Sold Out on Soul: The Corporate Annexation of Black Popular Music." *Popular Music and Society* 21, no. 3 (Fall 1997): 117–34.

Nell, William C. *The Colored Patriots of the American Revolution, with Sketches of Several Distinguished Colored Persons: To Which Is Added a Brief Survey of the Condition and Prospects of Colored Americans.* Boston: Published by Robert F. Wallcut, 1855.

Nelson, Dana D. "Representative/Democracy: The Political Work of Countersymbolic Representation." In *Materializing Democracy: Toward a Revitalized Cultural Politics,* ed. Russ Castronovo and Dana D. Nelson, 218–47. Durham, N.C.: Duke University Press, 2002.

———. *The Word in Black and White: Reading "Race" in American Literature, 1637–1867.* New York: Oxford University Press, 1992.

Nettles, Darryl Glenn. *African American Concert Singers before 1950.* Jefferson, N.C.: McFarland, 2003.

Newman, Richard S. "Black Shadow Politics in the Antebellum North." *Common-Place* 9, no. 1 (October 2008). On-line.

Newman, Richard, Patrick Rael, and Phillip Lapsansky, eds. *Pamphlets of Protest: An Anthology of Early African-American Literature, 1790–1860*. New York: Routledge, 2001.

Nixon, Nicola. "Men and Coats; Or, The Politics of the Dandiacal Body in Melville's 'Benito Cereno.'" *PMLA* 114, no. 3 (May 1999): 359–72.

"Notices." *Frederick Douglass' Paper*, April 28, 1854, 3.

Novak, Barbara. *American Painting of the Nineteenth Century: Realism, Idealism, and the American Experience*. 2nd ed. New York: Harper and Row, 1979.

Nussbaum, Martha C. *Upheavals of Thought: The Intelligence of Emotions*. New York: Cambridge University Press, 2001.

O'Meally, Robert G. "Frederick Douglass's 1845 *Narrative*: The Text That Was Meant to Be Preached." In *Afro-American Literature: The Reconstruction of Instruction*, ed. Dexter Fisher and Robert Stepto, 192–211. New York: Modern Language Association of America, 1979.

———., ed. *The Jazz Cadence of American Culture*. New York: Columbia University Press, 1998.

Otter, Samuel. *Philadelphia Stories: America's Literature of Race and Freedom*. New York: Oxford University Press, 2010.

Outkast. *Stankonia*. LaFace Records, 2000.

Painter, Nell Irvin. *Sojourner Truth: A Life, a Symbol*. New York: Norton, 1997.

Parliament. "Chocolate City," *Chocolate City*. Casablanca Records, 1973.

Patterson, Anita. "Jazz, Realism, and the Modernist Lyric." *Modern Language Quarterly* 61, no. 4 (1990): 650–81.

Pease, Don E. "*Moby-Dick* and the Cold War." In *The American Renaissance Reconsidered*, ed. Walter Benn Michaels and Don E. Pease, 113–55. Baltimore: Johns Hopkins University Press, 1985.

Peterson, Carla L. *"Doers of the Word": African-American Women Speakers and Writers of the North (1830–1880)*. New York: Oxford University Press, 1995.

Phillips, Dana. "Nineteenth-Century Racial Thought and Whitman's Democratic Ethnology of the Future." *Nineteenth-Century Literature* 49, no. 3 (December 1994): 289–320.

Phillips, Wendell. "Toussaint L'Ouverture." In *Speeches, Lectures, and Letters*. Boston: Lee and Shepard, 1894. 468–94.

Poe, Edgar Allen. "The Philosophy of Furniture." 1840. In *The Complete Works of Edgar Allan Poe*, ed. James Albert Harrison, 101–09. New York: T.Y. Crowell, 1902.

Portelli, Alessandro. *The Text and the Voice: Writing, Speaking, and Democracy in American Literature*. New York: Columbia University Press, 1994.

Powell, Richard J. *Cutting a Figure: Fashioning Black Portraiture*. Durham, N.C.: Duke University Press, 2008.

Price, Kenneth. "The Lost Negress and the Jolly Young Wenches." In *Leaves of Grass: The Sesquicentennial Essays*, ed. Susan Belasco, Ed Folsom, and Kenneth Price, 224–43. Lincoln, Ne.: University of Nebraska Press, 2007.

Public Enemy. "Fight the Power." Music from *Do the Right Thing*. Tamla Records, 1989.

Quarles, Benjamin. "Antebellum Free Blacks and the 'Spirit of '76." *Journal of Negro History* 61 (1976): 229–42.

Railton, Stephen. "'As If I Were With You'—The Performance of Whitman's Poetry." In *The Cambridge Companion to Walt Whitman*, ed. Ezra Greenspan, ed. 7–26. New York: Cambridge University Press, 1995.

Rancière, Jacques. *The Politics of Aesthetics: The Distribution of the Sensible*. New York: Continuum, 2004.

———. "Ten Theses on Politics." In *Dissensus: On Politics and Aesthetics*. Ed. and trans. by Steven Corcoran. 27–44. New York: Continuum, 2010.

Ramesh, Kotti Sree and Kandula Nirupa Rani. *Claude McKay: The Literary Identity from Jamaica to Harlem and Beyond*. Jefferson, N.C.: McFarland, 2006.

Rawls, John. *A Theory of Justice*. Cambridge, Mass.: Belknap Press, 1971.

Redding, J. Saunders. *To Make a Poet Black*. 1939. Reprint, Ithaca, N.Y.: Cornell University Press, 1988.

Redmond, Eugene. *Drumvoices: The Mission of Afro-American Poetry*. Garden City, N.Y.: Anchor Press, 1974.

Reid-Pharr, Robert. *Conjugal Union: The Body, the House, and the Black American*. New York: Oxford University Press, 1999.

Reilly, Bernard F., Jr. "Translation and Transformation: The Prints after William Sidney Mount." In *William Sidney Mount*, ed. Deborah J. Johnson, 135–61. New York: American Federation of Arts, 1998.

Remnick, David. "The Joshua Generation: Race and the Campaign of Barack Obama." *New Yorker*, November 17, 2008.

Remond, Charles Lenox. "An Anti-Slavery Discourse." *Liberator*, July 10, 1857

———. "For the Dissolution of the Union," *National Anti-Slavery Standard*, July 18, 1844.

———. "Resolved, That to Secure Funds." *National Anti-Slavery Standard*, May 3, 1849.

Reynolds, David S. "Politics and Poetry: *Leaves of Grass* and the Social Crisis of the 1850s." In *The Cambridge Companion to Walt Whitman*, ed. Ezra Greenspan, 92–109. New York: Cambridge University Press, 1995.

Robertson-Lorant, Laurie. *Melville: A Biography*. New York: Clarkson Potter Publishing, 1996.

Robinson, William. *Early Black American Poets: Selections with Biographical and Critical Introductions*. Dubuque, IA: William C. Brown Co., 1971.

Romero, Laura. *Home Fronts: Domesticity and Its Critics*. Durham, N.C.: Duke University Press, 1997.

Rorty, Richard. *Achieving Our Country: Leftist Thought in Twentieth-Century America*. Cambridge, Mass.: Harvard University Press, 1998.

Ruttenberg, Nancy. *Democratic Personalities: Popular Voice and the Trial of American Authorship*. Stanford, Calif.: Stanford University Press, 1998.

Ryan, Susan M. "Charity Begins at Home: Stowe's Antislavery Novels and Forms of Benevolent Citizenship." *American Literature* 72, no. 4 (December 2000): 751–82.

Sale, Maggie. "Critiques from Within: Antebellum Projects of Resistance." *American Literature* 64, no. 4 (December 1992): 695–718.

———. "To Make the Past Useful: Frederick Douglass' Politics of Solidarity." *Arizona Quarterly* 51, no. 3 (Autumn 1995): 25–60.

Samuels, Shirley. "Miscegenated America: The Civil War." *American Literary History* 9, no. 3 (1997): 482–501.

Samuels, Shirley, ed. *The Culture of Sentiment: Race, Gender, and Sentimentality in Nineteenth-Century America*. New York: Oxford University Press, 1992.

Sánchez-Eppler, Karen. *Touching Liberty: Abolitionism, Feminism, and the Politics of the Body.* Berkeley: University of California Press, 1993.

———. "To Stand Between: A Political Perspective on Whitman's Poetics of Merger and Embodiment." *ELH* 56 (1989): 923–49.

Schweninger, Lee. "*Clotel* and the Historicity of the Anecdote." *Melus* 23, no. 1 (1999): 21–36.

Scudder, Harold H. "Melville's 'Benito Cereno' and Captain Delano's 'Voyages.'" *PMLA* 43, no. 2 (June 1928): 502–32.

Scott, James C. *Domination and the Arts of Resistance: Hidden Transcripts.* New Haven: Yale University Press, 1990.

Shaw, Gwendolyn DuBois. *Portraits of a People: Picturing African Americans in the Nineteenth Century.* Seattle: University of Washington Press, 2006.

Sherman, Joan R. *Invisible Poets: Afro-Americans of the Nineteenth Century.* Urbana: University of Illinois Press, 1974.

Shields, John C., ed. *The Collected Works of Phillis Wheatley.* New York: Oxford University Press, 1988.

Shuffleton, Frank. "Thomas Jefferson: Race, Culture and the Failure of Anthropological Method." In *A Mixed Race: Ethnicity in Early America*, ed. Frank Shuffleton, 257–77. New York: Oxford University Press, 1993.

Sill, Geoffrey. "Whitman on 'The Black Question.'" *Walt Whitman Quarterly Review* 8 (Fall 1990): 69–75.

Simpson, Joshua McCarter. "The First of August in Jamaica." 1848. In Joshua McCarter Simpson, *Original Anti-Slavery Songs, By Joshua M'C Simpson, A Colored Man*, 13–15. Zanesville, OH: Printed for the Author, 1852.

Slaughter, Eric. *The State as a Work of Art: The Cultural Origins of the Constitution.* Chicago: University of Chicago Press, 2009.

Smith, James McCune. "Citizenship." In *Anglo-African Magazine.* 1859. Ed. Thomas Hamilton. 114–50. New York: Arno Press, 1969.

———. "Introduction." In Frederick Douglass, *My Bondage and My Freedom.* New York: Miller, Orton and Mulligan, 1855. xvii-xxxii.

——— (under pseudonym "Communipaw"). "Our Correspondence." *Frederick Douglass' Paper.* October 5, 1855.

Smith, Rogers M. *Civic Ideals: Conflicting Visions of U.S. Citizenship in U.S. History.* New Haven, Conn.: Yale University Press, 1997.

Sorisio, Carolyn. *Fleshing Out America: Race, Gender, and the Politics of the Body.* Athens: University of Georgia Press, 2002.

Southall, Geneva. "Black Composers and Religious Music." *The Black Perspective in Music* 1 (1974): 45–50.

Southern, Eileen. *The Music of Black Americans: A History.* New York: W. W. Norton & Co., 1997.

Spillers, Hortense. "Mama's Baby, Papa's Maybe: An American Grammar Book." In "Culture and Countermemory: The 'American' Connection." Special issue, *Diacritics* 17, no. 2 (Summer 1987): 65–81.

Spivak, Gayatri Chakravorty. "Can the Subaltern Speak?" In *Marxism and the Interpretation of Culture*, ed. Cary Nelson and Lawrence Grossberg, 271–313. Urbana: University of Illinois Press, 1988.

Stancliff, Michael. *Frances Ellen Watkins Harper: American Reform Rhetoric and the Rise of a Modern Nation State.* New York: Routledge, 2010.

Stanley, Sara G. "What, To the Toiling Millions There, Is This Boasted Liberty?" 1860. In *Lift and Every Voice: African American Oratory 1787–1900*, ed. Philip S. Foner and Robert James Branham, 285–87. Tuscaloosa, AL: University of Alabama Press, 1997.

Stauffer, John. *The Black Hearts of Men: Radical Abolitionists and the Transformation of Race*. Cambridge: Harvard University Press, 2002.

———. "Creating an Image in Black: The Power of Abolitionist Pictures." In *Prophets of Protest: Reconsidering the History of American Abolitionism*, ed. Timothy Patrick McCarthy and John Stauffer, 256–67. New York: New Press, 2006.

———. "Frederick Douglass and the Aesthetics of Freedom." *Raritan* 25, no. 1 (Summer 2005): 114–36.

———., ed. *The Works of James McCune Smith: Black Intellectual and Abolitionist*. New York: Oxford University Press, 2006.

Stepto, Robert B. *From behind the Veil: A Study of Afro-American Narrative*. 1979. Reprint, Urbana: University of Illinois Press, 1991.

———. "Storytelling in Early Afro-American Fiction: Frederick Douglass' *The Heroic Slave*." In *Black Literature and Literary Theory*, ed. Henry Louis Gates Jr., 175–86. New York: Methuen, 1984.

Still, William Grant. *The Underground Railroad*. Philadelphia: Porter and Coates, 1872.

Stowe, Harriet Beecher. *Uncle Tom's Cabin; or, Life among the Lowly*. 1852. Reprint, New York: Penguin, 1981.

Stuckey, Sterling. *African Culture and Melville's Art: The Creative Process in* Benito Cereno *and* Moby-Dick. New York: Oxford University Press, 2009.

———. "Cheer and Gloom: Douglass and Melville on Slave Dance and Music." In *Frederick Douglass and Herman Melville: Essays in* Relation, ed. Robert S. Levine and Samuel Otter, 69–87. Chapel Hill, N.C.: University of North Carolina Press, 2008.

———. "The Tambourine in Glory: African Culture and Melville's Art." In *The Cambridge Companion to Herman Melville*, ed. Robert S. Levine, 37–64. New York: Cambridge University Press, 1998.

Stuckey, Sterling, and Joshua Leslie. "The Death of Benito Cereno: A Reading of Herman Melville on Slavery." *Journal of Negro History* 67, no. 4 (Winter 1982): 287–301.

Sundquist, Eric J. "'Benito Cereno' and New World Slavery." In *Reconstructing American Literary* History, ed. Sacvan Bercovitch, 93–122. Cambridge, Mass.: Harvard University Press, 1986.

———. To *Wake the Nations: Race in the Making of American Literature*. Cambridge, Mass.: Belknap Press, 1993.

Sylvester, Charles H. *Journeys Through Bookland, Volume 6*. Chicago: Bellows-Reeve Company, 1922.

Tompkins, Jane. *Sensational Designs: The Cultural Work of American Fiction, 1790–1860*. New York: Oxford University Press, 1985.

Trachtenberg, Alan. "Democracy and the Poet: Walt Whitman and E. A. Robinson." *Massachusetts Review* 39, no. 2 (Summer 1998): 267–80.

———. "The Politics of Labor and the Poet's Work: A Reading of 'A Song for Occupations.'" In *Walt Whitman: The Centennial Essays*, ed. Ed Folsom, ed. 120–32. Iowa City: University of Iowa Press, 1994.

Trodd, Zoe. "A Hid Event, Twice Lived: The Post-War Narrative Sub-Versions of Douglass and Melville." Special issue, *Leviathan: A Journal of Melville Studies* 10, no.2 (June 2008): 51–68.

Truth, Sojourner. *Narrative* and *Book of Life*. Boston: Published for the Author, 1875.

———. "Dere Is a Little Weasel in It," *National Anti-Slavery Standard*, July 4, 1863.

"Turn This Mutha Out," *New Times Media*, September 13, 2006.

Von Frank, Albert J. *The Trials of Anthony Burns: Freedom and Slavery in Emerson's Boston*. Cambridge, Mass.: Harvard University Press, 1998.

Wagner, Jean. *Black Poets of the United States*. Trans. Kenneth Douglas. Urbana: University of Illinois Press, 1973.

Walker, Krista. "Trappings of Nationalism in Frederick Douglass's *The Heroic Slave*." *African American Review* 34, no. 2 (Summer 2000): 233–47.

Ward, Samuel Ringgold. *Autobiography of a Fugitive Negro: His Anti-Slavery Labors in the United States, Canada & England*. London: John Snow, 1855.

Warner, Michael. *The Letters of the Republic: Publication and the Public Sphere in Eighteenth-Century America*. Cambridge, Mass.: Harvard University Press, 1990.

———. "Publics and Counter-Publics." *Public Culture* 14, no. 1 (Winter 2002): 49–90.

Waterman, Christopher A. "'Our Tradition Is a Very Modern Tradition': Popular Music and the Construction of Pan-Yoruba Identity." *Ethnomusicology* 34, no. 3 (Autumn 1990): 367–79.

Webb, Frank J. *The Garies and Their Friends*. 1857. Reprint, New York: AMS Press Inc., 1971.

Weiner, Susan. "'Benito Cereno' and the Failure of Law." *Arizona Quarterly* 47, no. 2 (Summer 1991): 1–28.

Wharton, Edith and Ogden Codman. *The Decoration of Houses*. New York: Charles Scribner's Sons, 1897.

Wheatley, Phillis. "America." 1768. In *The Collected Works of Phillis Wheatley*. ed. John C. Shields, 134. New York: Oxford University Press, 1988.

Whitley, Ed. *American Bards: Walt Whitman and Other Unlikely Candidates for National Poet*. Chapel Hill, N.C.: University of North Carolina Press, 2010.

Whitman, Walt. *An American Primer*. Ed. Horace Traubel. Boston: Small, Maynard & Company, 1904.

———. *Prose Works 1892*. 2 Volumes. Ed. Floyd Stovall. New York: New York University Press, 1964.

———. "The Eighteenth-Presidency!" In *Notebooks and Unpublished Prose Manuscripts*, ed. Edward Grier, 6: 2119–35. New York: New York University Press, 1984.

———. *The Gathering of the Forces, Two Volumes*. Ed. Cleveland Rodgers and John Black. New York: G. P. Putnam's Song, 1920.

———. *Leaves of Grass*. Brooklyn, N.Y.: 1855. Online.

———. *Leaves of Grass*. Brooklyn, N.Y.: 1856. Online.

———. *Leaves of Grass*. Washington, D.C.: 1872. Online.

———. *Specimen Days* and *Collect*. Philadelphia: David McKay, 1882–83.

———. *Uncollected Poetry and Prose of Walt Whitman, Two Volumes*. Ed. Emory Holloway. Garden City, N.Y.: Doubleday, Page, and Company, 1921.

Wilder, Craig Steven. *A Covenant with Color: Race and Social Power in Brooklyn*. New York: Columbia University Press, 2000.

Wilson, Harriet E. *Our Nig; or Sketches from the Life of a Free Black*. 1859. Ed. Henry Louis Gates, Jr. Reprint, New York: Vintage, 1983.

Wilson, Keith P. *Campfires of Freedom: The Camp Life of Black Soldiers during the Civil War*. Kent, Ohio: Kent State University Press, 2002.

Wilson, William J. "Afric-American Picture Gallery." In *Anglo-African Magazine*. 1859. Ed. Thomas Hamilton. New York: Arno Press, 1969.

———. "A Leaf from My Scrap Book." In *Autographs for Freedom*, ed. Julia Griffiths, 165–73. Auburn: Alden, Beardsley, 1854.

———. ["From Our Brooklyn Correspondent."] *Frederick Douglass' Paper*. March 11, 1853.

———. ["From Our Brooklyn Correspondent."] *Frederick Douglass' Paper*. March 25, 1853.

———. "What Shall We Do with the White People?" 1860. In *Speaking Out in Thunder Tones: Letters and Other Writings by Black Northerners, 1787–1865*, ed. Dorothy Sterling, 242–44. Cambridge, Mass.: Da Capo Press, 1998.

Wilson, William J., William Whipper, and Charles B. Ray. "Report on the Committee on Social Relations and Polity." *Frederick Douglass' Paper*. July 29, 1853.

Wilson, William J., Stephen Smith, and John W. Lewis. "A Call for a National Convention of Colored Americans." *Frederick Douglass' Paper*. June 8, 1855.

Wolf, Bryan. "All the World's a Code: Art and Ideology in Nineteenth-Century American Painting," *Art Journal*, Vol. 4, no. 4 (Winter, 1984): 328–37.

Wonder, Stevie. *Innervisions*. Motown Records, 1973.

———. *Songs in the Key of Life*. Motown Records. 1976.

———. *Talking Book*. Motown Records. 1972.

Wood, Marcus. *Blind Memory: Visual Representations of Slavery in England and America, 1780–1865*. Manchester: Manchester University Press, 2000.

X, Malcolm. "The Ballot or the Bullet." In *Malcolm X Speaks: Selected Speeches and Statements*, ed. George Breitman, 23–44. New York: Grove Press, 1965.

Yarborough, Richard. "Race, Violence, and Manhood: The Masculine Ideal in Frederick Douglass's 'The Heroic Slave.'" In *Frederick Douglass: New Literary and Historical Essays*, ed. Eric J. Sundquist, 166–83. New York: Cambridge University Press, 1990.

Yellin, Jean Fagan. *Harriet Jacobs: A Life*. New York: Basic Civitas Books, 2004.

Young, Iris Marion. "Communication and the Other: Beyond Deliberative Democracy." In *Democracy and Difference: Contesting the Boundaries of the Political*, ed. Seyla Benhabib, 120–35. Princeton, N.J.: Princeton University Press, 1996.

Ziff, Larzer. *Writing in the New Nation: Prose, Print, and Politics in the Early United States*. New Haven, Conn.: Yale University Press, 1991.

Printed in the USA/Agawam, MA
March 17, 2014

586914.137